Youth in Prison

Youth in Prison

We the People of Unit Four

M. A. Bortner and Linda M. Williams

ROUTLEDGE
New York and London

Published in 1997 by
Routledge
29 West 35th Street
New York, NY 10001

Published in Great Britain by
Routledge
11 New Fetter Lane
London EC4P 4EE

Copyright © 1997 by Routledge

Printed in the United States of America on acid-free paper.

Library of Congress Cataloging-in-Publication Data

Bortner, M. A., 1948-
      Youth in prison : we the people of Unit Four / by M.A. Bortner and
Linda M. Williams.
          p.   cm.
      Includes bibliographical references and index.
      ISBN 0-415-91438-8. -- ISBN 0-415-91439-6 (pbk.)
      1. Juvenile corrections--Government policy--United States.
2. Juvenile offenders--United States--Public opinion. 3. Juvenile
justice, Administration of--United States. 4. Public opinion-
-United States.   I. Williams, Linda M., 1945-   . II. Title.
HV9104.B58   1997
364.36'0973--dc21   97-17823
                                                             CIP

Contents

Acknowledgments

We are indebted to the youths and staff members who made this research possible.

We are grateful to our friends and colleagues who have given graciously and critically to this work: Avery Gordon, Iyone Meyer, Anne Schneider, Lare Van Sickle, Jim Williams, Maria Allison, Lisa Bond-Maupin, Andre Brown, Carol Burgess, Barbara Cerepano, Jan Christian, Mary Fran Draisker, Gray Cavender, Kathleen Ferraro, Rocco Guzman, Portia Halbert, Mark Harvey, Nancy Jurik, Kay Korman, Gregory Lam-Niemeyer, Denis LeClerc, Kim Losey, Carol Chiago Lujan, Shelby Lunning, Melissa McDonald, Clara Moore, Michael Musheno, Joanne Nigg, Lee Overmyer, Kimmi Pallay, Diann Peart, Elizabeth Peck, Stephen Pfohl, Lucy Pope, Lisa Poupart, Alice Snell, Janet Soper, Richelle Swan, and Kerri Van Sickle.

We appreciate the ongoing support of Routledge staff, including Jayne Fargnoli, Ilene Kalish, Alexandra Mummery, Laura-Ann Robb, Anne Sanow, and Lynette Silva.

The Kept,
the Keepers,
the Social Order

We the People of Unit Four feel that an automatic level drop is too much of a consequence for some types of behavior, especially for those youth who have been able to make their levels in this program. Yes, we know what actions warrant a level drop and understand the rule, but we feel a youth that has been programming [participating successfully] deserves a chance on "level parole."

We are people and do make mistakes. We're not trying to make excuses for our actions; we just feel [that in these cases of minor rule violations] we deserve another chance to prove ourselves. For example, we feel if you're taking a three-month course in cooking and, two months into the program, you burn a meal, that doesn't mean you should have to start over. It simply means that you, as a human, made a mistake and deserve a chance to prove yourself again, because as people we make mistakes.

It's not important that we make mistakes; it's important that we learn from them. We are willing to do our best to make a change and prove that we don't need more time [within the institution]; we just need another chance.

—*Youths of Unit Four*

These "People of Unit Four" were twenty-four imprisoned youths. They were the first of 385 young men to participate in a model treatment program in two juvenile prisons during the two years of this research, 1992–1994. The model program was created in response to a class-action lawsuit against Arizona's juvenile prison system. The lawsuit detailed the abuse of imprisoned youths and condemned the prison conditions as unconstitutional. It characterized the prison environment as arbitrarily punitive, excessively coercive, and inhumane.[1] This occurred in a state with the nation's third-highest rate of incarceration for youths, and it called into question many justifications for that incarceration.[2]

The lawsuit described extensive and specific abuses: the use of handcuffs and leg irons on youths who refused to work or did not work fast enough; the use of solitary confinement for periods of up to two months, including cases where youths suffered from mental illnesses; "four-pointing" (spread-eagle shackling) of youths on beds with four sets of handcuffs or leather restraints for a minimum of two hours following what was viewed as disruptive behavior; and the shackling of youngsters on work details in full sun at temperatures of over 100 degrees.[3]

Unable to disprove the charges, state officials did not want to go to trial, pay heavy monetary damages, have the prisons shut down, or have a federal judge take control and run the prisons. They worked to reach an agreement, a consent decree, with those who filed the lawsuit. The settlement mandated changes within the juvenile prisons and specified conditions under which the state could continue to operate the prisons.

This research analyzes the model treatment program that was the center of the state's attempts to construct a new prison environment. The examination of this specific prison system is placed within the context of the more encompassing national controversies about crime, violence, and punishment.

Juvenile Crime, Public Fear, Political Symbolism

Widespread expressions of public fear, political rhetoric advocating increased punishment, and concern over the failure of prisons have become salient and seemingly permanent features of the contemporary landscape. These problems are magnified when the prisoners are young people, legal minors under the age of eighteen.

Overall, violence is declining in the United States, but youth crime has increased steadily and dramatically. Between 1985 and 1994, the rate of murders committed by adolescents aged fourteen to seventeen increased by 172 percent, and the number of adolescents killing with guns increased 400 percent. From 1989 to 1994, the adolescent arrest rate for the violent crimes of murder, rape, robbery, and aggravated assault increased 46 percent.[4] Many people fear that juvenile crime and violence are skyrocketing out of control, and they believe these trends reflect the destruction of the social fabric.

Delinquent youths and the perplexing question of how they should be dealt with are among the most widely discussed controversies in society today. There are insistent calls for increased punishment, especially for those youths who end up in prison. Incarceration in juvenile prisons and transferring youths to adult courts for prosecution are among the most prominent and strongly advocated "solutions" to the juvenile crime problem.[5] In contrast to traditional American images of young people as unsophisticated and meriting guidance and treatment, imprisoned youths are viewed as fully responsible "young adults" rather than children. The harsh punishment once reserved for hardened adult criminals has become a primary response to the young.

More than 55,000 young people are incarcerated in the United States each year at a rate greater than that of any nation in the world, and that rate continues to rise.[6] The number and proportion of youths imprisoned and the lengths of their stays in prison have increased dramatically in the past fifteen years as juvenile justice policies have shifted from an official emphasis on rehabilitation to one of punishment.[7] Unanswered questions include what happens in these prisons and, equally important, who imprisoned youths are. Prison conditions and youths' experiences within prisons are hidden from the public eye.[8] Juvenile prisons are less scrutinized than adult prisons, and youths have less access to the outside world than do adult prisoners.[9] Abuses are possible and occur even when rehabilitation is the rationale for juvenile prisons; the possibilities are magnified when institutions have a punitive mandate.

Our society has a long history of imprisoning young people. What has changed throughout the years has been the moral and political justifications for this imprisonment.[10] Always, power and ideology are at the heart of the incarceration of the young: systems of domination and belief are as consequential and real as razor-wire fences and locked cells.

Today, calls for increased punishment of youths contain powerful symbolism. Public figures gain political capital by portraying delinquent youths as a primary cause of societal problems and by advocating "get tough" policies as the answer to those problems.[11] Simplified and politicized images portray imprisoned youths as uniformly and singularly violent and as recalcitrant and inhuman monsters.[12]

While youth violence has increased greatly, two additional facts are equally important: (1) most imprisoned youths have not committed violent crimes, and (2) prisons have failed to combat youth crime. The image of incarcerated juveniles as predominantly violent, hard-core delinquents provides ideological and immediate justification for their imprisonment, yet it is an erroneous generalization. Nationwide, fewer than 20 percent of the youths detained prior to trial have been accused of violent offenses, and fewer yet—only 14 percent of those institutionalized after trial—have been found guilty of violence or serious felonies.[13] (In Arizona, 15 percent of young people committed to the juvenile prison system have been found guilty of a violent offense.[14]) Even in programs geared toward the most serious offenders, such as the model treatment program, only 37 percent of the youths have been imprisoned for violent offenses.

Three points are central to this analysis. First, important commonalities exist among imprisoned youths. They are disproportionately poor, male, and members of racial and ethnic minorities. For many, alcohol and drug use and/or gang membership are central to their identities. Most have histories of abuse, rejection, and failure within their families, schools, and general society. Second, great variation also exists among imprisoned youths in terms of their delinquency histories, personal propensities, and future possibilities. Finally, by virtue of their experiences on the streets and in prisons, imprisoned youths are unlike many other youths, but they are also similar to other youths in their immaturity, vulnerability, and lack of decision-making abilities.

Young people in prison share a similar fate; but they have individual human faces, and they vary considerably from each other and from the images that permeate society. There is a sameness, a similarity between imprisoned youths and other children. Simultaneously, there are differences and estrangements between imprisoned youths and others—estrangements of history, circumstance, social realities, and future probabilities. Imprisoned youths may not be "just like everyone else," but neither are they devoid of the characteristics and desires attributed to other members of society. This research demonstrates that imprisoned youths are childlike but also excluded from being children. Their situations can be explained, in part, by this disjuncture.

These understandings are important if we are to comprehend the complexities of youth crime and imprisonment. They are indispensable if we are to deal effectively with youths as well as with the widespread fear and anger that currently influence and are fueled by public policy. Until society acknowledges and grapples with the depth and complexity of these youths' lives, attempts to control crime and violence will fail.

It is crucial to scrutinize the social and political context in which the debates about delinquency, violence, and imprisonment occur. While it is important to address the controversies surrounding imprisoned young people, it is essential to do so in a manner that goes beyond abstract arguments and provides a more encompassing and intricate portrait of the human beings involved and the social structures that engulf them.

This book examines incarcerated youths' places in society as well as their lives in prison, focusing on their immediate environments and the larger social and economic context in which they live. It emphasizes the necessary link between a youth's imprisonment and eventual release, recognizing that most prisons prioritize compliance with institutional regimes rather than preparation for a successful return to society.[15] This is about youth in prison, those charged with their keeping, and the society that condones and demands this imprisonment.

Politics and emphasize the need to imprison delinquent y fact that those youths will eventually retur youths' prison experiences fail to provide them e survival strategies and fail to change their perspec- kely that their illegal behavior will escalate. It is impera- e far more selective about which youths are imprisoned and reate effective programs for those who are. We also need to have the courage to envision a society without prisons.

The model program that is the subject of this research merits attention because it provides a viable alternative to the abysmal failure of current prisons. It was an innovative attempt to stop wholesale incarceration, to make youths' prison experiences meaningful, and, thus, to decrease youth crime. It sought to change youths and to change their life chances by providing them with the skills necessary to survive and succeed in society.

One of the most unique and promising aspects of the model program was its explicit attempt to deal with power relations. Articulated in terms such as accountability, responsibility, and mutual respect, the program expressly dealt with power as it circulated among administrators, staff, youths, parents, and other members of society. The emphasis on mutual respect, participatory decision making, and the ultimate objective of enabling youths to succeed in the community represented not the eradication of power structures but rather an explicit recognition and critique of those structures. The program planned to enhance a sense of personal power for each youth, parent, and staff member by facilitating opportunities for human agency—that is, opportunities to affirm one's existence and the ability to act purposefully.

The program's philosophy emphasized protecting the public through effective services for youths and families. It acknowledged the pivotal role played by social institutions in the creation of delinquency and, simultaneously, emphasized youths' accountability for their harmful behaviors toward others. It attempted to balance a concern and respect for those harmed by imprisoned youths with respect for the humanity and potential of the youths. Such balance was envisioned as being integral to achieving meaningful change—change within that system of incarceration, change within the community, and change in the lives and futures of the youths.

Because imprisoning youths has become a major social policy, we must confront what happens within youth prisons. This research is relevant to any social change effort, but it is especially crucial for those engaged in creating policies and programs for youths. It is important to analyze how the model program succeeded during its early days and to analyze why it was never fully implemented. The problems included structural and political impediments, institutional and bureaucratic inertia, and individual failings. This analysis outlines what contributed to the program's demise, but it also affirms the model program's fundamental philosophy and structure. The research suggests that programs such as this could provide the basis for fundamental change in juvenile prisons. It also articulates the formidable political and ideological barriers to such change.

Going Inside the Prison

This book is the result of two years of intense interaction (twenty-five to thirty hours per week) with youths, staff members, and administrators of the prison, buttressed by fifteen years of juvenile justice research in Arizona. Uncensored access was a condition of the research, and thus access to the prison and its employees was made possible. Both administrators and staff members cooperated fully. Access to the youths was also part of the official agreement, but meaningful access to them in terms of their interest and participation was not automatic. This book exists primarily because the youths and staff members were willing to talk with us, formally and informally, and to interact freely.

In addition to extensive interactions within the prison, our research also scrutinized youths' histories and their involvements with the prison system. These included their family and educational backgrounds, the types of offenses with which they had been charged or convicted, the number of times they had been involved with the prison system, and the events that led to their current imprisonment.

We have attempted to maintain the confidentiality of youths, their families, and staff members and, as much as possible, to shield them from being individually identifiable.[16] It is less possible to mask the identities of several key officials because of their unique positions, for at any specific time there is only one director of juvenile corrections or one governor. But cloaking their identities is a lesser concern because they are elected or appointed public servants; their level of public accountability is qualitatively different from the line staff or the youths and their families.

The originators of the program, especially the director of juvenile corrections, wanted us to evaluate the program and wanted to be identified with it. They wanted the model to be explained and disseminated in order to reach a national audience—both inside and outside of juvenile prisons—that would assess and potentially adopt the program.

Although researchers frequently are at great pains to conceal the specific location of research, it is impossible to hide the identity of the state involved.[17] This is due to the necessity of providing the particulars of the lawsuit and consent decree central to the research. But the naming of Arizona should not encourage anyone to believe that this book is solely, or even primarily, about one state, for there have been twenty similar lawsuits nationwide since 1977.[18] The trends and controversies in this state are evident nationwide: this is about our entire society.

Throughout our analysis, we resist the euphemisms, the pleasant but misleading language and labels—however comfortable and comforting they may be—that are commonly used in the juvenile justice system. We call the institutions "prisons," not "secure schools." We call incarcerated youths "prisoners," not "students." We do this because the special language of juvenile justice denies the realities of prison conditions and perpetuates myths and untruths about what is happening to these young people. These youths, as well as many others, are imprisoned under conditions resembling adult prisons.[19] It is impossible to ignore the level of control, the razor wire, electronic gates, and the harsh and punitive nature of these institutions, historically and currently.

Although it is difficult to convey what prison is like, as much as possible we want to provide a glimpse of the inside and an opportunity to listen to youths' words about their imprisonment and their lives. We want to facilitate insight into these youths' complicated and controversial situations, including their own physical and sexual abuse, family lives, educational experiences, drug use and abuse, relationships with gangs, and the many factors that contribute to their sense of well-being and their sense of failure in society.

Change might be possible, if only each of us could experience this prison world through the youthful eyes, the bodies and desires, the experiences and longings, the dreams and nightmares of even one youth, or each youth in turn, or all of them collectively . . . to know them for even a brief moment, to experience a glimpse of all of this.

One
The Impetus and Hope for Change

CITIZENS HAVE VIRTUALLY NO INFORMATION ABOUT what happens to imprisoned youths. In those rare instances when events and conditions come to light, outsiders often denounce the neglect, inhumanity, and brutality that occur, while maintaining the need for prisons. Even those who view punishment as extreme deprivation may denounce "abuses of power," but it is likely that blame will be placed on individuals, not policies or politics. Least likely to be acknowledged is the fact that the deprivation and abuses that occur primarily reflect the power inequities inherent in total institutions such as prisons, especially those for the young.[1]

Abhorrent, inhumane conditions within juvenile institutions nationwide have been thoroughly documented in the past, and include a long list of abuses. Lawsuits record staff-administered beatings and tear-gassings, sexual assaults, the inhumane use of solitary confinement, physical brutality, and abuse;[2] padded cells without windows or furnishings, flush holes for toilets, and youths being denied access to all services or programs except a Bible;[3] inmates locked in solitary confinement, beaten, kicked, slapped, and sprayed with mace by staff; inmates required to scrub floors with a toothbrush; and youths subjected to such punitive practices as standing and sitting for prolonged periods without changing positions.[4] Court cases also tell of young people who have died in confinement.[5]

Although there had long been calls for change within Arizona's juvenile prisons, the primary impetus for mandated reform came from the case filed in U.S. District Court in 1986—a case that soon became a class-action lawsuit. *Johnson v Upchurch* charged that the "policies, practices, and conditions of confinement" at the juvenile institution near Tucson subjected youths to "cruel, unconscionable, and illegal conditions of confinement." These conditions violated their rights as granted by the First, Sixth, Eighth, and Fourteenth Amendments to the U.S. Constitution, by the Arizona State Constitution, and by federal and state statutes.[6]

The original case was filed on behalf of Matthew Davey Johnson by his father. Matthew had been imprisoned after "hitching a ride on a train" and, once imprisoned, "refused to perform hard labor on a work crew and insisted on receiving schooling."[7] Matthew would not participate in a work crew whose job was to "rake rocks"—that is, "continually smoothing out the desert landscape to remove traces of footprints and other indentations."[8]

Matthew's refusal to do this work and his arguments with staff members resulted in confinement in the prison's disciplinary unit.

> [Prison Superintendent] Upchurch established his authority by having youth who refused to do this work in the scorching Arizona heat, including Matt, shackled and handcuffed to the fence so they would have to stay in the sun with the rest of the work crews. . . . After a verbal altercation between Matt Johnson and a cottage supervisor, Upchurch decided that motivational hold [solitary confinement] was appropriate for Matt as well.[9]

Matthew had been incarcerated for over a year and reached age eighteen by the time his case became a class-action lawsuit incorporating seven other youths who were under eighteen years old and incarcerated at the time of the lawsuit.[10] Two of the youths were fourteen years old, one was fifteen, and four were seventeen. Importantly, the class on whose behalf the suit was filed consisted of "all juveniles who are now or who in the future will be confined" at the institution.[11] The lawsuit further stated that, because the injurious and illegal policies and practices were capable of being repeated as well as evading review, remedial measures on behalf of all confined youths were appropriate.

Those whom the lawsuit named as defendants, that is, the responsible and blameworthy persons, included both prison officials and the state's board of education and superintendent of public instruction.[12] The lawsuit described harsh conditions, arbitrary and capricious decision making, and an unduly punitive, unrehabilitative environment. It was a graphic portrait of deprivation and injury, focusing on the prison's internal disciplinary actions and conditions of solitary confinement. The "cottage" used for punishment consisted of sixteen 9' x 9' cells of concrete block construction with bare cement floors and heavy barred doors, fourteen of which had no furnishings except for a heavy metal bed frame stationed on metal legs; the remaining two contained uncovered institutional-style toilets and sinks as well. The cells were further described as inadequately heated in winter, inadequately cooled in summer, inadequately lighted, unclean, unsanitary, and unsafe.

The lawsuit documented youths' conditions of confinement and demonstrated prison officials' failure to acknowledge the punitive dimensions of the disciplinary unit.

[Prison authorities] confine juveniles as young as 11 years old in these cells for 24 hours a day with nothing to do. [Prison authorities] do not provide them with education, counseling, exercise, or recreation. They get no reading material. They eat all of their meals in the cells. They are not released to a day-room, and their contact with the outside world is restricted. When asked why juveniles are confined like this without programming or other diversions, the security captain replied:

When they are up here on disciplinary the theory is they're thinking about what brought them to disciplinary. They're talking about tomorrow, about why they're in disciplinary and hopefully that they won't have to return. If they're up here entertaining themselves I don't think those things—kind of things would be accomplished.

Defendants confine juveniles at [the prison] under such conditions in order to punish them so that they will reflect on their misdeeds and change their behavior. When asked what he expects juveniles confined under these conditions to do, [the director of prisons] replied:

I suppose that my expectation of what [youths in isolation] would do during the day is to reflect upon their current circumstances and to think about what they have gotten themselves into and to create that time for them to do some reflection of changes that they need to make in their lives. So I suppose I would summarize it as an opportunity to meditate.[13]

Youths were confined in these cells for periods ranging from several hours to weeks to months. The initial plaintiff, Matthew Johnson, had been kept there for eighty-three days, fifty of those days consecutively; another youth had been confined in the cells on at least seven occasions for periods as long as thirteen days; and another on at least thirty occasions for periods as long as seven days. The lawsuit stated that youths being disciplined were confined in the cells for twenty-four hours a day except for brief periods to use the bathroom or shower or for periods of forced exercise. Youths were permitted to shower only every other day and to leave their cells to exercise only after they had been in solitary confinement for five consecutive days. It was further charged that occasionally youths were denied permission to leave their cells to go to the bathroom and, of necessity, urinated or defecated on the floors of their cells.

The lawsuit also alleged that youths had not been provided adequate clothing. After being strip-searched, they were given only a jumpsuit to wear and, on occasion, confined with no clothing except underwear. The bedding provided was inadequate. Youths were given a mattress and one small blanket each night, which were removed from the cell each morning and, as additional punishment, might also be withheld at night.

Entries in staff members' "logs" were used to confirm that depressed, agitated, and emotionally disturbed children had been locked in solitary confinement without adequate measures to protect them against self-injury, which resulted in youths "cutting," hanging, and otherwise injuring themselves.[14] The abject conditions were described as follows:

> The [disciplinary] program and the conditions under which juveniles are held in the [unit] are psychologically damaging. Juveniles spend their time locked in small cells without even the relief from boredom and sensory deprivation that comes with work and school. Cramped quarters, unremitting boredom and sensory deprivation, perceived heckling, and increasing feelings of hopelessness and helplessness characterize [the disciplinary unit].
>
> Juveniles [in the disciplinary unit] have reacted to these conditions by cutting themselves with pieces of glass, metal, mattress buttons, tin foil, plastic, fingernails, and any other object they can find. They have attempted to hang themselves from nooses made from jumpsuits, shorts, socks, blankets, torn pieces of mattresses, and braided toilet paper. They have ingested toxic substances, foreign objects, and overdoses of medications. Juveniles confined [in the disciplinary unit] have eaten paint they have chipped off the walls, eaten bug spray they have scraped off the floor with paper, bitten themselves, and banged their heads against their cell doors, windows, and beds. They have become "hysterical," "cried," hallucinated that "bugs were crawling all over him," saved their own blood in cups, refused to eat, banged on the cell doors with their fists and/or feet, sworn at staff, spit at staff, broken ceiling light fixtures in the cells, urinated or defecated in their cells and thrown feces and urine, thrown food at staff, started fires in their cells, and flooded their cells.[15]

Suicidal youths were confined in the same unit as disciplinary cases, and staff working there received no suicide prevention training.

> The attempted suicide of [one of the youths in the lawsuit] on October 13, 1986, is an example of how poorly equipped and prepared [disciplinary unit] staff are to respond to juveniles on close observation. [The youth] attempted to hang himself with the seam piping from his mattress. The [staff member] who found him had no scissors and had to chew through the rope to get [the youth] down.[16]

In January 1988, a youth committed suicide. "[The youth] hung himself in a [disciplinary unit] cell while on close observation. A two- to three-minute delay in [the nurse's] initial examination of [the youth] was caused by the security captain's questioning [of the nurse] about how it could be determined whether [the youth] was 'faking it.' This delay possibly cost [the youth] his life."[17]

The lawsuit also charged that there were insufficient precautions in the event of fire. Cells were locked with individual padlocks, and there were poor evacuation plans. There were insufficient psychiatric and psychological counseling and other mental health services for youths, including those who had injured or attempted to injure themselves. Young people were not provided with educational programs, appropriate reading materials, rehabilitative treatment, or counseling programs. Youths had suffered and continued to suffer serious emotional and physical injury as a result of punitive confinement.

The lawsuit stated that, although there was a ten-day limit established for regular stays in the disciplinary unit, youths could be held indefinitely and subjected to unconstitutional conditions by placing them on "motivational hold."[18] The youths were usually confined to their cells continuously for the first week and then permitted to leave the unit only to perform hard labor or to attend school; sometimes they were denied the opportunity to participate in any educational program.

Contact between youths within the punishment unit and individuals outside the prison was greatly restricted. Only parents were permitted, and visits were limited to a half hour on Saturdays and Sundays—if at all. Youths were not permitted to communicate by telephone with family members. For example, Matthew Johnson was not permitted to visit with his father or to receive telephone calls from him for three months.

The lawsuit maintained that youths were subject to "cruel, excessive, harsh, and brutal punishments" for violations of institutional rules, including ones that were "petty, vague, and ambiguous." It decried the use of police-style handcuffs and leg shackles, solitary confinement, punitive segregation, and extending youths' sentences "for such rule violations as smoking cigarettes, swearing, 'staff disrespect,' 'excessive horseplay,' and 'rumor of AWOL.'"[19]

The lawsuit also objected to the routine use of handcuffs when any youth was taken to or moved from the disciplinary unit, calling the practice excessive and unnecessary because it was used even when youths offered no resistance and posed no threat to the security of the institution. Frequently, youths who had agreed to go peacefully to the disciplinary unit objected to being handcuffed, and staff were instructed to use whatever force was necessary to handcuff them.[20] Handcuffs, shackles, and belly-chains were also used on all youths leaving the prison for hospital or medical emergencies or appointments.[21]

A specific practice targeted for strong criticism was that of using handcuffs to bind youths' arms and legs to the corners of bed frames, a practice known as "four-pointing." A "routine part of the institutional environment," the practice was authorized for a wide range of behaviors, including when youths were "banging and disrupting their [living units]" and when youths in the disciplinary unit were "disruptive for more than fifteen minutes."[22] One of the youths in the lawsuit had been "four-pointed" and left on a metal bed frame for several hours because "he was involved in a fight."[23] Two methods of four-pointing were used:

Method 1 involves placing a [youth] face down on a bed and strapping his arms and legs to the bed frame with leather straps. . . . Method 2 involves handcuffing a [youth's] wrists to his ankles with metal handcuffs while he is seated on a mattress on the floor.[24]

The lawsuit reported that there was no policy regarding clothing or covering for youths who were four-pointed and quoted staff records stating that youths were four-pointed for hours while naked or clothed only in underwear.[25] Two hours was the initial period for four-pointing a youth, after which the handcuffs were removed and the youth was permitted to stand and to go to the bathroom. If the youth made a verbal commitment to cease the behavior that resulted in the use of restraints, the handcuffs were not reapplied. Refusal to make a commitment resulted in additional four-pointing for two-hour intervals until such a commitment was made. There was no requirement that medical or psychological staff be involved in the decision to reapply restraints, and, importantly, "there [was] no limit to the number of two-hour increments nor a maximum period of time that a resident [could] be kept in four-point restraints."[26] Staff logs and "use of force reports" revealed four-pointing of youths ranging from four hours to throughout the night.[27]

The lawsuit stated that no special training was provided for security officers in handling out-of-control, self-destructive, or severely depressed youths, nor were they instructed how to counsel youths to reduce or eliminate behavior that might result in the need for four-point restraints. This, combined with the fact that youths had to "make a commitment" to the same staff members who had four-pointed them, resulted in "restrained juveniles and security staff frequently [engaging] in power struggles while a resident [was] restrained with neither one willing to 'give in' to the other."[28]

A major issue raised by the lawsuit was the systematic denial of due process to youths in the meting out of punishment. According to the lawsuit, inadequately trained and supervised staff, as well as nonemployee volunteer "counselors," were authorized "to impose cruel and harsh punishments in an arbitrary and capricious manner."[29] Youths were punished without adequate due process, such as

M. A. Bortner and Linda M. Williams

specification of alleged violations or hearings adequate to determine whether the rule violation had actually occurred, whether the youth charged actually committed the violation, and what sanction was most appropriate. Nor was there an effective grievance or appeal process for those who had been subjected to "arbitrary, cruel, excessive, and illegal punishments."[30]

Specific accusations regarding the lack of adequate medical care charged that prison officials had failed to screen and evaluate youths' medical, dental, and mental health needs; to provide adequate and appropriate medical, counseling, and mental health services to youths who had cut, hanged, or otherwise injured themselves; to design and implement an adequate and appropriate treatment procedure for those who were injured or ill or to provide an appropriate facility to provide for their needs; and to protect youths from the excessive or inappropriate use of psychotropic and antidepressant drugs—specifically, prison officials were charged with administering such drugs in order to punish and control youths.

The prison system's educational efforts, most notably the lack of special education programs, came under harsh scrutiny and criticism in the lawsuit, especially in light of the fact the institutions received federal funds associated with the Education for All Handicapped Children Act. The lawsuit charged that the system did not adequately evaluate youths to determine whether they had special education needs and how such needs could be met and failed to develop appropriate individualized education plans for youths who required special education. One youth named in the lawsuit had a stuttering problem, and another with speech and language disorders had been diagnosed as seriously emotionally disturbed, and yet they were not receiving appropriate treatment.

In connection with this, the lawsuit also charged that the prison system failed to hire, adequately train, and supervise sufficient numbers of qualified personnel to meet the special education and related needs of juveniles. At the time of the lawsuit there were no special education classes at the institution, because the special education teacher position had been vacant for at least three months. The lawsuit also alleged that the system failed to monitor the institution to ensure that all eligible handicapped juveniles were identified, evaluated, and provided with appropriate and necessary special education and related services in a manner that complied with the requirements of federal and state statutes and regulations. Finally, the lawsuit accused prison officials of impropriety and illegality when they read, confiscated, and withheld youths' legal documents and communications with their attorneys, as happened to Matthew Johnson despite his objections and repeated requests that material be returned.

The lawsuit harshly criticized the state prison system for what it was doing and for what it was failing to do. State educational authorities were implicated as accomplices. Practices, procedures, and conditions at the institutions were condemned as arbitrary, cruel, and illegal, and the system was accused of not meeting its responsibility to provide individualized treatment for imprisoned youths and of failing to guarantee that such treatment would occur in a safe environment appropriate to each youth's needs.

The lawsuit claimed that many youths were inappropriately imprisoned and that their rehabilitation as well as public safety needs could be addressed in alternative settings. It offered as examples youths who were imprisoned for running away from a group home, for a probation violation involving loitering, and while awaiting the outcome of a joy-riding charge. It further alleged that, because the state had failed to design and implement an appropriate classification system, youths were arbitrarily confined to the institution regardless of their individual educational, vocational, psychological, or treatment needs.

The lawsuit asked the federal appellate court to order individuals in charge of the juvenile prison to stop "engaging in unconstitutional and unlawful acts and practices" and to begin fulfilling their legal responsibilities to youths. It also requested that the court take jurisdiction—that is, stay involved and be in charge—"until such time as the Court is satisfied that their unlawful policies, practices, acts, and omissions complained of herein no longer exist and will not recur."[31] In effect, the federal court had the power to close the state's juvenile institutions, to approve or disapprove suggested reforms, and, ultimately, to fine or jail responsible officials, including the state's governor, if illegalities continued or if a resolution via a consent decree was not negotiated or was violated.

◼ Negotiating a Consent Decree and Envisioning a New Era

The class-action lawsuit focused on solitary confinement in the "discipline" or "isolation" unit at the juvenile prison near Tucson and on those youths whom staff considered the most problematic, disruptive, and uncooperative—"the worst" of all incarcerated delinquents. The lawsuit did not allege that all youths in the prisons or even all youths subjected to disciplinary actions had been mistreated. Such allegations were unnecessary: the heart of the lawsuit was that abuses had occurred, some routinely and others occasionally, and that the prison structure, its policies and practices, made such abuses possible and probable. Accordingly, as the consent decree was negotiated, it applied to the entire system and treated the conditions of solitary confinement as representative or indicative of the overall conditions of youths confined in state juvenile prisons.[32]

After a two-year period of extensive investigation and pretrial discovery,[33] and at the direction of the appellate court, attorneys for the youths submitted a 268-page "Proof of Facts" document that described juvenile justice in Arizona as "a system run amuck" and disciplinary practices as "arbitrary and cruel."[34] Chief among the problems identified in the document was the fact that, because juvenile and adult institutions were run by the same state agency, "adult corrections continued to be funded at the expense of juvenile corrections," which obliterated the philosophical and operational distinctions between the two systems with adult correctional philosophy and procedures clearly dominating.[35]

The document stated that the disciplinary system at the juvenile prison was much like those in the adult prisons operated by the state Department of Corrections, "except the adult institutions are better."[36] Other criticisms included that the head of the prison system was unable to identify any significant differences between the juvenile disciplinary unit's cells and the cells in the maximum security adult prison, which houses the state's death row inmates.[37] The report also asserted that although prison officials knew that youths had harmed themselves, they had not analyzed the patterns of confinement in the disciplinary unit or the lengths of sentences.[38] Finally, officials acknowledged that, "because of the high incidence of attempted hangings in [the juvenile institution's disciplinary unit], staff began wearing scissors on their belts [approximately eighteen months after the lawsuit was filed]."[39]

Under the direction of the appeals court judge, seven years later a consent decree was negotiated whereby the state of Arizona agreed to extensive and specific changes in its juvenile institutions.[40] The negotiation process was detailed, arduous, and time consuming, but it was conducted in an extremely fastidious and thorough manner.[41] The case on behalf of Matthew Johnson, originally filed in April 1986, resulted in a model treatment program that was initiated in April 1992 as a major component of the state's efforts to respond to the lawsuit. On May 5, 1993, the official consent decree was signed by all parties.

The stipulations of the consent decree maintained that each youth has a right to individualized care and treatment in the "least restrictive setting consistent with the youth's needs and protection of the public." Accordingly, the diagnostic evaluation when a youth first enters prison was to include "a standardized, objective classification or risk assessment instrument" to determine what level of programming and confinement each youth requires. After the diagnostic period, only three categories of youths were to be kept in the locked, secure state institutions: those who pose a threat to public safety; those with histories of "persistent and delinquent offenses" that, as demonstrated through the use of other alternatives, cannot be controlled in a less secure setting; and those who have had their parole from prison revoked.[42]

The consent decree established specific population limits for the prisons that were significantly below the populations at the time.[43] It made an explicit commitment to decrease the prison population by returning youths to the community as expeditiously as possible.[44] Two primary beliefs underlay this priority. The first was that the majority of imprisoned youths did not need the maximum-security environment of the existing system, that is, they did not need to be in prison. The appeals court judge, youth advocates, and many prison personnel believed that these youths and the community were better served by community-based programs incorporating the principles of the model program.

The second belief was that greatly decreasing the prison population was imperative in order for the model program to be implemented successfully for those youths who were viewed as requiring incarceration in a secure setting. Intensive interactions between staff and youths, as well as the individualized educational and treatment programs, were inconceivable within the crowded, understaffed institutions.

The Model Program: Responsibilities, Rights, and Respect

The model program was conducted in specific living units within two juvenile prisons. Located in the desert beyond the metropolitan areas, the prison complexes are surrounded by twenty-foot chain-link fences topped with razor wire. Authorized personnel enter through two electronic gates in the fences, after being monitored by camera and cleared over the intercom. Signs on the highways announce, "Detention center. Do not stop for hitchhikers." In addition to housing units, each complex contains an administration building, schools, a gymnasium, outdoor playing fields for softball and football, a few basketball courts, a health unit, a chapel, a kitchen and dining facility, storage buildings, and a lockdown facility. The larger prison, located outside Phoenix, housed about 275 youths at the time of the research. The smaller prison, situated near Tucson, housed about 145 youths. The model program began in a single living unit in each facility.

Grounded both in accountability and change, the model program explicitly stated that it intended to respect and validate the very personhood of those involved, to build a sense of community, and to develop an environment of mutual support and empathy in which everyone involved endeavored to understand each other's roles, problems, and fears. "Collective problem solving" in an atmosphere of respect was to replace inflexible rules: the right to question and disagree was to be honored, and the free flow of dialogue was heralded as essential to change.

Personal application of the treatment ideals was the quintessential value, and the program was to constantly urge each youth to question, "What does this have to do with me?" The model officially prioritized continuity between the prison and the community, advocating an integrated and holistic approach called "a continuum of care." The program's proposed atmosphere of mutual respect, constant discussion, evaluation of approaches, and exploration of alternatives was to highlight the relationship between prison programs and the youths' lives upon their release to the community. The daily routine was designed to help youths acquire the competencies necessary to complete the program and return to their communities.

The model program acknowledged the tremendous influence of social forces on youths' behaviors. But it also proposed to instill a sense of agency in them, literally to proclaim that they existed and could act in a meaningful way to bring about change in their lives. The program sought to give youths a greater sense of control over their lives, to encourage them to affirm their own worth, and to engender hope for the future. The model program urged youths to address their past behaviors by emphasizing self-conscious efforts to know and understand their past motivations and present potential.[45]

The most essential objective was not that youths adapt to institutional life, learn to please staff, and "earn" release through compliance and conformity. Instead, their return to the community was viewed as the litmus test of the program, and the efficacy of the program was to be assessed in terms of its relevance to life on the outside. This commitment was evident in planning for family events within the prison, such as potluck dinners and holiday celebrations, in an active volunteer program linking youths with community members, and in setting up programs in the community for family members and youths released from prison.

Clearly, one of the program's most unique and visionary aspects was its commitment to dealing with youths' total needs, including the psychological, spiritual, and existential dimensions of their lives in the world. This included grappling with the enormous problems of "meaninglessness, hopelessness, and (most importantly) lovelessness" that result in a "numbing detachment from others and a self-destructive disposition toward the world."[46]

The model treatment program was envisioned as a participatory and reflective process in which mutual respect and collective decision making would be preeminent at all levels. Youths, "line staff" working directly with them, teachers in the institution, and the central administration were to be afforded respect and to give respect to each other. This was to occur in a safe, clean, adequately equipped physical environment that permitted a modest amount of privacy as well as extensive interaction and exchange. Although hierarchical dimensions were undeniable, the model program proposed an atmosphere in which all individuals were told they would be regarded as members of the "treatment team," permitted, encouraged, and expected to question what was happening on a day-to-day basis and to contribute to the ongoing development of the program.[47]

The program was conceived and designed by a thirty-person committee, which was composed of administrators and institutional staff.[48] The model embodied specific ideas of the new director and associate director as well as program elements proposed by outside experts.[49] It reflected the many years of experience of the participating staff members and administrators. The program was guided by a Code of Ethics and Philosophy Statement that captured the essence of the treatment model (see Figures 1.1 and 1.2). These statements embodied an alternative organizational model that contrasted greatly with the standard, traditional ways in which juvenile prisons and organizations in general have operated. Rather than emphasizing preexisting rules and viewing compliance with those rules as the primary objective, this model combined a collective formulation of values and rules with mutually recognized reasons for change and action.[50] The impact of this structure on the feelings, beliefs, and behavior of the individuals within the prison was the most important consideration. The primary concern was the extent to which the program influenced the youths, but inextricably bound to their fate were the staff members and administrators and, in a larger sense, the governor's office, the state legislature, and the community.

Figure 1.1 **Philosophy Statement**

We believe that:

- The Department is accountable to the people of Arizona for promoting the public safety through the development and implementation of individual treatment services for youth.
- The cooperative efforts of staff, youth, families, professionals, volunteers, and community services provided in a therapeutic milieu will make our vision a reality.
- All youth entrusted to our care regardless of race, creed, color, national origin, or sex are entitled to equal access to due process and to a quality continuum of services.
- Youth thrive in an environment which promotes dignity, mutual responsibility, self-esteem, respect, and joy.
- Youth must live in a safe environment, while providing the least restrictive care required to meet their individual needs.
- All learning occurs within a context of interpersonal relationships.
- Human interactions are too complex to become wedded to one theory or approach. Flexibility and a willingness to see with new eyes is crucial.
- Youth make their own decisions and that acceptance of this responsibility for choice is progress towards personal development.
- Youth should be held accountable for their actions; it is essential for youth to understand the effects of their behavior.
- The context for behavior includes factors within the youth's inner and outer environment.
- The assessment of needs must embrace all aspects of the youth's life.
- By completing outcome-based objectives in academic, vocational, and social skill areas in partnership with families and community resources, youth will be empowered to become productive members of their community.
- We have a responsibility to gather data, evaluate, and ensure the effectiveness of our program.
- Crisis is opportunity; growth occurs through successful resolution of crisis.

Arizona Department of Youth Treatment and Rehabilitation

Figure 1.2 **Code of Ethics**

The Department is committed to a Code of Ethics that will guide the performance, conduct, and behavior of employees entrusted by the State to provide care and a continuum of individualized services to committed youth.

This Code will ensure that our professionalism is reflected in the operation and activities of the Department and is recognized by all. In this light, the following principles are practiced:

- I shall uphold the tenets of the United States Constitution, its Amendments, the Arizona Constitution, Federal and State laws, rules and regulations, and policies of the Department.
- I shall instill in youth a sense of honesty and integrity, for it takes only a single instance of dishonesty to undercut the tenuous foundations of trust.
- I shall be firm, yet fair, with youth consistent with their individualized treatment needs. I shall treat others with dignity, respect, and compassion, while providing humane care void of retribution, harassment, or abuse.
- I shall instill a sense of caring in youth, realizing the most important thing that I can offer is myself.
- I shall instill a sense of rightness as adults are powerful role models. When wrong, I shall admit it. I realize if youth are to admit their shortcomings, that I myself, must acknowledge my own imperfections.
- I shall instill a sense of reasonableness, realizing that rules, regulations, and instructions should not be imposed in an arbitrary, authoritarian manner. As a role model, I shall display respect for youth by communicating why certain rules and consequences exist and are necessary without being drawn into a defensive posture.
- I shall instill a sense of dependability with youth as I realize the importance of keeping my word. If youth cannot depend on me to keep my personal commitments, to maintain my regular work schedule, and to act conscientiously, they have nothing to build on.
- I shall build a sense of mutual support with youth, fellow staff, parents, and other interested parties. I shall avoid overt staff conflict by communicating in a spirit of positive cooperation.
- I shall not accept or solicit from anyone, either directly or indirectly, anything of economic value such as gift, gratuity, favor, entertainment, or loan, which is or may appear to be designed to influence my official conduct.

Figure 1.2 **Code of Ethics** (cont.)

> ▪ I shall report without reservation any corrupt, illegal, or unethical behavior which could affect either youth, staff, the public, or the integrity of the Department.
>
> ▪ I will not discriminate against any youth, staff, or any member of the public on the basis of race, gender, creed, or national origin.
>
> *Arizona Department of Youth Treatment and Rehabilitation*

The model emphasized the importance that value systems play in the long-term treatment of youths. The program's objective was not to produce robots who could succeed within the highly structured institution; the goal was to encourage youths to develop values that transcend and outlast the prison structure.[51]

On a day-to-day basis, these goals were pursued through five basic programs: Keys to Innervisions, Limit and Lead, Therapeutic Crisis Intervention, Success School, and the Level System. These diverse components were intended to support and reinforce each other in the creation of a therapeutic milieu conducive to accountability, meaningful individualized treatment, and change. Each component and activity was to provide an essential treatment element and, together, they were to create a comprehensive, integrated system.

The Model Program's Essential Elements

The program's comprehensive emphasis on reflection and interaction was evident in the youths' daily routines. (See Figure 1.3 for daily schedules.) Their time was spent in intensive group sessions, individual counseling, and educational pursuits. Recreation, "responsibility time" (for chores and personal hygiene), and free time (for relaxation, letter writing, and television) were strictly monitored, and activities that dominated life in the other prison units, including watching television, were reduced to a minimum. Youths were constantly involved in goal-directed activities and all-encompassing group discussions. Days began and ended with youth-led "affirmation groups," in which individuals declared or reviewed their goals for the day and congratulated each other for behavior consistent with the program. These statements ranged from straightforward and brief comments such as "I want to thank Jorge for helping me" or "I want to make a commitment: I will do better in school today," to more extended statements about the day's events and declarations for the future.

Group discussions were the core of the program when youths were in their living units as well as in school. Originally led by members of the psychology staff, the Limit and Lead program later became the responsibility of all staff members and all teachers. It advocated a counseling strategy to integrate retributive and rehabilitative approaches by limiting youths' harmful behavior, holding them accountable, and helping them to develop new alternatives.[52]

Figure 1.3 **Model Treatment Program Daily Schedules**

Monday–Friday	
5:30 a.m.	Wake up—all youths in rooms cleaning rooms except those completing charges outside their rooms.
6:00	All showered and dressed, rooms cleaned, assigned charges completed, & cleaning supplies put away. Room inspections—checked for neatness & cleanliness (beds made, no wrinkles, tucked in); floor, counters, toilets/sinks clean; every item in its place; all trash in trash cans.
6:30	Affirmation meeting.
6:50	All youth to dress appropriately for line up & movement to kitchen for breakfast.
7:30	Back from kitchen, personal hygiene time.
7:45	All youth line up for movement to school.
11:00	A.M. school returns, limit & lead group.
12:05 p.m.	To kitchen for lunch.
12:45	Back from lunch; P.M. school begins.
3:30–3:45	P.M. school returns
3:45–4:55	Structured group (KIV, social skills, limit & lead).
4:55–5:05	Prepare for dinner.
5:15	Dinner in kitchen.
5:15–6:05	Back from kitchen & evening affirmation meeting.

Figure 1.3 **Model Treatment Program Daily Schedules** (cont.)

6:05–6:25	Evening clean up.
6:30	To recreation.
7:30	Back from recreation, responsibility time begins (showers, homework, & quiet time).
8:30	Evening group & activity.
9:00	Freshman level to bed (10:00 Fri & Sat).
9:30	Sophomore level to bed (10:30 Fri & Sat).
9:45	Junior level to bed (10:45 Fri & Sat).
10:00	Senior level to bed (12:30 Fri & Sat).
	Time between bed times is structured time to include groups, activities, huddle ups, etc.

Saturday

7:00 a.m.	Youths wake up, hygiene, showers, breakfast in cottage.
8:00–8:30	Inside cottage clean up.
8:30–11:30	Outside work crew (visitation takes place in unit from 10:00-11:30).
11:30	Clean up and prepare for lunch in kitchen.
12:00 p.m.	To kitchen for lunch.
12:30	Back from lunch.
12:30–12:55	Hygiene.
1:00–2:00	Structured activity (group games, contests, etc.).
2:00–2:10	Shift change.
2:10–3:15	Structured group (KIV, social skills, limit & lead).
3:15–3:30	Prepare for recreation.
3:30–4:30	Recreation.
4:30–5:05	Responsibility time (showers, clean up, phone calls, etc.).
5:15	Dinner in the kitchen.
5:50	Evening affirmation meeting.
6:15–7:15	Structured group (KIV, social skills, limit & lead).
7:15–8:00	Structured activity (group games, contests, etc.).
8:00	Free time begins.
10:00	Freshman level to bed.
10:30	Sophomore level to bed.
10:45	Junior level to bed.
12:30	Senior level to bed.
	Time between bed times is structured time to include groups, activities, huddle ups, etc.

Figure 1.3 **Model Treatment Program Daily Schedules** (cont.)

Sunday

7:00 a.m.	Youths wake up, breakfast in units.
8:00–9:00	Rooms/unit clean up.
8:30–10:00	Church services/unit free time.
10:00–11:50	Inside/outside work crew.
11:55	To kitchen for lunch.
12:30 p.m.	Back from lunch, free time begins (structured activities, movies, games, etc.).
2:10–3:15	Structured group (KIV, social skills, limit & lead).
3:15–3:30	Prepare for recreation.
3:30–4:30	Recreation.
4:30–5:05	Responsibility time (showers, clean up, phone calls, etc.).
5:15	To kitchen for dinner.
5:50	Back from dinner/evening affirmation meeting.
6:00–7:30	Visitation & free time.
9:00	Freshman level to bed.
9:30	Sophomore level to bed.
10:00	Junior level to bed.
10:30	Senior level to bed.

Time between bed times is structured time to include groups, activities, huddle ups, etc.

Arizona Department of Youth Treatment and Rehabilitation

During the daily Limit and Lead groups, each youth was briefly to discuss his behavior since the last session and to report on homework assignments, including ones dealing with his individual behavior cycles, offense cycles, victim empathy, and recidivism. The juveniles were encouraged to be self-critical as well as to critique each other. Following a roundtable discussion of current issues, the youths voted to determine whose problem would be the focus of the remainder of the discussion. Ideally, each youth would clearly identify and explain the issue, determine if the behavior was part of a pattern, develop alternatives, and make follow-up self reports. To conclude the session, staff members were to reinforce "positive interactions and initiatives" and to help youths "understand that their choices in life need not be self-defeating."[53]

During the sessions, unit staff and teachers were to limit "the use of delinquent strengths and weaknesses" and to lead youths "to use prosocial strengths in their place."[54] The chief of counseling described Limit and Lead as "a strategic program of behavioral change that emphasizes placing limits on the habitual thinking and behaviors of delinquent youth and, additionally, leads youth to the discovery of positive alternatives and options to getting personal needs met through modeling, teaching, and encouragement of positive problem-solving and behavior."[55]

Other groups were facilitated through a curriculum of self-study entitled Keys to Innervisions, in which the young men participated in groups and completed workbooks dealing with diverse issues such as drug abuse and violence. The exercises were intended to assist them in examining the impact of values, motivations, attitudes, and habits on their decision making. The chief of counseling wrote that the program "explores perceptions in the present and the associations to the past that determine the meaning and expectations of experiences. The evaluation of options, including past tendencies, allows for decisions that capitalize on past success and reduce the probability of repeating past failures."[56]

When an individual evidenced problems in dealing with his thoughts and emotions or difficulties in conforming to program guidelines, staff were to use Therapeutic Crisis Intervention, in which Life Space Interviews were conducted.[57] These one-on-one discussions were intended to defuse conflicts as well as to provide individualized attention and assistance to youths.

Specific problems were to be addressed in special groups called by either youth or staff. "Huddle-ups" were to be brief ten- to fifteen-minute groups called by youths or staff members to address activities viewed as disruptive. "Large groups," referred to as "marathons," were intended "to prevent activity that may result in others being harmed," specifically situations where weapons or escape tools were in the living unit, escape or assault plans had surfaced, pervasive problems existed that began as physical or sexual assaults, or contraband was present.[58]

One of the most original and pivotal elements of the model treatment program was the educational component. Many of the young men had experienced resounding failure within the public school setting, and the prison's school had done very little to address or alter the impact of those experiences. Indeed, the lack of appropriate and effective educational services was a major issue in the lawsuit, and the creation of a relevant, successful school system that could earn official accreditation was a primary tenet of the consent decree.

The model program's educational plan was one of the most visionary and promising aspects of the entire endeavor. The innovative proposal reflected an astute understanding of the needs of incarcerated youths and the manner in which traditional education had failed them. The central element of the plan, Success School, espoused a compelling philosophy of individualized and highly relevant education. The heart of the proposal was its commitment to capturing youths' imagination and tailoring the learning process to their interests, needs, and aspirations.

Fundamental academic skills were to be built around a specialized plan based on each youth's expressed goals for the future. The process was to begin with two basic questions, "What do you want to do in the future?" and "What do you need to know in order to do that?" Whatever the answers might be, teachers and support staff were to design an educational program grounded in each youth's current capabilities and the competencies necessary to fulfill his ambitions. Regardless of whether a youth said he wanted to become a firefighter or a rock musician, a plan was to be constructed to further that goal while teaching relevant academic and social skills.

The original design envisioned Success School as "a 60-day prevocational training component" that would prepare youths for further academic and vocational dimensions of the prison's educational system.[59] The compilation of a portfolio was to be the organizing feature of a youth's time in Success School. The portfolio attempted to individualize the acquisition of essential skills and to do so using a format that related realistically to the youths' experiences, at the same time meeting academic needs and encouraging occupational goals.

The requirements for completing the student portfolio were comprehensive. To achieve the first level of accomplishment a youth's portfolio was to contain a one- to three-page review of the results of diagnostic and assessment testing, a personal letter to a friend or family member discussing the value of gaining an education, a business letter to a member of the business community reflecting concern about attaining an adequate education to gain employment, a formal letter to the judge who sent the youth to prison discussing the subject of learning the skills and knowledge necessary to accomplish positive change, a two- to three-page autobiography, a two- to three-page book report on a biography or autobiography, a two- to three-page career exploration research paper, and a completed checklist of physical education competencies.

The second level required an additional five- to ten-page research paper profiling a successful individual in the student's career interest, a project demonstrating the applied scientific principles involved in at least one example of technology relevant to success in the type of career chosen by the student, and a certificate attesting to the youth's knowledge of at least one team sport and successful participation in intramural or tournament play.

The final level of accomplishment within Success School required a Personal Development Plan articulating one-month, three-month, six-month, one-year, and five-year goals, a resumé and summary of job development skills obtained to guarantee success, completion of three to five modules in the computer lab, completion of the computer literacy program, completion of Personal Leadership Development Training, and a certificate of service as a peer athletic team leader. According to the Success School program description, "completion of these documents . . . in the student portfolio will constitute approximately sixty classroom days within a ninety-calendar-day period."[60] At the end of the sixty days, youths were to transition to specific academic and vocational alternatives. Prior to being released from prison, each youth was to present his portfolio to a panel of representatives from education, the treatment team, and administration.

Another element of the model program, the Level System, was a point system used by staff to document youths' behavior and to measure their progress. The system's stated goal was to reinforce the ten conventional values stressed throughout the program: "responsibility, honesty/integrity, dependability, obedience/self-discipline, positive regard for others, industriousness, self-respect, good sportsmanship, altruism, and empathy."[61] The system contained six levels, four within the prison ("freshman, sophomore, junior, and senior levels") and two when youths were released on parole into the community. Higher levels brought increased privileges such as additional telephone time and extracurricular activities. Junior- and senior-level youths were also eligible for supervised activities outside the prison, greater unsupervised activities in and around the living unit, extra evening recreation when available, later bedtimes, and radio privileges. The junior level emphasized the importance of acting as a role model for other youths as well as taking responsibility for one's own actions, and the senior level emphasized the transition back to the community. When released from prison, if youths successfully gained the competencies associated with parole or "conditional release," they would be discharged from the supervision and authority of the prison system.

Youths were ranked on a scale of one to four points at the close of each staff shift. Advancement from freshman to sophomore level required an average of two points; advancement to higher levels required an average of three points. Youth petitions for level promotions, staff recommendations for level changes, and disciplinary issues were discussed at weekly treatment team meetings attended by the youths under consideration.

The disciplinary unit, so central to the lawsuit against the prison system, was reconceptualized and renamed the Behavioral Management Program. Likewise, the former prison guards responsible for disciplinary actions and institutional security were renamed the Crisis Management Team. Their role was now defined as providing "a structured environment for youth who cannot function successfully in the mainstream of the environment."[62] Each of the disciplinary unit's five levels was referred to as a Temporary Reassignment Adjustment Component (TRAC), and sanctions became increasingly restrictive as youths' behaviors were judged to be more seriously in violation of the program. Sending a youth to the disciplinary unit was intended to be an extreme action of last resort, and, given the interactive and cooperative philosophy of the model program, many staff viewed "calling security" as an admission of failure.

Surpassing Old Debates, Transforming Power Relations

Two major reasons the model program held enormous promise were its explicit commitment to change power relations within the prison and its advocacy of restorative justice. Restorative notions of justice emphasize the need to enhance individuals' abilities to live peaceably and productively within society, and these notions go beyond the dichotomy pitting punishment against treatment. In many ways, restorative justice steps outside the battle waged between champions of punishment and champions of treatment.[63] To incorporate restorative principles of justice, the program prioritized youths' accountability and "making things right."[64] It advocated a balanced approach that required community and victim involvement and attempted to prevent delinquency as well as to restore harmony to the community after delinquency occurs.

Traditional juvenile justice philosophy has emphasized the differences between youths and adults, contrasting the innocence and vulnerability of youths with the maturity and responsibility of adults. Accordingly, young people labeled as delinquents have been portrayed as deserving treatment because of their presumed lack of sophistication and receptivity to rehabilitation.[65] The dominant and consistent rationale or explanation for why youths were imprisoned has been their need for a structured, residential, *rehabilitative* environment. Most people working in the U.S. juvenile system, including judges, prosecutors, and prison personnel, had maintained that the primary issue is rehabilitation of the youths.[66]

Whether effective treatment existed is highly debatable,[67] but the fundamental premise regarding why youths were imprisoned remained consistent with the ideal of individualized justice espoused by traditional juvenile justice philosophy. Until recently, the most commonly asked question was not whether juvenile institutions should treat, but, rather, whether they could or were treating. Although U.S. Supreme Court decisions within the past three decades have provided greater due process and increased procedural rigor, such reforms have not challenged the fundamental assumption that treatment was the mission of the juvenile justice system.[68]

Today, benevolent images of *both* youth and the juvenile system are closely scrutinized and severely criticized.[69] Punishment is the most strongly advocated and enthusiastically embraced response to delinquent youths. Punitive rhetoric reigns, and punishment-oriented policies, such as increased imprisonment in the juvenile system and increased transfer of youths to adult courts for prosecution and punishment, are preeminent.[70]

Despite heated exchanges, what is meant by "treatment" or "punishment" is not always clear or consistent. Perhaps what is most important is what each term, "treatment" or "punishment," has come to represent or symbolize. At its most basic level, the debate revolves around the way in which youths are perceived and portrayed.[71] Those who champion treatment see youths, including imprisoned youths, as deserving nurturance and being capable of change. Advocates of punishment see delinquent youths, especially imprisoned youths, as committed to lawlessness, unlikely to change, and unworthy of treatment.[72]

This dichotomy and the tendency to view these alternative perspectives as absolute opposites fail to convey the complexity of the controversy.[73] Advocates of restorative justice, including the designers of the model program, view the punishment versus treatment debate as a false construction—a tired debate based on worldviews of the contestants rather than the lives and needs of youths and members of society. They maintain that, although the worldviews of those who espouse the models differ, the implementation of the models has been remarkably similar. Accordingly, youths and society have been damaged both in the name of treatment and in the name of punishment.

The Arizona model program did emphasize treatment more than punishment, but its notion of treatment embodied a restorative emphasis on both youths' and society's accountability as well as the necessity of creating change in communities. The program embraced traditional images of youths as needing and meriting treatment, but it also acknowledged and responded to criticisms that this emphasis had resulted in neither protection for society nor meaningful services for youths.

The restorative model of justice is greatly concerned with the questions of responsibility and protection of the public. The model program's creators were mindful of public fears and desires for protection, and they gave much consideration to which methods would bring about such protection. In particular, even when they felt incarceration was necessary because of the immediate threat posed by a youth, they saw punitive deprivation and isolation alone as doing very little to provide long-term protection for the community.[74]

The model program focused on questions of individual responsibility and accountability. Although it examined society's role in generating delinquency and viewed youths as less responsible for their acts than adults, the program philosophy maintained that "taking responsibility" for one's past acts and future behavior is an essential component of any effective treatment effort. A focal concern of restorative justice is how to get individuals to take responsibility and to change their behavior. Advocates maintain that punishment has great potential to generate bitter anger and nihilism, thus perpetuating or heightening the very behavior it purports to combat and change.[75] Restorative justice advocates argue that when youths return to society they will have been changed by their prison experiences, but the crucial question is *how* they will have changed. Accordingly, the isolation and deprivation of prison itself is sufficient punishment, and what happens during youths' prison time should be rehabilitative—not exclusively or excessively punitive.[76] The image of restorative justice inherent in the model program made it possible to acknowledge and confront issues of power within the prison.

Prisons evoke strong images of old-fashioned power, physical coercion, and subjugation—all of which lack subtlety and finesse. On an immediate and urgent level, the power exercised within prisons is supreme—brutally and nakedly sovereign. Youths are subject to the vulgar, obvious power of imprisonment: it is by definition isolation and deprivation, and it has great potential to be demeaning and abusive. There is no denying the possibilities and potentials of physical imprisonment and emotional deprivation.[77] Being in prison means that you are always confined and controlled, locked up, and told what to do; it also means that you can be disciplined, belittled, yelled at, sworn at, shoved, pushed, handcuffed, locked down, isolated, beaten up, brutalized, and raped. Someone can try to kill you, and you can be driven to try to kill yourself. They or you may succeed.

All this is true, but power relations within prisons are more encompassing than the "heavy hammer" image suggests, especially in prison programs such as the model program that are officially committed to maintaining a safe environment and containing physical coercion. Power within a juvenile prison is as complex as it is everywhere else; it is polymorphous and ubiquitous—that is, it takes many forms and is everywhere.[78] The true intricacy of power is found in its multitudinous expressions, especially as revealed in the experiences and interpretations of the least powerful individuals, including imprisoned youth.[79] Power in prison is about these adolescents' bodies, their desires, their dreams, their nightmares. It is about the many and diverse ways in which power is exercised over them, but it is also about the forms and methods of power they seek, possess, and exude, as well as those they are denied.

In order to come to grips with the experiences and realities of youths, as well as all the adults involved and implicated in their imprisonment, it is essential to grasp the fluid and all-enveloping nature of the power relations in which they are engulfed. These encompass the process as well as the organization of imprisonment, including the multitude of disjunctions and contradictions.[80]

Although the power exerted by the legal system and its agents over the lives of imprisoned youths is extensive and immeasurable, it is crucial to try to comprehend its limitations as well. Most importantly, prisons seem especially powerless to effect lasting change in youths' lives. It is possible to lock youths in their cells, deny them basic needs or privileges, inflict pain upon their bodies, and engender humiliation and anger in their psyches. It is possible to get youths to espouse beliefs they do not hold or promise changes they will not make. But this does not amount to altering them or their futures. Powerful adults can force young people to do many things, but they cannot force them to adopt a specific view of themselves or the world.

The fundamental coercive power exercised by the state in its imprisonment of adolescents is clear and consequential, particularly in the profound manner in which that power may be inscribed on the bodies and psyches of young people. But this coercion is not unlimited, and other methods of power lie outside the purview of the prison's ability to dominate. The state power inherent in imprisonment is qualified and frequently incongruous with, and less important than, more powerful forces that saturate and control youths' lives. Some youths endure while others flail within the prison routine; they are impacted but rarely in a positive, transforming way. Imprisoning youths fails to produce the desired "intrinsic modifications" or to persuade them to identify with or incorporate prison authorities' depictions of their immediate situations or future lives. The forces that lie beyond prison walls seem the most monumental and influential to the youths: on an interpersonal level, the power of families, friends, neighborhoods, and gangs; on a societal level, the power of the economy, politics, mass culture, and social inequity;[81] and, on an individual level, the power of youthful anger, pain, and, perhaps most damning, despair.

The magnanimous challenge faced by the model program was to disrupt patterns of power and to create new methods of survival for delinquent youths. The original model held potential for meeting that challenge. We will discuss the program's strengths and limitations in depth, but first it is essential to know the individuals for whom the program was designed, to address the important question of: "Who are these prisoners, these kids?"

Collective and
Individual Identities

Two

Who Are These Prisoners,
These Kids?

THE RANGE OF PERSONALITIES AND POTENTIALITIES
among youths in prison is considerable, as evidenced by the youths'
histories before they entered the model program, their responses to
the program, and their lives after they returned to their communities. The individuality is illustrated throughout this book by the
backgrounds and experiences of eight members of the original Unit
Four in the model program. Each individual's story is unique, but
together they reflect a variety of patterns that are repeated among
the 385 imprisoned youths.

Kevin, an Anglo youth imprisoned four times before his eighteenth birthday, exemplifies youths who have been imprisoned
repeatedly although they have never been involved in serious delinquency.[1] Kevin's imprisonment was not so much the result of needing to be incarcerated as a lack of alternatives. He literally had
nowhere else to go, and the juvenile justice system found nowhere
else to send him.

Kevin's childhood and adolescence were highly volatile. His parents separated when he was six months old, and Kevin went to live
with his paternal grandparents until he was six. For the next two
years he lived with and was abused by his father. At least once, the

child's injuries were so severe that he was hospitalized. For the next four years, between the ages of eight and twelve, Kevin returned to live with his grandparents. When he was twelve years old, his grandmother became ill and he went to live with his mother. Throughout his childhood, Kevin had problems at school and was diagnosed with emotional problems.

Kevin's first referral to the juvenile justice system at twelve years old was for running away from home; he ran away six additional times in the next year and a half. At age fourteen, he was caught shoplifting a carton of cigarettes, was adjudicated ("found guilty") for that offense, and was placed on probation. He continued to run away from home, and seven months later he was charged with technical violation of his probation due to the repeated runaways. Kevin's mother told the judge that there was no point in taking him home because she was unable to control him, and he was imprisoned based on the violation of probation.[2]

Kevin spent six months in prison that first time. Then he was sent to a foster home and, a week later, to his mother's home. When difficulties arose between Kevin and his mother, a woman who was a former volunteer at the prison offered to have Kevin stay with her and was appointed as his guardian. The forty-year-old woman and fourteen-year-old Kevin became romantically and sexually involved. When his mother discovered this, she took Kevin back to her home. Soon Kevin ran away again and was subsequently sent to a residential treatment facility from which he ran away three times in one month. He went to another residential facility, but when he ran away within five days he was returned to prison. Three weeks later Kevin became a member of the model program in Unit Four.

Nick was also an Anglo youth; his delinquency history was limited, but his offenses were more serious than Kevin's. His childhood was extremely unstable and his father was abusive. When Nick was three years old, his parents were divorced after his mother discovered that his father was also married to another woman. Nick was sent to live with his grandmother and stepgrandfather for several years; when his grandmother had cancer, Nick was "the one pretty much to take care of her." After his grandmother's death, he lived with his stepgrandfather and his stepgrandfather's woman friend. He returned home to his mother upon her remarriage when he was eleven years old. This marriage, as well as a subsequent one, ended in divorce. Throughout this time, Nick was often left to care for himself.

Nick's first arrest and referral to court came when he was fourteen years old after he exposed himself to an eight-year-old boy and a ten-year-old boy and convinced them to expose themselves. Nick was convicted of child molestation, sentenced to prison, and served twenty-three months. While Nick was incarcerated, his family moved to another state; when he was released from prison, they were unwilling to have him join them. He was sent to a residential facility in the community and, unwilling to tolerate the rules, he ran away.

While Nick was on the streets, a friend he met in prison introduced him to a white supremacy gang, the Fourth Reich. The gang took him in, gave him a place to stay and, Nick insists, a sense of belonging. They also involved him in a number of bank robberies from which the gang members gained most of the profit. (In the following exchange and throughout the book, our questions are in italics.)

Who approached you about the robberies?

They did.

How did they know you?

Through somebody else. . . . See, I met up with someone [I knew] in here, you know, all by accident. That was by accident, meetin' up with him. It was like we started partyin' together. . . .

When you got out—

I didn't have nothin'. . . .

Only eighty-six days after he had been released from prison, sixteen-year-old Nick was arrested and subsequently reimprisoned for armed robbery. He had served seven months in this second sentence when the model program began and he became one of the original twenty-four residents of Unit Four. Nick had helped with painting and refurbishing the living unit for the new program and said that "just knowin' the satisfaction that I had helped paint it and did most of the work" was the main reason he was willing to be in the program.

Bernardo, a Mexican American, lived with his mother in Arizona and had little contact with his father in Mexico. His life outside the home seemed to bewilder his Spanish-speaking mother, and she was often frustrated with Bernardo and unable to deal with him effectively. Bernardo was first referred to juvenile court at ten years of age when he was accused of burglary of a commercial establishment but was not formally charged, and no court intervention was ordered. Four and a half years later he was referred to court on three allegations of vehicle theft, two counts of residential burglary, and one count of trespassing. He was not found guilty of any of these charges, but was found guilty of resisting arrest and was placed on probation.

Nine months later Bernardo was referred to court for violating his probation, but this was dismissed. Two weeks later he was referred to court for vehicle theft and violation of probation. This time, at age fifteen, he was found guilty and sentenced to prison. Two months later he became one of the first youths to enter the model program. He said he volunteered because, among other things, staff said the youths could have their girlfriends visit them and because the program was supposed to be "something fun."

Bernardo had completed eighth grade but tested below his grade level and was not attending school prior to his imprisonment. His file indicated "no evidence" of past substance abuse, but officials "suspected" both substance abuse and gang involvement. Although he identified himself as a gang member, Bernardo stated that the offense for which he was imprisoned was not gang-related. "I didn't come in here because of my gang. . . . It was *my* choice to go out and steal a car—not them. I did it by myself."

Two years before the model program began, Mitch was a thirteen-year-old seventh grader with one referral to juvenile court for giving a false report to police. He was a middle-class Anglo child with a history of family problems. His father and mother divorced when he was an infant, and Mitch's relationship with his stepfather (his mother's fourth husband) was conflictual. He had run away from home four times, and the family had been in counseling following accusations that Mitch had stolen money and weapons from his stepfather.

While his mother and stepfather were out of town on separate business trips, Mitch and his thirteen-year-old girlfriend were at his home alone. In the course of a game, he pointed one of his stepfather's guns, a .357 Magnum, at her head and fired. When the girl's body was found a day later, the media reported that Mitch was not considered a suspect, but police were looking for him to "check on his welfare and possibly get more information on [the victim's] death."[3]

Mitch had used his mother's credit card to get an airplane ticket to his uncle's home in another state. Three days later police picked him up and he was returned to Arizona. He told the police he had shot his friend accidentally, became scared, and fled. The shooting was interpreted in numerous ways. Initially, police investigators called it an "unintentional discharge" and stated that "[the youths] were sitting there talking, and he thought the gun was on an empty cylinder. For some unknown reason, we don't know exactly what the conversation was at this point or why the gun was pointed at her, but it was. The gun discharged, and she was killed."

A neighbor described Mitch as "a nice, intelligent kid" and viewed the shooting as the result of "bad judgment." The girl's father called Mitch "a friendly, normal kid" and indicated that he was most upset with Mitch's parents: "To leave guns with a youngster and then leave the state, that's ignorance as far as I'm concerned. I kind of feel sorry for him. He's got to live with the shooting for the rest of his life."

When prosecutors decided to charge Mitch with murder and to request he be transferred to adult court, police received numerous calls from citizens who were angered by the charge. The victim's father also expressed surprise: "The boy made a stupid mistake, but, from what I know, it didn't seem intentional . . . Jesus, he's only 13."

In a rare move, the prosecution charged Mitch with both first- and second-degree homicide, leaving it to a judge to decide which charge to pursue and whether Mitch would be tried as an adult or juvenile. The judge decided that Mitch would stand trial in juvenile court for second-degree homicide. Mitch later pled guilty to the charge and was sentenced to juvenile prison.

The presentence assessment depicted Mitch as an emotionally troubled, argumentative youth with few friends and low self-esteem. It also suggested that he would require long-term therapeutic intervention. Twenty months after being imprisoned Mitch entered the newly established model program. Due to his conviction for second-degree homicide he was classified as the highest risk to public safety. He also had the highest IQ score, near the genius range.

Larry came from a very stable home; his parents had been married almost thirty years. He had completed tenth grade and tested above grade level. When his parents moved out of state, Larry remained in Arizona, got a job, bought a car, and lived independently with a roommate. A middle-class Anglo, he was referred to court for shoplifting when he was fourteen and again for shoplifting two months before his seventeenth birthday. His case was handled informally both times and no court intervention was ordered.

Two weeks before his seventeenth birthday, Larry was arrested for aggravated assault. He and a friend, David, were "horseplaying" with a .38 caliber Smith and Wesson revolver. While "roughhousing," the youths struggled for the gun, it discharged, and a bullet entered David's head below the right eye and exited behind the right ear. He was blinded in the right eye, partially paralyzed on his right side, and required twenty-four-hour medical care.

Larry's file said he had previously used alcohol, marijuana, crystal-meth, and cocaine, and had experimented with LSD. He was convicted of aggravated assault and sentenced to prison. Three months later Larry entered Unit Four.

Daniel, an African American, lived with his mother and had no contact with his father, who lived in the Midwest. When Daniel was fifteen, two years prior to his incarceration, his mother remarried.

Her new husband was six years younger than she, and Daniel resented his stepfather because he was less than ten years older than himself. Daniel went to live with his uncle. He was suspended from school due to a history of truancy, and official records stated that he used crack, marijuana, and alcohol.

Gang membership was a major part of Daniel's identity and he portrayed the gang as a substitute for family life:

> If you don't got a family, best you gonna go to a gang, because they're just like a family. . . . Some people join because they been getting child abuse or sexual abuse or something. . . . When people got problems with their family, and they don't want to go live with their mom somewhere—they gotta get on the streets and then learn to work the streets and all of a sudden they're gonna try to get in the gang. . . . Some people steal because it's fun. Some people steal to get money for their drugs, and that's the only way they can get their money, so they steal. That's the only way to get their clothes and to eat. . . . Back then [when my parents and uncle were growing up], it wasn't like that. It was just like—he's my friend and he's my friend and everybody was just friends. Nowadays, you got enemies.

Prior to his imprisonment, Daniel was deeply involved in gang activities. He viewed gang membership as part of everyday life, and depicted many gang activities as "just fun." Like most of the youths, Daniel depicted cruising rival neighborhoods ("out looking to start trouble") as gang banging, but he distinguished between general conflict and serious violence. "Gang banging is just fun. It's just fun. But killing other people is scary." The violence included drive-by shootings: "We did a drive-by at twelve o'clock in the morning, in the daytime. . . . And then we, like, we shot some Bloods. We shot and killed some Bloods that jumped [our homeboy]. . . . [You have to] get them before they get you."

Daniel expressed clear understandings of gang values related to violence:

What values are important in the gang?

We are like—like Crips, they don't kill babies. We're not ever supposed to kill babies.

Tell me, how old is a baby?

Like 1, 2, 3—4.

How about an 8-year-old?

An 8-year-old? That's a gang banger.

Daniel also portrayed drug use as ubiquitous and fully integrated into casual gang life as well as gang violence.

Well, see, like we Crips we smoke something called "shiner." Like we don't go through a job unless we smoke shiner.

What's that?

It's like angel dust and PCP. . . . It's like a cigarette dipped in embalming fluid or horse tranquilizers. . . . It slows your heart down in beats, and if you get shot, it's like you're already dead, so you won't feel it. And I got an O.G. [original gangster], and he was on shiner and he got shot. We call him "O.G. Black Lazarus," because he got shot and he was on the table and he died, but then he just woke back up.

So you take this drug, because you don't feel the pain? Or it's because it slows you down enough so that you think you have a better chance of surviving the gun shot?

It slows you down.

What does it do as far as your judgment and your reflexes?

It makes you strong. It'll take a lot of people to get you down.

The first time Daniel was arrested was the day before his seventeenth birthday. He was accused of aggravated assault, weapons misconduct, and possession of narcotics. The last two allegations were dismissed, but he was convicted of aggravated assault and sentenced to prison. His victim was a pregnant young woman from a rival gang who had "disrespected his hood."

> So she disrespected my hood, and then I said, "You disrespect my hood, and I'm either gonna kill you or you're gonna be shot." And then my cousin [her boyfriend] grabbed my arm before I could shoot her in the head, and I just shot her in the thigh.

Although this was the first time he was arrested, Daniel was a violent youth and a hostile prisoner. Staff talked him into being in the model program because he thought it would be more fun and that it would help him get out of prison sooner: "They told us that this program is gonna be a lot of fun and we always gonna be doin' something, and that we'd get out in three months."

Tomás, a Mexican American, had a difficult home life. His father left the family when he was three and he had no contact with him. His mother's boyfriend had been living with the family for ten years; the boyfriend abused alcohol and drugs and he also physically abused Tomás's mother and her children. Tomás viewed this man as an "intruder" and was also deeply angry with his biological father for abandoning the family.

Tomás ran away five times, starting when he was thirteen. When he was thirteen, he was on the streets for three months but no concerted effort was made to find him.[4] That year Tomás also was found guilty of theft and placed on probation. Over the next two years, his probation was continued twice for additional charges of theft and violating the conditions of his probation. On one occasion when he was fifteen, Tomás fought back against his mother's abusive boyfriend and was referred to the court for domestic violence. The charges were dismissed.

At age sixteen, when he reappeared before the court on charges of theft and burglary, Tomás was found guilty and committed to the juvenile prison. His previous offenses were nonviolent and relatively minor, and he was not considered a danger to the community. Nevertheless, perhaps because he had been referred to court six times in three years, after less than a month in the prison's diagnostic unit, it was determined that Tomás would be kept in prison rather than returned home. He was assigned to the new program in Unit Four.

Marcos, a Mexican American, was a baby when his father left the family. During Marcos's childhood, both his father and mother were in and out of prison numerous times for possession and sale of drugs. Marcos lived with his maternal grandmother and in foster homes; he was moved frequently and attended six elementary schools in his first seven years of school.

Marcos was an intelligent child and prospered in foster care during one period when his mother was imprisoned. He was on the honor roll, played on the basketball team, and, through his academic work, won a trip to fly over the Grand Canyon with the governor. Once when Marcos's mother was not in prison, she worked two jobs and provided a secure home for Marcos and his brothers and sister. But when she and her new male partner became deeply involved in drug use, Marcos's situation deteriorated.

Marcos sniffed paint with his uncle, cousins, and brothers when he was eight years old, and by age thirteen he joined his grandfather and uncles in smoking marijuana and crack cocaine.[5] Cocaine use became a central part of his life: "This high was all I knew about and cared about in life. I thought it was the best thing I had ever experienced."

Marcos's first referral to juvenile court was for petty theft two weeks after his twelfth birthday. His referral was handled informally and no court intervention was ordered. Two and a half years later, at fourteen, he was referred to court for robbery, theft, and burglary of a commercial establishment. He was found guilty of the robbery and placed on probation.

A year later allegations of vehicle theft were dismissed, as were allegations of burglary of a commercial establishment four months after that. Marcos was arrested for vehicle theft and violation of probation nine months later, and, just after his sixteenth birthday, he was sentenced to prison and entered the model program.

Three months before he was charged with the vehicle theft that resulted in imprisonment, a juvenile court report stated, "This is a case that cries out for intervention on the Court's part in terms of placing Marcos in a [drug] treatment center." This recommendation was never followed.

These brief introductions to the lives of eight youths from the original model program unit demonstrate the necessity of placing youths' delinquent behavior and their imprisonment in the contexts of their lives. This is true for each of the 385 youths who participated in the program during the two years of this research.

Identity and Imprisonment: "Lots of Us Inside These Walls"

Each youth's individuality is apparent within the prison setting, but there are also striking commonalities. A randomly selected juvenile prisoner is likely to be a minority male, between fifteen and seventeen years of age, from an impoverished neighborhood. As one youth said, "There are lots of us inside these walls!" The matrix of gender, class, and race, with its confluence of maleness, poverty, and racial or ethnic difference, is crucial.

Race and social class are key elements in the youths' collective identity. It may appear that almost all imprisoned youths are poor African Americans or Latinos, but in fact many imprisoned youths are white: in this prison, 38 percent of the youths. True, this is considerably less than their 64 percent in Arizona's population, but the numbers counter the common misperception that all imprisoned youths are minorities. And the further youths become integrated into the juvenile justice system, the more skewed is the racial and class representation.

Nationwide, minority youths are in the majority in juvenile prisons. In fact, at all stages of the juvenile justice process, the percentage of minority youths is higher than in the general population. This includes arrests, referrals to court, and pretrial detentions. Juvenile court researchers in Arizona's largest county estimate that 71 percent of African-American males are likely to have court records by age seventeen, compared to 43 percent of Mexican-American males and 39 percent of Anglo males.[6]

In Arizona, Latinos, almost exclusively Mexican Americans, comprise about 30 percent of the youth population but account for 44 percent of imprisoned youths. The disparity for African Americans is even greater; they are only 4 percent of the youth population but account for 15 percent of imprisoned youths. American Indians comprise 2 percent of the youth population and 3 percent of imprisoned youths.[7] The racial and ethnic identities of youths who participated in the model program closely paralleled those of the state's youth prison population.[8]

Systematic statistical information about the social class of these imprisoned youths is not available, but it is clear that youths from economically deprived backgrounds are most likely to be imprisoned. Nationally, half of imprisoned youths' families are headed by single mothers and have annual incomes below the poverty level.[9] This was true of the majority of the first twenty-four youths in Unit Four. Despite a lack of systematic information about the social class of all 385 youths in the model program, comments in their case files as well as observations and interactions with them in their homes and communities bore out that many came from impoverished homes and neighborhoods.

Race and ethnicity often act as surrogates for social class in U.S. society, because class and race are so closely linked and racial and ethnic minorities are disproportionately poor. Within prison there is even less class diversity than racial or ethnic diversity. An overwhelming number of both the minority youths and white youths are poor. A few youths come from middle-class homes, and there is the occasional youth from an affluent suburban neighborhood, but poverty is apparent in most of the youths' backgrounds. Homes are in disrepair, and neighborhoods are in decline. For some youths who live in large modern apartment complexes, a small one-bedroom apartment frequently houses seven or eight people, with several family members sleeping on the floor.

Gender and age also influence imprisoned youths' identities. There is a far greater percentage of males than females in prison, despite the nearly fifty-fifty distribution in the youth population.

Only 9 percent of those sentenced to Arizona's youth prisons are females and, at the time of this research, all youths in the state-run prisons ("secure facilities") were males. The females were held in a locked, "secure" residential facility in the community.[10]

Although the ages of imprisoned youths ranged from twelve to seventeen years of age, about 87 percent were fifteen and older. Less than 1 percent of the imprisoned youths were twelve years old, and 3 percent were thirteen-year-olds. Eleven percent of the youths were fourteen years old, 21 percent were fifteen, 32 percent were sixteen, and 34 percent were seventeen-year-olds. The age distribution of youths in the model program approximated that of the overall prison population.[11]

To say imprisoned youths are disproportionately male, poor, and minority members is an accurate description, but it does not explain why these particular youths are in prison. To address that crucial question it is necessary to examine the social context of those characteristics within contemporary society—that is, to explore what it means to be male, poor, and a minority. This involves two distinct yet related issues: why these youths are more likely to be delinquent, and why they are more likely to be incarcerated than other delinquent youths.

To be male, poor, or a racial or ethnic minority enhances the likelihood that youths will become involved in delinquency. One level of explanations lies in the differences between these youths and the rest of society. They lack the privileges and support systems that higher income levels make possible, such as adequate housing, food, clothing, medical and dental care, quality educational opportunities, safe neighborhoods, and nurturing extracurricular activities. The lack of support and opportunities has been exacerbated by extensive cuts in funding for youth social programs that once augmented families' and communities' meager financial resources.[12]

The consequences of class status pervade these youths' lives. Deprivation of basic necessities, psychological and emotional difficulties, and restricted options dominate their life chances. Many of the youths worry about the poverty that surrounds their families, and many feel responsible for their mothers and younger siblings. Youths' feelings of hopelessness and powerlessness are reinforced by their inability to find work, as well as their observation of the adults in their neighborhoods—some of whom have worked a lifetime at menial tasks with little reward, and others who are stigmatized as multiple-generation welfare recipients. Some youths express disillusionment, others disdain, for the "straight" work world and the injustices they perceive in the lack of meaningful, dignified, well-paying jobs.[13] Although the youths do not use terms such as "economic deprivation" or "marginalization," they are acutely aware of their standing in the economic and racial hierarchies of U.S. society.

These social and cultural forces influence youths' behaviors, but they alone do not fully explain their delinquency. Obviously there are thousands of poor, male minority youths who are not involved in any serious illegalities and who will never be imprisoned. The issues of individual socialization, self-concept, and identity must also be taken into account. The racial, class, and gender dimensions of youths' identities are related intricately to their delinquent behavior. They all affect how the youths make sense of the social world and their places in it, including how they see themselves and how others see them.

There are many alternative conceptualizations of what it means to be black or Latino or American Indian, even as there are alternative notions of being poor or male. The identities of many imprisoned youths incorporate specific and similar interpretations of these attributes, with most emphasizing their race or ethnicity. Indeed race is likely to be preeminent in youths' descriptions of themselves, for their self-concept as well as life experiences are permeated by racial and ethnic distinctions. Minority youths are especially aware of the racialized context of their existences.

Some white youths become more overtly race-conscious while in prison. For many of them, the experience of being in the minority in prison highlights the racial dimension of their identities. Some imprisoned white youths are members of a white supremacy gang, the Fourth Reich, and others, like Nick, are influenced greatly by them. Nick viewed the white gang as providing support and protection.

What does the Fourth Reich stand for?

Like white pride, you know. Like not letting them all [minority youths] disrespect [you] and get away with it. . . . Whites, you know, don't really stick together like blacks and Mexicans. . . .

What does "disrespecting" mean?

Like saying, "Fuck you," you know, or "You ain't nothin." You can use all different terms.

Nick said that a major value of the white supremacy gang was the importance of "keeping the white race pure." When asked to be more specific, he said that he didn't "like to see like a white lady with a black man," but that he personally would not attack or initiate conflict with an interracial couple.

So are you against blacks and Hispanics?

No, but I think, you know, if God wanted us to be together, He would have made us all the same. I think He may not believe in racism, you know, but I think He'd believe in separation.

Do you see the black or Hispanic culture as being less valuable than the white? Or lower?

I'd say there's some [that are lower] and then there's others [who are not]. . . . They'd probably say the same thing about all the whites, too.

Race and gender are foremost in youths' expressions of identity. They act in ways that are distinctly and stereotypically masculine and heterosexual. Some undoubtedly have a homosexual orientation, but there is little tolerance or support for alternative sexual orientations within their neighborhoods or the prison world. A maleness that emphasizes control, aggressiveness, and sexual prowess is most prevalent. This image includes a defiant stance toward a hostile world as well as bravado and a readiness to do verbal and physical combat. Conflict is viewed as a given, and "being a man" informs strategies for prevailing and dominating.[14]

Masculinity, including an actual or assumed sexual sophistication, is a salient element of the youths' identities. Although they are adolescents, a significant number of the imprisoned youths have fathered children, as had eight of the twenty-four individuals in the original model unit. Their relationships with their children's mothers varied from committed relationships, including plans for marriage, to very casual relationships where the young men proudly displayed pictures of their children but assumed no responsibility for their well-being and evidenced little intention of providing support for their children's mothers.[15] The young men's attitudes toward women in general are characteristically patriarchal, demeaning, and insensitive. The youths' relationships with adult women contrast with their disregard and lack of commitment to women their age. Many have close and respectful relationships with mothers and grandmothers, as well as convivial and respectful relationships with women staff members.

Some of the youths clearly do not evidence an accentuated masculinity, but most do. This includes codes of behavior on the street, in gangs, and in prison. Although evident, aggressiveness and machismo were somewhat muted in the model program because the environment did not require or encourage them. The extreme caricature of masculinity was mitigated by the control exercised by the prison staff and by youths' realization that such behavior was not rewarded routinely and would not help them get out of prison.

Interactions and Interpretations

It is not just that poor, minority males are more likely to be imprisoned because they are more delinquent than other youths.[16] While their illegal activities contribute to their imprisonment, many of these youths have similar offense profiles to individuals who remain in the community on probation or in private and public treatment facilities.

It is the context of youths' behavior that is paramount: in most cases who they are is as consequential as what they have done. The expectations and responses of powerful adults increase the probabilities that these youths will be viewed and treated as serious delinquents and eventually imprisoned.[17] This interactive matrix is crucial to understanding imprisoned youths' experiences and life chances.

Youths' social identities impact their interactions throughout life, including their involvement with the juvenile justice system. The responses of powerful decision makers, such as school, community, and juvenile justice personnel, are frequently influenced or conditioned by youths' social identities, including their neighborhoods, families, school records, social class, culture, race and ethnicity, and gender. In particular, the lack of resources within their families and neighborhoods intensifies the juvenile justice system's involvement in these youths' lives, and decision makers' perceptions of "future probabilities" play a role in determining these youths' fates.[18] It is not simply a matter of overt prejudice and discrimination, although this occurs, but also of the intricate web of scarce resources and lowered expectations for these youths.

Assessing the impact of race, class, and gender on social identity and individuals' interactions within society is a vast undertaking that occupies many. Numerous researchers have attempted to analyze the interactive effects of youths' behavior and society's responses. For example, during the time of this research within the juvenile prisons, another statewide study found statistically observable impacts that resulted in further juvenile justice intervention in the lives of minority youths.[19] For example, minority youths were more likely than Anglo youths to receive outcomes that increased state intervention and moved them further into the system. These differences were present at some stages of the juvenile justice process even after relevant "legal" factors, such as seriousness of offense and delinquency history, were taken into account. This suggests that race and ethnicity have independent and negative effects on youths' fates, even when we include those factors most commonly used to explain why specific youths received harsher penalties such as imprisonment.

The findings of this analysis of more than thirty thousand case histories were highly relevant for imprisoned youths. The research found that: (1) the effects of differential treatment are cumulative—

that is, when race influences decisions at one stage it also influences subsequent decisions; (2) the distinction between legitimate and illegitimate influences on case outcomes is often blurred—factors frequently considered legitimate in decision making may be highly correlated with race and lead to severe punishment; and (3) it is important to examine the extent to which process (i.e., the structure of the decision-making system itself, including options available) influences case outcomes.

In addition to the statistical analysis, researchers conducted 185 interviews with minority youths, parents, community activists, and juvenile justice personnel.[20] All had strong impressions and opinions regarding the treatment of poor and minority youths. These interviews provided insight into those places where racial and ethnic identities appear to have an inordinate influence both statistically and substantially on the lives and experiences of minority youths, families, and communities.

There were widespread perceptions that minority youths were discriminated against throughout the juvenile justice system. Many of those interviewed maintained that individuals working in the juvenile system lacked an understanding of minority cultures and were increasingly withdrawn from contact and involvement in minority and poor neighborhoods. Resources in the justice system and the community were a major concern. Many acknowledged the problem of limited justice system resources and the critical need for improved coordination among agencies in the allocation of resources. There was a universal acknowledgment of the acute lack of resources—including educational, vocational, cultural, recreational, employment, medical, and behavioral health—for minority youths.

Many of those interviewed criticized the lack of family-oriented treatment for minority youths and argued that the justice system did not facilitate parental advocacy on behalf of their children who were involved in the system. Community members expressed much concern that justice officials were quick to label minority youths as gang members, and that the officials lack an understanding of the reasons for gang involvement. They also maintained that the juvenile justice system needs to involve youths and families directly in system policymaking.

One of the most revealing findings of this extensive community study was widespread acknowledgement of a "two-track" juvenile system:

> Two tracks exist for [youths involved in the juvenile justice system]—one for those of families, largely middle- and upper-class Anglo, with means to afford private behavioral health treatment services, and a second for the children of low-income families, largely African American, Hispanic, and Native American children living in single-parent homes, perhaps surviving through public assistance, children whose parents know of no treatment options to suggest to juvenile justice decision makers.[21]

Individuals working at all levels in Arizona's juvenile justice system told researchers that "given the prevailing economic situations of the families and neighborhoods of youth of color, system decision makers are much more likely to view those referred to the system as 'young criminals' deserving punishment." One experienced administrator stated, "It goes again to the unwritten, unspoken word that an Anglo kid who's got in some difficulty with the law can be treated . . . and minority kids are delinquent, they're thugs, they're tough kids, and they need to be punished."[22]

Numerous imprisoned youths in our research echoed those sentiments, including Richard:

> When the cops see you . . . like they see a group of Mexican kids together like us, you know, they're going to think we're a gang. Five or more people, you got—you don't need to be causin' trouble or anything. You can be walkin' down the street, they'll stop you. . . . They look at you like that—like they automatically assume that you're guilty of something by the way you look.[23]

The relationship between gang members and police is particularly volatile. The youths are angered when they believe police stop, question, and search them because of their ethnic background and their assumed gang affiliation. As elucidated by Richard here, youths say they are certain that any questions they ask will only lead to retaliation, harassment, or a loss of freedom.

> Whew! They treat you like a second-class citizen—lower than second class—they see you like you're trash. . . . You'd be hanging out, even at like a pizza place, you know, just sitting there eating. . . . They'll come and harass you, man. They'll like sit next to you and start talking to you. They'll say, "Hey, come outside. I'm gonna check you guys." They constantly get at you. And the gang thing—you'll be walking down the street. I was walking down the street to school—they stopped me, and I was late for school, because they just stopped me—'cause I was walking down the street, you know? They want to take pictures of you, ask you what your name is, where you live—

> *Why?*

> I don't know, 'cause as if they don't have enough pictures of me already. I don't know how many pictures the police department has of me, just from walking around. . . . "Listen to me, or you're goin' to jail!" I don't want to go to jail for no reason. If I do something, I'll take my punishment, but just to be bothering me when I didn't do nothin', that's not right. They do it all the time.

> *And is that based on tattoos, gang colors, your ethnic background?*

> It's like your ethnic background, too—and gang colors. So if you wear your colors and have your tattoos, it doesn't necessarily mean you're going to start trouble in the community, you know? You could just be minding your own business, and they'll just stop you, man, like it's some game. They think it's funny when they like—when you get mad, too. When you get frustrated, they think it's funny. . . . You're at their mercy when they stop you. They can make up a lie, and the other cops will back them up. You're at their mercy, so you can't say anything

in your defense, or they'll run you in, man. Like when they stop me, I never say anything bad to 'em. I never say like, "You're not supposed to do this to me." If I say it, they'll run me in, man, so I just say, "Well, whatever." I do what they tell me to do.

Such police actions reinforce youths' bitterness and their perceived need to band together and to develop a sense of identity and solidarity through the gang.[24]

Life on the Streets: Friendship, Loyalties, Protection, Economics

Life on the streets, including gang membership, is a common feature of imprisoned youths' identities. It is a symbol of profound social forces at work, such as poverty and discrimination, as well as youths' needs to establish a sense of identity and community. One of the model program's greatest challenges was to recognize the centrality of gangs and drugs for many of the imprisoned youths, and to prepare them to return to society in light of those realities.

Life on the streets is a lifestyle generally characterized by truancy, unemployment, economic disadvantage, and innovative, sometimes illegal, behavior. It includes a search for food, clothing, shelter, safety, friendship, purpose, self-esteem, and fun. This lifestyle is *not* necessarily driven by or synonymous with gang membership, crime, or violence, but it may involve these aspects. It often leads to further victimization.[25]

Kevin never became a gang member, but as a "chronic runaway" he was adept at life on the streets. Occasionally, sympathetic adults offered food and shelter "until he could get a job and get on his feet." When he stayed longer than they anticipated, they gave Kevin a little money and asked him to leave. Kevin would move on, prevailing on the goodwill of other people. When such opportunities were not available, he usually found alternatives to actually sleeping on the streets. At least once he stayed in a hospital's intensive-care waiting room. The waiting room was equipped with chairs that folded out into single beds so family members could be available for emergencies. Kevin "adopted" an elderly patient as his grandfather for a couple of days, appearing too upset to engage in any lengthy conversations with hospital personnel.[26]

Imprisoned youths gave diverse reasons for resisting gang involvement when they were on the streets: gang membership was not an available option when they needed support; the fear of violence associated with gangs deterred them; when their support could be cultivated, adults were more capable of providing needed financial assistance; and gang affiliation might interfere with other survival options. This last reason was offered by one young man who was "jumped out" of the gang in order to extend his drug dealing to a wider market, since he felt that gang membership limited his ability to sell to everyone willing to buy. Thus, his decision to leave the gang was based on his economic interests and entrepreneurial ambition.

Gang membership *is* of major importance for many imprisoned youths, a matter both of identity and of survival. However, imprisoned youths' understandings and descriptions of gangs are complex and diverse. The structure and sophistication of gangs vary significantly, and there is notable individuation among the gang members serving time in juvenile prison. The decision to resist, embrace, or renounce gang membership, and strategies for surviving on the streets, differ from one youth to the next.

Not all young men who join gangs are engaged in criminal activity or seeking violence.[27] Gang members who commit crimes most often act alone or with one or two homeboys—not in a gang-related capacity. Many of those who have been involved in violence experience internal conflicts about their values and priorities, conflicts that result when they confront the fear of dying, the desire for "the rush" they associate with fighting, the remorse they sometimes feel when they think about their victims' suffering or their mothers' hopes for them, and the impossibility of simply "trying not to think about it."

Gang membership is inextricably bound to youths' deep desires for "respect." This includes issues of pride, status, fairness, equity, and trust; civility, dignity, integrity, and acceptance of cultural differences; recognition of loyalties; and freedom from abuse and harassment. Respect is central to youths' motivations for joining gangs, but their interpretations of "respect" differ, and they give respect only to a select few.[28]

Many of the youths suggested that gangs are formed initially for protection *against* violence or injustice. One youth said, "The rebels who fought for democracy during the Revolutionary War were a gang tryin' to protect themselves against the injustices of *their* day." Gangs provide safety in numbers—friends who are willing to stick up for each other against threatening odds.[29]

In a gang, what are the . . . things that you feel are really important?

Your set. Your hood. Your homies. Your life. That's it.

Neighborhood youth gangs develop as kids grow up together and identify with a particular geographic area, often supported by a common ethnic heritage. In older, more stable neighborhoods, membership in a specific gang sometimes is associated with family pride, with second- or third-generation family involvement.[30] As one youth, Terrence, described it, "Some people just was raised over there, like me. . . . I was just raised over there." Gang membership for these youths is about establishing relationships, seeking support for the frustrations and hardships they face, and attempting to fit into the larger culture.[31]

Most of the youths "slide into gang membership" through their involvement in a gradual progression of activities and relationships within their neighborhoods.[32] Their main purpose for coming together is "when the neighborhood gets down—parties, stuff like that." Gangs are appealing: young people in the neighborhood enter the ranks of "wannabes," ripe for membership, and eventually a significant number are initiated.

Did you have to go through anything in order to be jumped in?

I grew up with 'em.

So you didn't have to do anything—or get beaten up or anything like that?

It's like people that haven't grown up with anybody from the neighborhood and nobody knows them, *they* have to be jumped in. They don't have to steal anything or anything, but if you don't grow up there and nobody knows you, you have to be jumped in.

Becoming a gang member is not uniformly violent nor does it usually involve violence against nongang members. When youths join gangs within their own neighborhoods, it is more likely to be gradual rather than dramatic. In contrast, for outsiders or relative newcomers, those who grew up in a different neighborhood, being "jumped in" is a violent ritual to renounce their loyalty to their old friends and neighborhood and pledge their commitment to the new.

Although life on the streets frequently can be an escape from poor family relationships,[33] many youths did not join gangs for this reason. A significant number of the gang members expressed great respect and caring for their families, and they often referred to the positive influence of a particular family member, like a mother or a grandmother. When they first joined the gang, many youths did not perceive a conflict between family and gang loyalties, nor did they acknowledge the potential for danger to their families.[34] One such youth stated:

> I value my family—and myself. That's my biggest priority. I'd say—I'd say I'd take my family over a gang any day. . . . And then like—you may wonder why I want to be in a gang if my family is there for me. I don't know, it's more or less where I grew up, my friends. I also value friendship, you know? My friends—I never let my friends down.

Few imprisoned youths said they joined gangs to become a part of the violence and criminal activity associated with the gang culture.[35] Grant explained:

When did you get started in the gang?

About six and a half years ago [at age ten].

And how did you get started?

Well, I was going to get beat up this one day—get jumped by these guys—and this guy came by and saved my butt. And we became good friends and, you know, he's "gang-affiliated. . . ."

Tell me, is the main reason that you got involved with the gang that you liked this guy, you hung around with him, and, like you said, he saved your butt? So is it for protection, friendship? What was the biggest reason?

First, it was for protection, then friendship, and then it became like family. We always did everything together and always got along, and we just had fun together.

Even "hard-core" gang members initially turned to the gang for protection, security, recognition, self-esteem, a sense of belonging ("kickin' back with my homies"), and the opportunity to "meet girls" and to "party." Some were "jumped in" while inside the prison, and their reasons were similar.

In contrast to the majority of gang members, these hard-core gang members provided insight into the less numerous, more sophisticated gangs that are violent both in their initiation rituals and routine activities. Daniel explained:

People like my hood. Everybody want to be from my hood, 'cause they hear that my hood's strong. . . . If you're gonna be from this hood, you gotta show your loyalty for this hood. You can't be no little punk. . . . Some hoods, they'll make you kill somebody or do something else or—it's just a test. . . . If you're going to get into our hood, you're gonna pay for it.

It is more than "just a test"—it is also a commitment. Richard explained, "You gotta be trusted, you know. They have to know you're down for it [the gang], 'cause there's no time for a part-time gang member, you know? You gotta be down. When it comes down to it, you gotta be down . . . whatever happens."

Once young "wannabes" have committed serious crimes in order to prove their loyalty to the "hood," they are not likely to change their minds about gang membership. They have new enemies and are in danger of arrest or retaliation. After years of violence, some (like Angel here) express regret, grief and fear when they reflect on the high price of gang membership in their lives and the lives of their friends.

You have tattoos. Tell me why—is there any meaning behind the tattoos?

Any meaning?

Well, let's start with the teardrops [tattooed below your eye] . . .

See, you have dead homeboys, commit a murder of some sort, or it's like how long you've been locked up. . . . It's a long story. I don't think I want to talk about that.

Okay . . . you can't tell me what they mean then?

I still have—I still have bad feelings about that sometimes.

That's okay. But the general purpose of the teardrops—is it pride? Is it grief? Is it—is it self-inflicted punishment? Is it—

It's more or less like grief, like—like you can't cry for who you—or what you did, so you have something there to remind you of the bad that you did, most of the time. It's not like punishment, it's like crying without crying, you know? You can't really feel anything, 'cause you didn't know them. You didn't know their family or anything like that, most of the time.

What does it tell you—when you see them in the mirror?

It reminds me, a lot of time, of what I did.

How does that make you feel?

It makes me feel like I don't want to do it again. . .

You have another tattoo by your other eye.

That's for my dead homeboy.

How long ago did that happen?

About two years ago.

And how did that happen?

He killed himself.

He killed himself? . . . Was he on anything when he killed himself?

Well, I think he was drunk. He was.

Do you know why he killed himself? Do you have any idea?

I think he was just tired of his life—the way it was going. Things weren't right.

Despite their grief and fears, the benefits youths associate with gang membership often are most important.[36]

> I'm not gonna lie to you and say I don't get anything out of it, 'cause I, you know, I kinda like it. . . . You get that adrenaline when you know that somethin's goin' to go down, you know? But it's not like you're not afraid to die or anything—'cause I think about that almost every day. . . . It's a sense of like who's the bigger man when you fight somebody—who's the best. It's like a name—like you get a reputation on the streets—like they hear my name, so "He does this," you know? Or, "He beat this guy up," or "He's known for doing such and such."

Ironically, gang membership frequently intensifies problems that individual members are seeking to escape—personal danger, insecurity, and disrespect. Adolescent gang members' distrust and fear of others match society's distrust and fear of *them*. The symbols of their collective social identity—tattoos, tagging (gang graffiti), and certain types of clothing (Dickies, colors, and sagging pants)—are transformed in the public mind into indicators of "social collapse," explosive anger, and impending violence.[37] Adolescent rebellion is escalated by declarations of war by politicians—war on the symbols and the meanings ascribed to youths by a fearful public. As a result, youthful behavior is defined and redefined to fit the focus of the current battle being waged.[38]

▉ The Perpetual Specter of Drugs

A major subtext for nearly all incarcerated youths is the prevalence of drugs and alcohol. Since as young as the age of eight, most of these young men have used and abused drugs, ranging from paint to alcohol to crystal-meth and acid.[39] Some learn this behavior at home and some on the streets. For many, the potential and likelihood of substance abuse was established long before they entered the juvenile prison and often several years before they were accused of crimes. Few experts would say drug use *causes* delinquency, but the two become intertwined and inseparable for most of the youths.[40] As Carlos explained:

> I was high twenty-four hours a day. I'm sayin' the truth. I would barely wake up sometimes, you know—you'd watch me—the first thing people wake up they go to the rest room, wash their face, brush their teeth. Well, I'd do that, but I'd wake up, you know, light up a joint—and then while I walk over there to brush my teeth. . . . It's like—it's like a sickness. . . . And that first time that I got locked up . . . because of . . . probation violation, I fainted. That's—that's crazy. Every time I'd eat, I'd throw up. I'd be shakin' and all of that. . . .

Drugs are ubiquitous and integral to the youths' everyday lives. Drugs are seen as a vehicle for entertainment as well as an escape from the disappointments and hardships of everyday life. For some youths, the months spent in prison are among the few that they have been "straight" in recent years. For, unlike most adult and juvenile prisons, the model program units were primarily drug- and alcohol-free during this period. One sixteen-year-old reported, "I haven't been straight since I was thirteen, except for the last six months. I'd really like this to be an option when I go home."

Although the levels of involvement and the motivating factors vary, some youths, like Carlos, regret ever starting to use drugs.

Smoking a joint, drinking some beer. It's stupid. It's bad stuff. After my mom and dad got divorced . . . all this stuff started happening, so I just stopped going to school, stopped getting like As and Bs. It's bad—just started rollin' joints. That's all I see myself doing—rolling joints, selling pot, just getting money. Because it's like I had everything from my dad, and when my dad got sick and couldn't work anymore, it's like my mom couldn't get—she was goin' through a hard time . . . That's when I started getting messed up.

A few youths had succeeded in getting off drugs prior to entering the prison, but they were a small minority. The determination to change their lives and strong support from friends or relatives were the common threads in their accounts. Richard described his transition:

You said you don't do drugs. So drugs aren't big in your gang . . . or is it just with you?

Not big with me. . . .

Okay. Alcohol?

I used to drink—a lot, a long time ago, but not no more—not when I got out this last time. I stopped.

Why?

I felt like a bum. I feel dirty when I do that stuff—you know, afterwards. I'd say, "Well, it's worth it," you know? It feels good when you're doin' it, but afterwards you feel like a bum, so I don't want to feel like that. So I stopped.

Richard's experience is exceptional among imprisoned youths. Some are unconvinced that drug use is problematic. The vast majority acknowledge the dangers, but they view drug use as inevitable and quitting as impossible, especially in light of the pressures of life on the streets.

Widespread images portray imprisoned youths as uniformly violent and dangerous. But the offenses for which these youths were imprisoned and the prison system's assessment of their risk to public safety do not confirm such assumptions. Less than half were currently imprisoned for violent offenses, including 10 of the first 24 youths in the program (42 percent) and 138 of the total 385 youths (36 percent). An additional 29 percent of the first 24 youths and approximately 43 percent of the 385 were imprisoned after being convicted of property felonies. Fifteen of the youths (4 percent) were currently imprisoned for drug offenses ranging from possession of marijuana to sniffing paint to sale of narcotics. The remaining 68 youths (18 percent) had been imprisoned after being convicted of misdemeanors.

Sixty-one percent (233) of the youths in the program over the two-year period were in prison for the first time. Comparable figures for the total prison population are not available for that time period, but in late 1995 a similar proportion, 62 percent of the total prison population, were first timers.[41] In contrast, 39 percent of the youths in the program were placed there after their parole had been revoked. These youths had been imprisoned previously and they were reimprisoned after being arrested for new offenses or for technical violations of parole—behaviors such as curfew violation, consumption of alcohol, truancy, or failing to meet with their parole officers. Of the 152 youths in the program as a result of parole violations, 20 (13 percent) were originally imprisoned for violent offenses, 86 (57 percent) for property felonies, and 46 (30 percent) for misdemeanors.

The youths recommitted to prison after parole violations had been imprisoned an average of three times with the actual number ranging from once to seven times (there was one youth in the latter category). In many parole violation cases, determination of guilt regarding the newly alleged offenses was uncertain because the youths never went to court. Some charges were reduced or dropped, while others were simply used as evidence of parole violations for which the youths served additional time, as determined by prison officials.[42]

The consent decree negotiated after the lawsuit stipulated that "a standardized, objective classification or risk assessment instrument" must be used in diagnosing youths committed to prison to determine if public safety required their continued incarceration.[43] The task force on juvenile corrections, charged with responding to the lawsuit, created the risk assessment instrument, which focused on the delinquent behavior of youths and the issues that many consider the most important indicators of danger to the community and the likelihood of recidivism.[44] It examined: (1) the past and present offenses for which the youth had been adjudicated (found guilty in court); (2) aggravating factors that may have been associated with the offense, such as using a dangerous weapon, causing serious bodily harm to the victim, or committing any sexual offense; (3) the number of delinquent adjudications within the past year; (4) the total number of delinquent adjudications on record; and (5) the age of first adjudication.

Like most risk assessment instruments, there was little attempt to contextualize the "risk score" through reference to social factors that may have contributed to the creation of delinquency. Thus, the risk assessment score represented a summary of a youth's history of official delinquency. The scores were intended to be used for two purposes: to identify youths whose imprisonment was necessary for public safety, and to identify youths for whom community-based alternatives were most appropriate in light of their low risk to public safety.

Review of the risk scores of these imprisoned youths clearly demonstrates that many imprisoned youths represented little risk to public safety. Over the two years of our study, no more than half of the youths in the program were classified as presenting high levels of risk to public safety, due to offenses such as multiple burglaries, multiple vehicle thefts, aggravated assault (including drive-by shootings), armed robbery, sexual assault, and homicide.[45]

In contrast to youths convicted of violent offenses or multiple property offenses, there were 16 percent (60 of the 385) for whom it is difficult to support the argument that they needed to be imprisoned. They were classified in the low-risk category based on objective assessments of their delinquent behavior, including involvement in such activities as shoplifting, simple assaults, trespassing, and disorderly conduct. An even higher percentage, 46 percent (11 of the first 24 youths), in Unit Four were classified as low risks to public safety.

During the two years of the study, 34 percent of the youths who participated in the program (131 of the 385) were classified as medium risks to public safety, based on their involvement in offenses such as burglary, vehicle theft, narcotics charges, sexual abuse, and manslaughter. Seven of the first twenty-four youths to enter the program (29 percent) were classified as medium risks to the community.

Although half of the program participants were classified as medium or low risks, some of the youths confirmed the images portrayed by media hype and political rhetoric. These youths were typically included in the high-risk category. Of the first twenty-four youths, 25 percent were so classified. A larger proportion of the 385 youths who participated throughout the two-year period, 40 to 50 percent, were classified as high risks to public safety.

But being classified as "high risk" to public safety did not mean that youths could not return to and succeed in society. "High risk" is not synonymous with diagnoses of psychopathy or sociopathy, and juvenile justice professionals consistently maintain that an overwhelming majority of juvenile offenders are capable of responding to treatment. Clinical psychologists diagnose an extremely small percentage of imprisoned youths, 1 to 3 percent, as psychopaths or sociopaths not amenable to treatment.[46]

Contextualizing Their Offenses

It is important to know the offenses for which these youths were imprisoned, but it is equally essential to place the youths' offenses and lives within the social context that engulfs them. These young men's experiences, problems, and potentials are inseparable from their life circumstances and positions within society.

Manny's arrest on charges of theft cannot be understood fully without acknowledging that his family lived in poverty in the barrio, with both parents working long hours at hard labor for substandard wages. These economic conditions bear a direct relationship to Manny's lack of supervision, gang affiliation, and commitment to the juvenile prison, despite a minimal delinquency history.

It is impossible to address the charges of child molestation against Brandon adequately without recognizing the impact of his own sexual abuse that occurred routinely over an eight-month period at age nine. Matthew's repeated aggressive behavior cannot be dissociated from the fact that four years ago, at age nine, he saw his mother brutally murder his two half-sisters, six months and eighteen months of age. The knowledge that she also intended to kill him, slashing his throat and bashing his head repeatedly, devastated Michael. The additional strain of being sent to live with a father with whom he had had no contact since age two was overwhelming.

It is not enough to know that David raped an elderly woman without also acknowledging that early intervention might have prevented it. David himself was brutally raped and molested seven years earlier, at age eight, at the hands of a violent stranger in a parking lot near his home. The rapist was caught and convicted, but the full and lasting impact on David is unknowable. The unavailability of public treatment resources and his parents' inability to pay for private counseling and treatment were significant.

Some of the youths have supportive families and friends; many are not strongly gang identified; a number have limited delinquency histories; and few have received treatment or rehabilitative services in the community prior to imprisonment. And, from an early age, the majority have been exposed to varying degrees of violence, abusive treatment, neglect, and alcohol and substance abuse (by family members as well as themselves). As other analysts have observed, these youths generally have had difficult and deprived lives and have experienced the underbelly of contemporary society.[47]

There are also youths who more closely approximate the stereotypes: youths who have been involved in extensive violence, are committed to gang lifestyles, are heavily drug dependent, and are generally scornful of and isolated from conventional society. There are youths who are hardened, for whom repeated imprisonment is a badge of courage or a rite of passage to full respect and membership within gang culture inside and outside the prison. Several can be crass and foul, others become disrespectful to staff and other youths when frustrated and angry.

Within this prison environment the individuality of the youths is evident, their talents and propensities as well as their limitations. In fact, these young men frequently exhibit personal traits that are highly admired in conventional society.[48] Kevin's poetry is expressive and poignant. Tyrone's musical talent at the keyboard is impressive. Grant's ability to develop thought-provoking word pictures is extraordinary. Many of the youths are articulate, interesting, and engaging, and a substantial number display an adolescent charm and attractiveness. A number of them demonstrate an astute ability to discern what behaviors and language are appropriate to a situation, and, without exception, they respond positively to those adults they respect.

The youths' lives reveal a highly complex set of factors enmeshed in an intricate pattern of frustration and failure. A complicated web emerges from the specifics of the youths' lives and behaviors, the philosophy and practices of the juvenile justice system, and the prevailing national and local political climate.

The majority of the youths had problems prior to their first referrals to the juvenile justice system. Difficulties ranged from special education needs to severe psychological and emotional disorders to extreme cases of abuse and neglect. Behavioral problems, family histories, academic test results, treatment issues, and psychological diagnoses demonstrated a series of failures that generally began at an early age.

Very early in their lives, many were casualties of school systems with inadequate resources to address their needs.[49] They were labeled as "disruptive to the normal classroom setting" (often accompanied by a diagnosis of Attention Deficit/Hyperactivity Disorder), "learning disabled," "emotionally handicapped," or simply "not normal." Of the first twenty-four youths to participate in the program, four had histories of chronic truancy, six had dropped out of school prior to the offenses for which they had been imprisoned, and three had been expelled or suspended more than once.

The pattern of difficulties in school often masked the intellectual capabilities of these youths. Although the reported IQ scores for the first twenty-four varied widely, from 68 to 138, even this limited indicator of ability disclosed extensive potential. Most fall into what is considered "the normal range" (85–115), with an average IQ score of 96. But many of these youths had attended six or seven schools over an eight-year period, contributing to the significant number of those functioning below appropriate grade levels.

More importantly, numerous youths say that at some point they came to understand that they were somehow inferior to others who were able to demonstrate success in meeting the expectations of the classroom or society.[50] Some responded to this denigration with defiance, bravado, and hostility; most, like Carlos here, fled the school setting but retained a continued sense of failure.

> I like school, 'cause it's like—I used to be—well, I *am* smart, but it's like after a while I just dropped out of school. And everybody tripped out, because I dropped out—because I was using drugs. I started wantin' to get back into it, but I can't. . . . It was bad.

> *So when did you drop out of school?*

> Six months—a year—two years ago. It's like—I decided to drop out my freshman year, but I'd go back just to mess around. So my mom didn't say nothin'. (He pauses and continues wistfully)—But I would have graduated next week if I had stayed in school.

Although schools are the most common site of early and re-peated feelings of failure for these imprisoned youths, the clues that point to their views on the "real" world and to the circumstances leading to their imprisonment extend throughout their entire lives. Most come from families and communities that have experienced deep-seated problems in a state where more than one-fifth of all children under eighteen years of age and one-third of all minority youth live in poverty.[51] It is also not atypical for these children to have experienced physical, sexual, or emotional abuse.[52] The youths frequently mentioned drug and alcohol abuse within their families as well as physical abuse. Their case files revealed beatings from family members who used fists, extension cords, wire hangers, belts, and water hoses. In one case, child protective services was called to a youth's home twenty times in fourteen years. Assault, rape, molestation, murder, imprisonment, suicide, drug addiction, and abandonment are realities familiar to a substantial number of these youths, within their communities and within their own families.

Youths inside the prison repeatedly expressed their conviction that "most people don't understand" what they face in their own neighborhoods "on the outs." Readily available weapons of all kinds, widespread distrust, fear and death, kill or get killed—these are recurring themes in the lives of these young men.

Almost without exception, these imprisoned youths share a common bond of poverty, physical and emotional abuse, disastrous school experiences, and deadly boredom with a way of life that offers little opportunity to participate in meaningful and interesting activities. They express wariness about adults who have let them down in a variety of ways—family members, teachers, child welfare agencies, and juvenile justice personnel. Despite the desensitization that frequently accompanies these types of experiences, quite a few of the youths are able to express their feelings of frustration and anger in powerful metaphors.[53] Some are remarkably optimistic, many are at least open to opportunities for change, and most are not cynical or caustic. Ironically, many of the youths "volunteered" for this program because they believed their imprisonment, the end of the road, signaled that something would finally be done to change their lives.[54]

Never Children, Still Children

Larger social forces have stripped most of these young people of any meaningful childhood. The precarious nature of their existence is exacerbated by current political strategies that essentially deny their youthfulness. In fundamental ways, they have never gotten to be children and now they are being cast as nonchildren.[55] *Yet they are still children.* It is a tremendous irony. These youths have not been afforded the protection presumed to be part of childhood, and yet the harshness of their lives frequently is disregarded or minimized, even while their presumed responsibility and guilt worthiness are used to justify punitive responses to them.

Most of these youths have not had the experiences traditionally viewed as part of childhood. They often have not been provided with the basic necessities of food, shelter, and care. They have not been protected or shielded from life's cruelty and abuse. They have not known the nurturance and tolerance that encourage personal growth and development. They have not known adolescence as a time of learning and gradual accumulation of experience and understanding. They have not been granted opportunities to feel needed or to make valuable contributions to their families and to society. They have seen little evidence of the "promise of the future."[56]

Even as they are denied experiences once assumed to be fundamental aspects of childhood and adolescence, these youths are deluged with experiences and knowledge from which the American Dream suggests they should be shielded, that is, the harshness of the adult world. Poverty, hunger, drugs, and death are very familiar to most of these youths. They know sexual and physical abuse and exploitation. They live the tragedy and despair once thought reserved for adults.

In recognizing that these youths have been denied the innocence of childhood, it is important to acknowledge the extent to which all youth, regardless of privilege and circumstance, may be exposed to the vicissitudes of adultlike awareness and experiences.[57] It is also likely that the innocence of childhood in past generations has been overstated. We have underestimated and hidden the extent to which all generations have observed and experienced the conflicts and weaknesses of their parents and other adults, especially family violence, alcoholism and drug addiction, and sexual violation.[58] Many children survive such experiences, others do not.

Nevertheless, the experiences of the youths in this book contrast starkly with the images of a protected and nurtured childhood and adolescence and are in sharp dissonance with the experiences of most children within society. With few exceptions, these children's lives have been adultlike in the intensity of their experiences and the depth of their deprivations.[59] Many have seen walls splashed with blood, and the vast majority have experimented with or been controlled by drugs and have known what it is to be considered and feel like a failure.

Yet there is still an enormous vulnerability in them. They retain childlike characteristics: lack of experience in relationships; lack of opportunities to develop decision-making abilities and mature judgment; a sense of humor and playfulness; and a hopefulness. These youths are not uniformly violent, adultlike, cynical, recalcitrant, irredeemable, or committed to crystallized, lawless lifestyles. Many reflect an incongruous combination of street sophistication, because of what they have experienced and "seen" so soon in life, and a striking naivete and guilelessness about other aspects of life. What appear to be contradictory attitudes and characteristics coexist, residing simultaneously within most of the youths. A few have none of the assumed characteristics of imprisoned youths, most have some, and yet others approximate the stereotypes. But almost all exemplify the uneasy mixture of being a kid and premature social aging.

These youths' potential has not solidified to the extent commonly assumed. Most are impressionable and malleable and embody those qualities ascribed to youth by traditional American beliefs. It is a crucial fact that these young men are also children. The vast majority do not have the sophistication, the intent, the malice, or the evil designs of which adults are capable. The portrayal of imprisoned youth as "monsters" is not accurate,[60] but it is politically expedient and necessary in order for a society officially and ideologically committed to its children to vilify, chastise, disregard, devalue, and abandon *these* youths.

It would be an act of romanticization to portray imprisoned youth as rebels or individuals defiant in the face of power. More importantly, it is essential to grasp the great extent to which they are like all of us. Their lives—experiences, imaginations, dreams—are enmeshed within power structures and relationships, and, like so many of us within society, their actions are not so much those of rebels as reflections of their everyday multiple and contradictory realities.[61] Perhaps what is most important about the model treatment program is that, because it viewed extreme, hierarchical forms of power as counterproductive and useless in changing youths' lives, it sought to offer spaces of resistance to domination and opportunities for change.

The Program's Early Success and Eventual Demise

Three

The Early Days of Intense Effort, Initial Triumph

The reform of the juvenile prisons was based on a legal mandate for change brought about by the class-action lawsuit. This included the separation of the juvenile and adult prison systems and the selection of a nationally prominent director for the agency.[1] The task force created in response to the class-action lawsuit conducted a national search for a director and recommended an individual not tied to juvenile corrections within the state; the governor accepted their recommendation. The new director recruited a talented and accomplished administrative staff. In addition to hiring a dedicated associate director and relying on the highest caliber of existing leadership and experience within the agency, juvenile corrections combed the state for respected and innovative individuals from a variety of backgrounds. They persuaded staff from the state supreme court's administrative offices and the state's office for children, as well as private practitioners, to join "the team for change." These individuals left established positions because of the director's persuasiveness, the attraction of the challenge of such an innovative endeavor, and the opportunities for professional and personal fulfillment and reward.

The composition of the central administrative staff reflected the ethnic and racial communities of the youths they were to serve. The director was a Mexican American, and there were more African Americans and Mexican Americans in decision-making positions than ever before in the agency's history. While the staff within the institutions remained predominantly white, increased efforts were made to recruit and retain individuals from racial and ethnic minorities. Women continued to be a strong presence among the institutional staff and assumed positions of leadership and authority, but the majority of central administrators were male.

The role of the "line staff" in creating and giving life to the model program cannot be overemphasized. Many of these staff members were long-term employees within the juvenile prisons, and they were well acquainted with the vulnerability of juvenile corrections to political fashion and opportunism. Many of the staff members had outlasted multiple changes in leadership and numerous philosophical and programmatic shifts. Despite meager compensation, they were assigned major responsibility for designing the new program and generating the motivation and enthusiasm necessary for its initiation. At the beginning of the program, when only one of the fifteen living units within the two institutions was designated as a model program unit, the program staff also endured the cynicism and rivalry of other staff members not chosen to be involved with the program.

In the earliest months of the program, staff members' enthusiasm and dedication, as well as satisfaction with the program, were evident. One experienced staff member said, "You can see that the kids are really gaining something out of it. . . . And it's not going to be one out of a thousand, maybe, that you make a difference with." Another staff member expressed similar feelings:

> I *enjoy* [my job]. Days go by real fast for me. . . . And I hear some of the kids who are saying, "Boy, it's that time already! [incredulous that time passed that quickly]" That's nice, because it's structured, and you don't have all that free time and you're not sitting back thinking, "Why am I here?" . . . What I like the most

is the ability to tell a kid something and see it click, and the honesty that comes from a kid when he actually has a breakthrough. . . . That gives me the opportunity to say something that he is actually going to hear and remember.

In many ways, the lawsuit against the prison system permitted staff members a unique opportunity to initiate change that was otherwise impossible. Crucially, the majority of these staff members *wanted* to work with youths, despite their own sense of disillusionment with their jobs. Six months after the model program began, we surveyed the thirty-eight staff members most closely associated with the program and found a strong majority who reported that the youths were the major reason they stayed even though several had to work a second job in order to do so. For several staff members within the prison, the model program was the long-awaited opportunity to offer these young people what they believed had been missing.

In the first six months of the program, the youths, staff members, and administrators were enthusiastic and intensely participatory. The eagerness and hopefulness was obvious, and references to specific program values, objectives, and methods were constant. Despite their occasional defensiveness and authoritarianism, staff members worked diligently to follow the program's principles.

When the first twenty-four youths entered the model program, they were apprehensive, curious, and guardedly hopeful. Their concerns ranged from immediate details affecting their daily routines to the long-term potential of the program. They hoped that the program would be less boring, that the promised Ping-Pong table would materialize, that they would be released sooner, and that legitimate help would be offered that might really make a difference.

The youths were intensely involved in "doing the program." Many seemed to take the program at its word, evidenced by the way they acted toward each other and staff. Although in the beginning they had reservations, most of the youths reacted very much the way the model had envisioned. While their behavior, of course, reflected individual temperaments, the youths responded well to being treated with respect; living in a clean, well-equipped, and pleasant environment; and being regarded as individuals worthy of the responsibility to participate in the program.

The group orientation and interactive philosophy of the model were highly successful in getting the youths to "buy into" the new program and to consider seriously the possibility of making changes in their lives. Youths who previously felt they had been treated with little respect, or with much disrespect, responded positively to their inclusion in decision making. The youths displayed considerable potential for collective, communal action in support of the program's principles. As Nick commented,

It was like the first eight people were together . . . like the first ten days. . . . Then . . . the next group came in and it was just like a slow process of [building], and by the time all twenty-four people was there, everybody was, you know, "Well, let's go do this, let's do that." Yeah, *together*.

Mutual respect and trust emerged gradually but steadily. Youths who had been in prison for several months prior to entering this program offered comparisons of life before and after their introduction to the model program. Their comments, like Mitch's below, reflected the hope that things could be different.

It's like [the youths] have respect not to go into other people's rooms and all that. Over in the other cottage, you turn your back on your door—you're standin' right at your door with your back against the door lookin' down the hall, you know, for about thirty seconds, and you look back in—and if you don't catch 'em in the act, you're gonna notice that there's somethin' missin' off your desk, and you just can't place it. There's somethin' that's not there, and then you figure out what it is, and then you're like, alright, he's got it.

Tell me again why you think it's different here.

Just people—it's just like they came in here, and they told everybody, "This is a different program, and we don't steal in this program. You can keep your door open. People won't steal from you." So they're like, "Well, they're not stealin' from *me*," you know. "Let's be cool and not steal."

The vastly improved physical environment was significant, for it symbolized the new beginning represented by the program. Many of the youths had transferred from existing units at the prison to the newly renovated one. The units they left were bleak, smelly, poorly furnished, crowded, and covered with graffiti. The model unit was freshly painted and pleasant. Each youth had his own cell-like room, and the common areas contained new and comfortable, although modest, furniture. The walls were adorned with contemporary posters supporting program principles, and, after initial problems were overcome, the showers and laundry facilities functioned fully. Once they arrived in the unit, the youths became actively involved in the ongoing improvement of their residence. They planted trees and greenery outside and meticulously cleaned and maintained both the inside and outside of the unit. For many, Unit Four was both a matter of responsibility and pride.

Several incidents demonstrated that the youths had begun to identify with their unit as a place of support and community, as "the home" staff members encouraged them to make it. In one instance, a youth overheard a visitor denigrating his barrio background and responded by telling the visitor to "Get out of *my home!*"

Many of the youths demonstrated pride in Unit Four, including their "rooms." Carlos was one of those who kept their cells absolutely spotless and meticulously organized. He displayed his attractive bulletin board and said that this was the first time in his life that he had a room of his own. Prior to his imprisonment he lived in a tiny apartment with several members of his extended family, and he usually slept on the couch.

The bulletin boards hung in each youth's room displayed pictures of girlfriends, family members, and, often, the youths' children. Some youths tacked up profuse drawings and poetry, and many, especially Latino youths, displayed crucifixes. Initiated by the director of the prisons, the bulletin boards illustrated the program's attempts to support youths in expressing their identities and in creating a space, even in prison, that was their own. Despite the restrictions and lack of freedom of the prison environment, the model program had the potential to provide a reprieve from the constant struggles outside and inside.

These early days did not witness a miraculous, total transformation of youths and staff members, but they did constitute a time of change and engagement at a level previously unexperienced. The first twenty-four youths, unlike those who followed, had volunteered to be in the program, and they were "willing to give it a chance" for a variety of reasons. They thought it would relieve the boredom and vacuousness of their routines, hasten their release from prison, and, perhaps, help make a difference in their lives. Despite images of imprisoned youths as recalcitrant, belligerent, and hostile, the great majority of these youths were not hardened, and many still maintained a belief, a hope, that their lives could get better. Some did well in the program from the beginning.

Quiet and cooperative, Tomás was predisposed to doing well in the program. He received no special attention, but completed the prescribed tasks without problems. He presented little difficulty for the staff, but was seldom recognized as one of the "stars." Considered "a good kid" from the beginning, his progress was not seen as dramatic. He did not publicize his good behavior, and, although he was among those who did well in the model program, on many occasions he seemed to fade into the background and to become almost invisible. Perhaps because of his difficult home life, Tomás was relatively content to remain in the institution. He neither flattered staff nor annoyed them. Other youths who were extremely solicitous or demanding of staff received more attention.

Bernardo was initially reserved and hesitant during group activities. Quiet and lacking self-confidence in a way that seemed inconsistent with his large physical presence, he frequently distanced himself from activities in Unit Four. Emotionally withdrawn and sitting alone, he often observed the others and appeared to weigh the risks of joining the group. But within the first month Bernardo began to be more comfortable in the program and expressed fondness for his room, several of the youths, and some staff members. He worked on his GED, and, although he was not one of the youths who talked routinely during group sessions, he was pleasant and cooperative in program activities. When asked, "What should this program be like to do kids the most good?" Bernardo responded, "It should be like this, how it is right now, but [fewer] groups and [penalties] that are not that high."

Within the first six weeks, most of the youths responded positively to the program. Although their actions were tinged with incredulity and amusement at what they were involved in (constantly talking everything out, "commending" each other for behavior reflecting program principles, and verbalizing explicit "affirmations" of their goals for the day), most of the youths embraced the program. In the main, they behaved in ways that suggested they took the program seriously, especially the crucial notion that they were valued participants, not passive prisoners. They were cooperative and good-humored, and many assumed the responsibility to help each other, to lead and engage actively in discussions, and to grapple intensely and extensively with their past experiences, current problems, and "the future."

Two months into the program, a teacher described the change:

The atmosphere is much better. . . . The only thing I can say is every bit of work I've ever given them, they take very seriously. These are the same kids that would not be in public schools, or if they were, they would be holy terrors. And now when we give them—one of them walks in every morning and says, "Give me my book. I'm ready to get started." And they're constantly asking me, "How's this going to help me? You tell me and I'll do it, but you show me how it's going to help me." And they're learning about how to budget, and they're learning how to get out there and try to live alone and how to get a decent job and what that job's going to pay them.

In part due to the stimulation and recognition associated with being selected for a new and highly visible program, the youths contributed, questioned, exhibited respect for each other and staff members, interacted in a cooperative yet critical way, and encouraged each other to set and achieve goals. Numerous incidents demonstrated that they felt they had a right to question perceived injustices, inconsistencies, or "inappropriate" situations. They could and did say things such as "This rule does not make any sense," "I'm angry," or "Just because you're an adult, you think it's okay for you to lord it over me and to make me do things I don't like." Many had a great deal to say and felt they could say anything they wanted, as long as they did so within the established guidelines—that is, without becoming physically aggressive or using abusive, disrespectful language.

One exchange, illustrative of the early days of the program, took place between Larry and a staff member. The youth's response to the incident was legitimated and encouraged by the program but inconceivable in a "normal" prison environment. Larry was challenging a staff member's interpretation of a specific program rule. As the discussion continued, the staff member had become extremely angry with Larry and "had lost it," as other youths remarked later. He was yelling loudly at Larry, looming physically much larger over the small youth. Embodying the program ideal, Larry then attempted to calm the staff member: "Mr. Carpenter, I think we can settle our problems, talk this out in a peaceful manner. That's what this program is about."

It was clear to youths, staff, and the researcher that this exchange did not represent pure fulfillment of program principles. The staff member's behavior was not idyllic nor unambiguous, for although he contained his anger and lowered his voice, later he violated the program when he ordered the youth to his room, even though Larry had followed program principles. To a certain extent the precocious youth enjoyed the fact that the program legitimated opportunities "to be right." But the most significant point of this exchange was that Larry had comprehended the principles and, in some measure, believed that if he acted in accordance with the program's philosophy, including assuming responsibility for himself and others, the program would work, both to his short- and long-range betterment.

During the initial six months, the discussion groups (youths with youths and staff, as well as staff with staff) were intense and focused. Likewise, the youths participated in reviewing institutional policies, especially those they viewed as unjust, and were afforded a significant role in negotiations and decision making. They prepared and presented requests and petitions; in open sessions they expressed their perspectives and clearly expected that these would be discussed and considered.

Many youths acknowledged that the model program differed significantly from their experiences in other prison units, particularly in the level of concern expressed by most staff members and the concerted efforts to accomplish things cooperatively. Nick commented:

> More of the staff here will sit down and talk to you than they did in [the other unit]. You know, they'll sit and they'll talk to you if you got a problem. Most of them will sit down and explain to you what you're doin' wrong. . . . Now I'm willin' to stop and learn. Before it was just like it's gotta be what I want and, you know, "No matter what, I ain't gonna listen to you. . . ." There's a *lot* of positive things [about the program].

The youths acknowledged benefits from the program that reached beyond education and employment goals. They expressed their appreciation for learning new ways to look at old situations. Of vital importance was the opportunity for many to learn how to control anger more effectively, to deal with conflict without physical aggression, and to consider consequences before acting. Many youths made statements such as, "I *changed*. . . . I used to get mad and wanted to tear stuff up" or "[Before] when I got mad, I used to go in my room alone and cool down, and now I talk to the staff about exactly what's bothering me" or "I think it helped me, 'cause . . . often you don't think before you do [something]. That's how I was. I didn't think before I did it."

It seemed that many of the youths seriously considered the possibility that there was hope for their futures. Kevin was one who wanted to succeed in the program. He expressed his thoughts in poetry:

> I look out the window of life,
> And the thunder sounds in the distance,
> And the lightning lights the black sky,
> And I see a storm beginning in my life—
> A storm in which all elements represent something.
>
> As the thunder screams,
> I realize that the thunder is my anger screaming inside me.
> And as the lightning flashes,
> I realize it is my frustration exploding inside my mind.
> And as for the black sky,
> I realize it is the feeling of emptiness and hopelessness in
>   my heart.
>
> And as I think of these things,
> I do not realize that the rain has stopped
> And that the sun is shining
> And that the storm is over.
> And the rain was the tears I was crying—
> With the pain of realizing these things—
> And now I must do something about them.

Although they were unaccustomed to and somewhat embarrassed by positive attention, the youths also appreciated it. They enjoyed and thrived in the activities tailored to their individual situations. Once he was comfortable enough to reveal that he could not read, Tyrone, a seventeen-year-old who had shown little enthusiasm for the program, worked steadfastly with a personal tutor to gain this crucial skill. Several youths who were more academically prepared for community college visited campuses and filed the necessary paperwork to determine their eligibility for financial aid. Encouraged to finish high school or obtain their GED and go on to college, many were seeing their futures in a positive light for perhaps the first time in their lives.

Some youths reported they were considering the possibility of pursuing community college degrees in counseling, because they might have something to offer other young people in similar positions. Several became excited when prison personnel said they might establish peer counselor positions and hire these youths part-time while they attended college. The hopelessness and confusion that the youths had expressed about their futures when they first entered the program were mediated by their desires to obtain good jobs, own homes, and have families. For many of the youths, academic and vocational aspirations were a high priority when they were in the model program.

During the early days, the program's fluid approach allowed for the youths' ambiguity and complexities. It did not punish them for expressing or exploring contradictory emotions. It tacitly acknowledged the enormous irony of the youths' simultaneous exclusion from childhood and their longing for it. Staff members dealt with youths' street-smart dimensions as well as their vulnerable, childlike dimensions.

It often seemed that perhaps the one place these youths were permitted their childhood was within the prison walls, such as when staff organized relay races or hung a piñata. Masks slipped away as seventeen-year-old, "hard-core" gang members joined thirteen-year-old, giggling youngsters in line, waiting to be blindfolded for their turn before the piñata. Once the piñata was broken, and the candy scattered on the ground, it was a scene of childhood play, with all the youths laughing and scrambling to retrieve the prizes. Despite their occasional sophisticated behavior, the youths also acted like immature, inexperienced, "goofy" adolescents. How else do you describe a fifteen-year-old kid shuffling blindly down the hall uttering muffled pleas for help after getting his head and shoulders stuck in his wastebasket? The explanation: he just "wondered what it would feel like in there."

The program gave the youths the chance to have new types of interactions with each other and members of the community. It supported the expression of emotions and responses that received little recognition in their regular lives within society. Openness and trust became conceivable for many as they were encouraged to develop their identification with, and sensitivity to, others.

One particular evening session with guests from the community demonstrated the complexity of the issues dealt with by the youths. It highlighted the magnitude of their abilities, within a nurturing environment, to confront life's difficulties and their troubled pasts. It also demonstrated the youths' capacity to empathize with and support others, even strangers. Our fieldnotes tell about the session:

> Unit Four has scheduled an evening presentation and discussion on drinking and driving. Their guests are two white women probably in their late twenties. The first speaks passionately about losing someone she loved, her much younger brother, because of a drunken driver. She tells the youths about the incident in great detail: her brother's scout troop on a bicycling trip, a blind-drunk driver barreling down a narrow road after nightlong partying, and the virtual massacre of two fourteen-year-old boys. She has carefully prepared remarks, but, grief-stricken, she becomes barely audible and weeps as she sits down.
>
> The second woman has come to speak not of the loss of a loved one, but of the indelible experience of being the drunk driver and causing the death of another. She, too, tells her story in great detail: the alcohol consumed, the envisioned quick trip to the store, the running of the stop sign, the horrendous sound of the collision, and the mangled human being no longer breathing. She tells the youths she was imprisoned, she has lost her children, and her life is ravaged; and that this devastation is second only to the nightmares of endlessly reliving that deathly moment.
>
> Throughout these remarks, the youths sit on chairs and couches, quietly, respectfully, and attentively. Some look directly at each speaker, while others look steadfastly down, many with their hands folded in their laps.

It is possible to imagine imprisoned youths—all of whom know violence, some of whom have been violent—responding defensively or defiantly to such remarks. It is also possible to imagine imprisoned youths—many of whom are racial or ethnic minorities and many of whom are poor—being indifferent to or derisive of two unknown white women, one of whom is clearly affluent. It is possible to imagine imprisoned youths—most of whom have never enjoyed the rewards of conventional respectability—failing to relate, especially to a presentation about a white, privileged Eagle Scout and a presentation geared to a middle-class white audience. It is possible to imagine such responses, but in this instance such imaginings would be mistaken. The youths' comments and questions following the presentations displayed a sensitivity and kindness rare for any group, regardless of age or circumstance, even as they revealed the depth of their familiarity with pain and tragedy.

Shawn asks the woman whose brother died if she believes in reincarnation. He says he is not certain how he feels about it, but that he has asked because, if she believes, it might help. Straightforwardly and very quietly, Luke, known for being streetwise and tough, states that he has had someone die. His little brother, born the first week of November, died at Thanksgiving. Gently he says, "I don't think about it like he's dead, I think about it like he's gone away."

These young men have known violence, and they are sharing their understanding of how to deal with being violated. They are trying to somehow provide comfort by sharing survival strategies. They are simultaneously talking about and dealing with their issues and making gestures of decency and concern to this woman whose brother was killed. They knowingly, yet with the innocence of youth, suggest how she might deal with her great loss.

Armando tries to address the woman who has been imprisoned, but what he says is unclear except for something about "I drink and I drive." It seems she might think he is proud of this, and he cannot explain his thoughts. A few minutes later he tries to explain that he isn't proud of it at all, and, finally, he asks the staff, "May I please be excused? I'm saying things that are inappropriate." After receiving permission, he goes to his room. When the session ends another youth, Carlos, goes to talk with him.

When Larry asked, "What rumors did you hear about the accident?" the women did not know that he was pondering his own experiences. Subdued and distant, he continued, "I was involved in something, and there are lots and lots of stories or rumors you get."

As the discussion concludes, another youth says, "I really appreciate you coming. It would be very hard to do, and I don't think I could do it." As they had done when the guests were first introduced, the youths applaud loudly as the session ends.

Throughout the presentation and discussion, it is clear that the youths' comments are grounded in their life experiences. Shawn saw his best friend murdered. One evening there was a knock at Shawn's door, and intruders gunned down his friend. Sitting outside Unit Four, Shawn tells this to a small group, including the guest who has been convicted of vehicular homicide. He says the friend who died was really good to him, taking him to his drug treatment meetings, not allowing him to do any more drugs, and paying the rent for his mother and him. Then this "wonderful friend" who made a difference "gets blown away."

Carlos returns after talking with Armando. He tells the staff supervisor that Armando "is doing okay," and that a friend of his was paralyzed "because of drinking and driving, [influenced by] peer pressure and everything." Armando had told Carlos—a member of a rival gang who has become a friend while living in Unit Four—all about this. Armando said he "just couldn't get it out" in the session. Carlos says that Armando is so sad and maybe "he just couldn't say that this had happened."

Mitch's past is already known to the woman whose brother was killed. They had met at another session where she told her story, and they had befriended each other. This evening Mitch was chosen to escort the guests from the prison reception area to Unit Four, and, upon seeing him, she had hugged him like a brother. They share the grief of losing a loved one. Recently Mitch talked with staff members about the additional grief he carries because he is responsible for the death of one he loved. . . . Staff members say that Mitch had refused to discuss any of this before coming into this program.

▀ Holding the World in Abeyance

During its earliest days, the model program evidenced considerable success in confronting major issues youths face in the world beyond the prison. The intense efforts to follow the program model also held several crucial dimensions of ordinary prison life at bay—in other words, the tremendous focus on this new way of existing and relating caused major conflicts to be mitigated or held in abeyance. Most, if not all, of the youths held stereotypic and prejudiced notions based on race and ethnicity. These biases were frequently evident in casual, informal, and private conversations and, more heatedly, in moments of conflict between youths of different races and ethnicities. Remarkably, issues of race and ethnicity, although highly salient elements of the atmosphere and of youths' identities, were not major barriers during the first six months of the program.

One possible reason for this is that the youths and staff members had agreed to be in a program that demanded cooperative efforts, and, perhaps, this was sufficient impetus for tentative association. When racial confrontations occurred, the program's assumption that issues would be discussed openly and candidly prevailed with astounding facility.

Calvin: He called me "nigger," and I got mad and went after him.

José: But you call each other "niggers."

Calvin: You aren't one of us. You can't do that. You just can't.

Another related and potential source of conflict, gang rivalries, was also held in abeyance by the intensity of the program's early days. In adult and juvenile prisons nationwide, racially specific gangs provide the basic foundation for the social order.[2] Within the regular, nonprogram units of this juvenile prison, gang membership and identity were obvious and volatile. Youths swaggered, signed, and spoke in the language of their outside worlds, even when they were not dedicated to a gang.

In contrast, gang rivalry diminished in the model program. Gang graffiti, gang dress codes, and "throwing gang signs" (a system of hand signals) were explicitly forbidden. Some youths thought the staff to be sincerely concerned yet grievously naive about gangs. They joked about the staff's misplaced emphasis on and prohibitions of gang dress and symbols. Nevertheless, they clearly understood that they could not "display colors" nor claim allegiances. Occasionally and subtly some did, but in many ways they also signaled relief for the respite from "all of that," including the constant cloud of rivalry and challenge. A few perpetuated their gang loyalty as their primary identity, but most gang members only performed minute, unoffending rites, and a notable number of the youths were not affiliated with any gang. Unlike the outside, gangs did little to assist survival in the model program.

In addition to staff and youths' intense participation, the early months of the program were also characterized by a higher degree of support from the central administration. Despite the fact that it was a half hour drive from their offices near the state capitol, early on several administrators maintained an active presence in the institution. A few attended treatment team and staff meetings, talked with youths directly, and participated in the newly established social events, such as potluck dinners, that brought youths' families to the prison. Even after such participation in the life of the model program declined, one or two administrators remained dedicated to this day-to-day involvement.

Disinterest, Reluctant Participation

Although most of the youths participated in program activities, it became apparent that some of the twenty-four youths, including

Marcos, Daniel, Mitch, and Nick, were not engaging in the program consistently. They were frequently disinterested or disruptive, balked at the intensified structure and routine, complained because so little television watching was permitted, charged that false promises had been made to them about the new unit, and expressed alarm that the program could require longer to complete than they had anticipated. As Daniel said, "I would have been out in five months [in a nonprogram unit]." The youths' behavior vacillated considerably, and they were often engulfed in conflicting and contradictory responses, such as proclaiming their disdain for staff members one moment and joining in activities and discussions the next.

Marcos's behavior vacillated considerably. Sometimes he felt the program "was fun," and he enjoyed leading small group discussions. However, he also derided the program, showing both a keen sense of humor and a reluctance to cooperate. He sometimes jokingly belittled other youths for taking the program seriously, but he was not confrontational with staff. At the first potluck dinner, when he was one of a few youths with no family present, Marcos participated enthusiastically in the youth-staff softball game. His continual joking was good-natured even toward staff members whom he disliked.

Initially, Daniel did not cooperate with or participate in the program, and he was one of the few to be sent to the disciplinary unit during the program's early days. He appeared cool, experienced, and tough, yet he occasionally displayed interest in program activities. He constantly invoked his gang affiliation with the other youths and was recognized universally as a "hard-core" gang member. He was cleverly belligerent and quietly hostile toward some staff members, yet obviously friendly toward others.

Approximately six weeks into the program, Daniel began to participate fully in group activities. He attributed this change to an awareness that he would not be released until he cooperated: "I just started behavin' 'cause I wanted to leave. So I'm just gonna go with the program so I can leave." Daniel and staff agreed upon a behavioral contract, which Daniel explained as: "I've gotta be respectful to staff. I can't sag my pants. I gotta obey staff immediately. I gotta—I can't be intimidating. If I do, I gotta go to [the disciplinary unit] . . . isolation."

Mitch had been in the prison for twenty months before the model program began, and, during the first two months of the program, his behavior was erratic and generally uncooperative and disruptive. He was "sick of" the prison and felt he did not need to be there any longer. He said, "I've proved again and again and again and again and again that I'm ready to leave. I've told everybody, let me out. Give me a chance. I will not be back. I won't disappoint you. And they never listen to me, so now it's like, 'Well, you all say I'm not ready to leave [prison]. I'll show you *not ready to leave*, if that's what you want to see.'" Mitch also expressed scorn for the self-righteousness he perceived in many adults:

> This is why I don't like society, and I'll say it straight up and holler if they're not looking. . . . They have this big high-horse attitude of, "Oh, we're good. We're perfect." You know? "We don't do things wrong." And some kid, you know, somebody goes out and drinks one beer, and then somebody rear ends them, but the alcohol shows up on their breath. So, of course, *they* backed into them, because they had it in the wrong gear or something. And everybody just like flips their lids over stupid little things like that, or simple everyday mistakes that cause major trauma and that. They just totally—"Oh, God! Criminal! Criminal! Criminal!" And I'm willin' to bet that nine out of ten people out there, in that general society, have done things and messed around like that, but it didn't go bad on 'em, and they didn't get caught. So they're up on this big high horse. . . . They've done all that. They know they've done it and gotten away with it, but they're up on this high horse. "Oh, we are society. We are citizens of the United States of America. We are perfect. We don't do things wrong."

Mitch depicted his situation during these early days: "They brought me here so I could make the program look good and make myself look good and get out. And I've pretty much done the opposite. I've made the program look stupid. I've made myself look *com-*

pletely stupid." He repeatedly lost his temper, rebelled at the intense programming, and accused staff of misinforming youths when they were recruited for the program. At a deeper level, Mitch was unconvinced that the program components were relevant to his life:

> If there was actually a point to the groups and they let the kids know what the point was before the groups started, they could get somewhere with it. You might get—all this cheesy [psychological] crap right here—Nooooo! . . . It's just like they're telling you, "You have the power to do everything." [If a youth says] "That person just pisses me off!" [staff say] "That's giving away your personal power. You're saying they control you." And when [staff say], "You're mad." And you become mad. [Then I think,] "Excuse me? Bullshit!"

So some of it just doesn't make sense to you?

Some of it? All of it makes sense to me, but some of it is flat out a crock of shit. (Laughing) I'm being straight with you. It sucks.

Do you think somebody really believes that life is like that? And that they don't understand what it's like to be a kid? Why would people write things like that? And why would the staff have you—

Uh, they're escapees from [a mental hospital]. I don't know. I don't know why they would do something like that. I'm thinking I'm still a kid. Maybe when I grow about twenty more years, I'll understand all this. God, I hope that day *never* comes.

Mitch frequently refused to attend group discussions and, unconcerned with failing to progress in the level system, would return to his room to sleep. This continued until one staff member brought the discussion group to Mitch's room. The refusal of some staff members to be swayed by Mitch's obstinacy was one factor in his eventual agreement to participate in the program. Other factors included constant pressure from his parents, his embarrassment at failing, and, most importantly, the realization that he had no hope of being released unless he "did the program." Mitch began to participate and to succeed.

Although Nick liked most of the staff, he said that his first month in the model program "was dedicated to tryin' to get kicked out." Much of Nick's difficulty was because he had been imprisoned for most of his adolescence and was truly "institutionalized." Staff agreed with him that he was the creation of the prison system: "I said [that] before a staff meeting [and] one of the staff members was like 'Dang! You know, you're right.' About, you know, how they created me. And now they're like, 'What do we do with him?' You know, it's like, 'What *are* you going to do with me?' That's where I'm at. There ain't nothin' I can do, regardless of what you all do for me."

Nick's experiences, inside as well as outside prison, caused him to be extremely distrustful of others:

> And I don't feel comfortable to ask for help. No offense to you, but I'm not a trusting person. . . . I've got just one fear—trusting somebody. The next thing you know, you turn around, and they stab you in the back. I ain't saying that would happen to you, that you would do that, but, for some reason, especially bein' in here, a lot of people, you know . . . I've been raised pretty much in here, pretty much, you know.

Within six weeks Nick realized he would not be "kicked out" of the program. This, coupled with his realization that being in the model program saved him from being transferred to adult court, caused Nick to cooperate. Within the second month he said he was pleased with the program. He enjoyed some of the group discussions, attended church services, and especially liked working with the maintenance crew: "I like to work! I mean, since I've been small, I've been raised around working. But it's got to be something I like to do, you know. It can't be somethin', you know, like diggin' holes or pulling weeds." While he was eventually more hopeful about the program than many youths, Nick was more likely than many others to voice his complaints and less successful than most in communicating with staff:

> The staff think that I'm the negativest person around . . . . They keep saying I'm improving, but 'cause I'm the one that ain't

scared to state what's on my mind, [staff don't like] exactly how it comes out of my mouth.

So they think that's negative? Is it negative?

The way it comes out, but what I have to say ain't. But the words that come out are.

There were early signs of considerable promise in the model program: youths responded positively, they were willing to cooperate and contribute, and they confronted their problems. Nevertheless, the model treatment program was never fully implemented during the two-year period. The program was undermined by political opposition, bureaucratic exigencies, and individual inadequacies. We turn now to a discussion of that process.

▇ The Program's Demise: A Dream Diminished

The ultimate reversal of the program's direction and its stagnation were not the inevitable outcome of a faulty model or ideal, but, rather, a reflection of the magnitude of the opposing forces. It was the result of endless roadblocks, political abandonment, structural impediments, the albatross of prison tradition, and a wearing away of individual resolve.

Intricately interwoven societal, organizational, and interpersonal realities are all implicated in the deterioration of the program. Although it is impossible and unnecessary to unravel the threads, perhaps it is most accurate to say that the great individual and collective efforts of youths and staff members were defeated by organizational inertia and lack of political support. Ultimately, this led to individual cynicism that the obstacles were insurmountable and resignation to a greatly diminished vision of how a prison might be transformed to care for troubled youths.

The program components were ineffectively implemented and never worked in harmony to create the comprehensive system envisioned by the model. The model program was intended as a holistic system, one in which all participants in all components shared ethical and organizational principles, worked in unison to promote those principles, and constantly reinforced and strengthened the collective efforts. But the implementation of each component evidenced major limitations, and an integrated system never existed.

The heart of the model program was to be its innovative educational system, centered on the concept of "Success School." This crucial component was intended to transform one of the youths' foremost failures—their education—into a relevant, engaging, and rewarding experience. The inability to accomplish this goal figured prominently in the demise of the model program, and the educational system's weaknesses mirrored those throughout the program. There was a lack of understanding of fundamental principles, lack of commitment to a unified team approach, narrow conceptions of responsibilities, ineffectual leadership, premature and perpetual changes, and unsuccessful relationships with the youths.

Throughout the two-year study, many teachers never evidenced a clear or in-depth understanding of Success School. In part this can be attributed to their lack of enthusiasm for a school that deviated from traditional practices, especially in its focus on individualized portfolios and an open curriculum.[3] These dimensions were intended to be the school's greatest strength, but, rather, became highly contested symbols of its difficulties. To a considerable extent, the school's ineffectiveness stemmed from the fact that the model was communicated poorly and modified continually. The constant state of flux and uncertainty clearly affected the teachers, the living unit staff, and, ultimately, the youths.

Two months after the model program began, a teacher expressed these concerns:

> My major problem is that we haven't had enough guidance on the Success School, and we've been told many conflicting things. . . . These students were going to stick around until they have fulfilled what needs to go into the portfolio. And yet we really don't know—we haven't gotten one portfolio. We have no idea what is supposed to go into it.

Sixteen months later, a year and a half into the program, another education staff member expressed the same sentiments:

> Why we're in this chaos is that there's too much going on at one time, because nothing has been established so that we have any guidelines to go by. Very little is in place. . . . I know within a three-month period, the program changed four times.

Why?

> Because there was something new that [the superintendent] wanted to do differently. And so there is constant change. There is no settling in, and so people . . . to keep their mental health, they don't keep hitting their head against the wall. You don't put a lot of effort into a new classroom, because it's going to be changed. . . .
>
> And that's prevalent of what happens here. You've got a goal, you're set, you're working on it, and somebody comes in with a bomb . . . something crazy. . . .
>
> We need to decide which three or four things we need to concentrate on and the rest of the stuff, yes, we want that to happen, but let's just decide on four things and get that going, so we have some credibility, because we have *no* credibility. . . . Let's have some successes. Let's have some celebration. Let's have some recognition of what we *are* doing. Let's keep talking about solutions as opposed to do what I've just been doing, saying what the problems are.

Quite clearly, educating imprisoned youth is a demanding task. Youths acknowledge the benefits of furthering their educations while imprisoned ("When you hit the streets, you ain't gonna want to go to school. So while you're in here, you might as well go to school and get some more education"), but they are easily deterred from that objective. Many have not been in school for a period of months or years, and they present a complex combination of capabilities and needs. These include language barriers, illiteracy, a variety of learning disabilities and special education needs, patterns of below-grade-level functioning, behavioral disorders, and mental and emotional health concerns.

Within the prison, classroom difficulties were increased by the policy of assigning all youths from a specific living unit to the same classroom, despite the wide range of their academic abilities and accomplishments.[4] While attempts were made to provide work appropriate for each youth's abilities, the tremendous range frequently resulted in teachers focusing on an imaginary "average student" that bore little resemblance to a substantial number of the youths. Maintaining classroom discipline often became the overriding issue, and individualized attention was nearly impossible. Pablo was one of many youths who were frustrated.

> They don't teach us nothing, man. That makes me angry, because everything you've learned in the past is just going to waste. Because you forget. Some of what I learned at school on the outs, I forgot half that stuff, because I'm sitting in here doing fourth-grade work. . . . Not everyone's as smart, not everyone's at the same level as others . . . the work here ain't high school level, it's elementary level.

Youths' classroom behaviors varied greatly. They behaved in an exemplary manner when they considered specific teachers to be fun, personable, or genuinely concerned about and respectful of them. In at least one instance, they explicitly discouraged disruptions because they did not want the teacher to "get in trouble" if security had to be called. But many teachers did not evoke such loyalty or consideration, and school continued to be a site of boredom and misbehavior. Most youths found it uninteresting, unhelpful, and essentially like the regular schools in which they had experienced overwhelming frustration or failure. The changing guidelines and proliferation of rules reflected the uncertainty and insecurity of the adults involved, including their attempts to respond to youths' disruptive and uncooperative behavior. In turn, youths' behavior reflected not only their propensities but the fact that the school failed to capture their imaginations, to challenge them, or to meet their needs.

Success School originally was portrayed as the first phase of the educational system. After completing basic skills, youths were to move on to other educational endeavors tailored to their specific needs. Success School was to be the *precursor* to vocational education or preparation for obtaining an eighth-grade diploma, a high school equivalency degree, or for entering college. Instead, it became the entire curriculum, and specialized elements were never developed fully due to continual difficulties in the school.

Bernardo's comments were typical. He originally enjoyed school, but after being in the program for three months he was no longer working on his GED and found the school much less worthwhile. "I used to like it, but I don't like it that much no more. 'Cause they just, they don't even teach you nothing. All they're concerned about right now is just doin' their job in helpin' us do that portfolio." Although Daniel said that at least one teacher cared about and tried to help him, he echoed Bernardo's sentiments:

And even the education ain't any good no more.

Here?

Yeah. They teach you—they don't teach you nothing.

Are you still working on your GED? Are they doing anything about it?

Not no more. They was at first, but not no more.

What are they doing now?

Samo, Samo. . . . They don't do nothing.

One promising attempt to provide qualified youths with college-level classes failed due to insufficient communication and coordination with the community college. The individual working with the imprisoned students was certified to teach at the community college and felt the youths were making considerable progress, but the course monitor at the college became concerned about possible collaboration among the youths. The teacher inside the prison offered assurances that youths were working independently and producing original assignments, and the school superintendent met with community college representatives, but the dilemma was unresolved, and all the youths were withdrawn from the course by the community college.[5]

As a group, the teachers were ambiguous about their involvement in the model treatment program, despite their centrality to its success. At the outset, living unit staff members and teachers participated in joint training, including team building and conflict resolution exercises. By the time the third unit was opened seven months later, living unit staff and teachers were not being trained as a team, and exposing teachers to all the program's elements was de-emphasized in light of continual understaffing and difficulties within the school. Likewise, early in the program a representative teacher participated in weekly treatment team meetings, but attendance became irregular, and by the end of the two years, teacher participation was minimal and confined to discussion of a youth's school problems, not the total treatment picture.

Although the teachers' abilities and motivations varied, most viewed their contribution exclusively as teaching academic subjects. They were far less prepared for, or comfortable in, their roles as classroom disciplinarians and "members of the treatment team." They viewed their jobs narrowly, and some were reluctant, unwilling, or unable to maintain discipline in the classroom. Many teachers suggested that they were "there to teach," and that if they spent their time disciplining delinquent youths, they could not fulfill their teaching responsibilities. Most wanted and needed someone else, namely staff from the living units, to undertake the considerable task of maintaining order while they taught.

A few teachers cooperated effectively with living unit staff, but many never saw themselves as part of the overall treatment effort. For example, when they were required to supervise youths returning from school to their living units, many teachers implied they were "above" such activities. Their reluctance and ineffectiveness as counselors and mentors also reflected a serious lack of training for these roles.

An example of the combination of unwillingness, ineptness, and poor administration occurred when Limit and Lead group sessions were integrated into the school day, rather than being conducted solely in the living units. In order to achieve national accreditation, the school needed to lengthen the school day, and incorporating group sessions into the curriculum appeared to provide a meaningful avenue for doing so. But most teachers were unsuccessful in their attempts to lead the groups and violated fundamental principles, such as participatory decision making, and permitted the sessions to become ineffective and superficial "time fillers." While resistance came from some teachers who considered this an inappropriate aspect of classroom teaching, more problems arose from many not having been trained in the counseling method.

Some teachers intimated that having to teach within a prison was stigmatizing. Similarly, because they were college graduates some teachers viewed less-educated staff members as less capable. The gulf between teachers and other staff members was increased when teachers received a pay raise and living unit staff did not. The consent decree's emphasis on the educational system included a stipulation that teachers, heretofore underpaid, be placed on a salary schedule commensurate with public school teachers of similar training and experience.[6] While staff members acknowledged the need for such parity, they also objected to pay increases being awarded so selectively. Teachers needed the raises, and it was a significant accomplishment for the school superintendent and prison director to obtain them, but this further distanced them from other staff members and exacerbated conflicts.[7]

Another perceived inequity was that teachers were provided with planning time in their daily schedules, a luxury never enjoyed by the living unit staff. Planning sessions are, of course, essential to the routine operation of a school system, especially an embryonic one. But, unlike schools within the community, when prison educators scheduled planning sessions, other staff members had to attend to the youths. Especially when teachers were allotted several days for planning, staff within the living units covered for the teachers' regular school time *and* maintained their own full-time responsibilities. Importantly, by taking care of the youths, it was impossible for living unit staff to participate in the school planning.

Although officially everyone employed in the model program was considered a member of the treatment team, those who worked in the living units were commonly viewed as *the treatment staff*. They repeatedly had been promised opportunities for retreats and planning sessions, but this never occurred. In the earliest days, the director suggested that central administrators would come to supervise youths during a retreat for the living unit staff, and the appeal of such an arrangement was apparent. It would have encouraged and supported the unit staff in their efforts to reflect upon and improve the treatment program in a thoughtful and purposeful manner. Central administrators would have benefitted by spending time with the youths, experiencing the challenges faced by staff, and being exposed to the "big picture." It also would have provided a significant gesture of support to youths and staff members from administrators.

Difficulties in providing alternative education (AE) for youths who disrupted regular classrooms also reflected the program's inability to address the full range of youths' educational problems. The content of the alternative education setting varied: sometimes youths were given packets of academic "busy work"; at other times youths brought specific, individualized assignments from their regular teachers; and, when AE was located in an unoccupied unit, disruptive youths frequently spent their time in locked cells waiting to talk with staff.

The complexities surrounding classroom disruptions seemed endless. At times, despite the fact that being sent to AE automatically resulted in a two-week demotion in the level system, program youths would misbehave purposefully in order to meet and "hang out" in alternative education with their friends and homeboys from other living units. During a period when staff members conducted one-on-one interviews with youths in an attempt to intervene and prevent the need for further sanctions, several youths overtly sought this attention and the opportunity to talk intensely with a staff member *while escaping the classroom*. This became so widespread that staff did not have sufficient time to conduct half-hour interviews with all disruptive youths, and the approach was suspended.

The lack of financial and instructional resources made it a formidable task to fulfill the consent decree's requirement to provide education and vocational services for all imprisoned youths *based on their individual needs*. For several months the lack of resources, coupled with the admonishment to individualize instruction, made it necessary to teach without books and to copy lessons for each day. Grants were obtained for major expenditures, such as a computer lab, but basic needs were often met out of teachers' own resources.

The education system's considerable difficulties were further magnified by the continuing lack of rapport between the teachers and the superintendent of the prison schools. Many teachers lacked respect for the superintendent's skills as an educator or leader, and his repeated inability to communicate his educational vision made it difficult for him to generate support for the program. Many teachers were uncertain whether their opinions were honored or given a fair hearing. Even when they or their representative (the principal) were consulted regarding curriculum changes or the ongoing operation of the school, the teachers frequently felt ignored or irrelevant because they believed the superintendent had already finalized decisions.

Perpetual Change, Ineffective Treatment Groups

The treatment groups were as crucial to the model program's success as the educational system. Organized yet open-ended discussions were envisioned as the primary vehicle for holding youths accountable for their decisions, providing alternatives to aggressive or violent resolution of conflicts, and creating opportunities to confront the past and plan for the future. To be effective, the "groups," as they were called, needed to be purposeful, honest, and engaging; staff needed to provide sensitive leadership while enhancing democratic participation.

When they were implemented as planned, group discussions

were intense, stimulating, and rewarding. Youths were motivated and mutually supportive; they were learning enhanced reasoning and verbal skills and being afforded opportunities to practice new approaches to interacting with other youths and adults. Frequently, the sense of pride and accomplishment they experienced during the sessions was highly visible.

Facilitating discussion groups required enormous energy and commitment from staff members, and, when job pressures or personal preoccupations overshadowed this demanding task, the sessions became ritualized, rather than spontaneous, and superficial, rather than penetrating. The effectiveness of sessions vacillated throughout the program's two years, but by the sixth month the overall quality had declined significantly.

The perpetual modifications that were characteristic of the educational system were also evident in the organization and content of group discussions. In several situations it would have been beneficial to retain procedures while systematically assessing them. Instead, the constant changes made it difficult to connect day-to-day crises with underlying structural problems, and it was thus impossible to know which of the program's components caused the problems and needed to be altered. The rapid changes went beyond the flexibility advocated by the program philosophy and, at times, approached chaos.

The tendency to make constant and premature changes may be attributed to numerous things, including many administrators' fundamental lack of security in their organizational standing. Quite a few decisions appeared to be influenced heavily by a fear of being chastised by superiors. Activity was deemed preferable to inactivity, and covering one's position was essential. Many thought it far better to be able to say, "I saw this wasn't working, and I've already implemented change," rather than risk continued lack of success. This reflected a general lack of confidence in longer trial periods that would demonstrate positive aspects or enable informed changes. It also reflected staff perceptions that top administrators preferred spectacular or dramatic action, for, as one staff member suggested, "They're into home runs."

Constant changes were particularly disturbing to youths, who needed the promised structure and stability of the original program. The following example from our fieldnotes typifies youths' dismay when an established group they appreciated was eliminated:

> Once again the kids are concerned about the perpetual changes. One youth, whose life has been filled with constant disruptions, came over to a staff member to ask why another group had been rearranged. He said they really like the volunteer who does the group: "OK, we've got a group we really like, and it's going to change. Now they're going to change it."
>
> The staff wants eight youths in each group, and their group has more. Also, a psychologist has completed her special training and wants her original group back. The staff member said the expected things, but the youth was unpersuaded. When the staff member said, "Well, change isn't all bad," the youth responded "Well, if it's around me, if I'm involved, it'll change." And, when the staff member asked, "What if nothing ever changed?" the youth said, "Maybe I'd be happy."

The use of special groups—marathon groups intended for crisis situations in which staff members were attempting to prevent activity that might result in youths harming others[8]—was problematic. Originally these were intended to augment daily groups and serve specific functions in maintaining the treatment atmosphere, but they ended up being used to maintain general control or to punish an entire unit, with all of the youths forced to attend for prolonged periods of time. As Mitch ruefully commented, "You'll be sittin' in that room, sittin' in a circle, going—I mean, you're going to have saddle sores from sittin' still. That's how long they sit you in there. They'll sit you in there for weeks on end if they have to." This misuse occurred even when the problem was as amorphous as general disrespect among the youths in the unit or when only a few youths were involved in the problem. For example, the first marathon session in Unit Four resulted when a youth carved gang graffiti on the television. All twenty-four youths were forced to attend the three-day marathon session.

The deterioration of the groups included failure to respect and abide by "group rules" established at the beginning of the program by staff and youths. These included courtesies such as taking turns, raising hands and not interrupting others, and, more importantly, the principles of encouraging expression and respectful, reciprocal discussion and listening. Many of the youths had responded well to this structure and demonstrated a willingness and, sometimes, an eagerness to facilitate the sessions. But as the program declined, these guidelines were violated. Staff members' attempts to exert excessive control, dictate issues, or exempt themselves from group rules evoked critical and hostile responses from the youths. When staff members were unprepared for discussions or failed to hold them regularly and on time, the crucial objectives of the groups were undermined. It clearly affected the extent to which groups played a positive role in the youths' experiences. Rather than providing stability and structure, the groups became an erratic, disorganized symbol of the program's ineffectiveness.

Further Component Limitations

Significant problems were evident in other program components, including the level system. This system originally was envisioned as a vehicle for providing youths with continual feedback regarding their progress within the model program. They were scored several times throughout the day and were keenly interested in how staff made decisions. Their primary complaint about the system was that they were not assessed consistently and fairly. For example, the criteria used to score youths in the classroom differed greatly from the criteria in the living units. In the living units the highest scores were intended for youths who not only accepted responsibility for their own behavior but also provided leadership for other youths, including intervening in a mature, appropriate way when others were not following program guidelines. Scoring criteria within the school was much more lenient, and frequently teachers gave youths the highest marks in exchange not for exemplary behavior but for promises not to be disruptive.

Youths protested the fact that they were given scores even during the nightly graveyard shift. Because they were asleep, they could not display the exemplary behavior necessary for high marks that, in turn, were essential to progress in the level system. These "average" marks lowered their overall scores. In the beginning, staff only assigned numbers without written explanations, and, too often, when they met with youths to explain the scores, they could not remember their reasoning. Later, when the system was changed to require written explanation of high and low scores ("4s and 1s"), staff tended to give out midrange scores because those did not require time-consuming written justification.

Youths also protested the imbalance between the stellar behavior necessary to advance a level and the minor violations that resulted in level losses. The youths understood and did not contest the "major violations" or most of the "moderate violations" that resulted in automatic level drops. But they considered several of the moderate violations too minor to deserve demotion, including being in another youth's room without staff permission, lending or borrowing personal possessions, and "horseplay"—defined as "rough, boisterous fun; minor physical contact designed to aggravate but not cause injury."[9]

As demonstrated by the petition that begins this book, youths felt that the hard work and accomplishments of several weeks could be wiped out by a small mistake, "like having a little pillow fight." As Bernardo explained, "Somebody's just sittin' over there, and you get a pillow and just throw it at him. And they call that horseplaying, and you get a level drop—both you guys. Even if you're just innocent, doing nothin'." Staff members responded to this specific concern by initiating two-week level suspensions rather than immediate level drops.

Another area of concern was the prison's security unit, particularly in light of the fact that disciplinary practices were a primary focus of the original lawsuit and the consent decree. Due to former abuses of power and mistreatment of youths, the model program mandated extensive changes to reform the approach of those individuals charged with maintaining prison security. Although the title of "Security" was changed to "Crisis Management Team" (CMT), changes often appeared to be cosmetic.

Staff members, formerly called "officers," from CMT did not receive the same training in the new program as others. Their exposure to the program's components was even less comprehensive than that afforded several of the teachers. This resulted from CMT members' reticence as well as their low priority in the training schedule. Few CMT members appeared to understand the basic principles of the model program, nor did they show a commitment to its treatment philosophy.[10] The staff members generally acknowledged the difficulty of CMT tasks, including their ultimate responsibility for highly charged incidents. Situations in which CMT personnel became involved were potentially dangerous and, in many ways, provided stringent tests of the program's consistency and philosophy. Nevertheless, other staff members expressed considerable frustration with a small number of CMT staff who repeatedly violated program principles when dealing with youths. Others often viewed CMT personnel as needlessly inflexible, disrespectful of youths and staff, and unwilling to consider any deviation from their previous routine without specific instructions "from downtown," that is, from central administration. CMT staff members' resistance to the new program and their resulting defensiveness may have also been fueled by the knowledge that their jobs had been a critical focus of the class-action lawsuit.

A memo from the head of the Crisis Management Team to his staff members exemplified the problems. Seventeen months after the model program had been initiated, members of the unit had to be admonished for their reliance on adult-prison terminology and their failure to use language appropriate to the model program. They were instructed to stop referring to various members of the crisis management team as "captain," "lieutenant," and "officer." They were also directed to refer to the facility grounds as a "campus" rather than a "yard." The memo concluded, "I will be monitoring this and will correct you if you forget and use the wrong word. If you do it over the radio, I will correct you over the radio. Hope it doesn't embarrass you but you need to get it straight. You have certainly had enough time and have been told too many times. Thank you for your cooperation and understanding."[11]

The Crisis Management Team was used minimally during the early days of the model program, but their involvement increased as the quality of the program deteriorated. During the first year of the model program, there were an average of 9.6 calls to security per month. This increased to an average of 14.1 calls per month during the second year.[12] Equally important, some security staff members' resistance to the new program's philosophy and their unwillingness to change their orientation and approach to youths limited the model program's success.

As suggested previously, inadequate and uneven training of the staff damaged the delivery of the model program immeasurably. Some staff members never received sufficient exposure to grasp the complex endeavors in which they were engaged. Others were motivated and prepared by early training, but did not receive refresher courses or additional instruction and guidance due to the need to train new personnel. Some staff members seemed poorly equipped to understand and implement the program, while others were qualified and capable but uninspired to do so. Several youths made critical observations:

> There are some of the staff in here that I know are not goin' to be too good for the program. They're not designed for this program. They cannot do this program. . . . Like Miss Truro [a living unit staff member]. When I first saw her a couple weeks ago, I thought, "Oh, no!" I didn't know who she was—I didn't know her *name,* but I knew who she was, 'cause over in the gym I've seen her and—when she used to be in Sunrise [Unit]. . . . I've seen the way she reacts and stuff, and then I saw her that day . . . she just started tellin' me that I couldn't say nothin', to listen to her, and I said, "That's not the way the program's run." And she said, "Don't tell me how to run the program! I just got out of training, and I know how." And I said, "Whew!"
>
> And you got staff comin' in here that *are* taking into consid-

eration that this is a new program, and it's not like the other cottages, but then you've got staff in here that don't believe that it can change, you know, so they're still gonna treat us the way it was in the past. Yet they're still gonna have—they still went through the training, so they're gonna *expect us* not to swear and not to do this and not to do that, but they're still gonna *treat us* the old way.

Following his altercation with Mr. Carpenter (discussed earlier) Larry felt that the staff member needed to pay more attention to the program:

> *You said to another kid that one of the things Mr. Carpenter needs is to pay attention to the training that you've gotten, the Limit and Lead training. What did you mean by that?*

He's the way . . . that I kinda was when I first got here, that anytime somethin' happens that I always felt that I was right, and everybody else was wrong. . . . You know, he was right and, no matter what anybody else would say, he was still right . . . . I feel that *he* needs to go through training, and he needs to go through the stuff that we do to realize that there are other alternatives besides he's God or he's always right. Or, I'm not going to say *always* right, but he's 100 percent right *in that situation*. He needs to get the big picture instead of, you know, he only sees one thing and that's what he's going to stick to, no matter what.

"Doing the Program": Variation Among Youths

Youths who had committed more serious crimes and those with extensive past involvements in the system tended to be most successful in adapting to and succeeding within the regular institutional environment *and* within the model program. This was attributable to their sophistication and prowess in dealing with—and manipulating—an often hostile world. These youths "do" institutions very well. Imprisoned for such crimes as aggravated assault (including drive-by shootings), armed robbery, and multiple vehicle thefts,[13] several admitted that, after spending a few weeks familiarizing themselves with the program, they learned how to "play the game" in order to "get out" as quickly as possible.

While the model program's goal was to effect lasting change, several youths said that playing the game was key to advancing in the level system. Larry portrayed the situation vividly:

> I'm just learning to play the game better. . . . Because, I mean, to a certain extent you learn things, you know, behaviors like not going off. But some things you learn are that you'll get things easier and you get more things if you don't yell. . . . When I first got here, I used to cuss out the staff, and anything I didn't like I used to voice my opinion. And then I got my sophomore level, and I started thinking, "Wow!" you know, "I gotta get my junior to get out of here."
>
> And what I did is I took a look at Carlos and Jorge and Bernardo; they were juniors. And I said, "How are they doing this? What did they do to get their junior levels?" And then we'd be in the groups, and I'd look at them and they'd be just sitting there. And I'd look around at everybody else, and they'd all be talking, and I'd look back, and they'd just still be sitting there.
>
> So I'm like, alright, when I want to voice my opinion—I won't! I'll shut my mouth. When I have a problem with staff, I won't say anything. I'll shut my mouth. And I should be getting [promoted to] my junior [level] today! . . . They want us to go and voice our opinions, but if we do, then we'll never get out of the program.

Perhaps because staff members felt that some youths' pride and bravado prevented them from embracing the program, the youths were even encouraged by some staff members to cultivate this passive strategy for getting through the model program. This was combined with the belief that, in the name of "playing the game," some youths would be more cooperative in groups and willing to listen to staff and other youths. They would not be disrupting youths who were more committed to the activities, and, staff hoped, the youths' patterning of program activities might be the beginning of more lasting changes. In practice, this did not always work, as Bernardo made clear:

> They're just playing the game. (Laughing) I know a whole bunch of people who are.

> *And so what they're doing—they've learned what it takes to get out. Is that it?*

> Yeah. They say they're going to use it, but they ain't. They say, "I can't wait 'til I get out. I'm gonna drink and smoke weed and all this."

> *Is there anybody who seems to be serious about it?*

> (Laughing) No. Unh-unhh. . . . Well, that's what they *told* us to do—play the game, so you can get out of here. That's what Mr. Carpenter told us.

> *Mr. Carpenter told you?*

> Yep, he told us that.

A review of program youths during the two-year study revealed that more sophisticated youths categorized as high risks to the community had averaged six and one-third months inside the juvenile prison. (High-risk youths included those convicted of multiple vehicle thefts or multiple burglaries, as well as violent offenses.) The prison system's sentencing guidelines recommended they serve six to fifteen months, followed by six to ten months in community programs. But the results differed for a subset of youths imprisoned for high-profile violent crimes, such as murder, manslaughter, negligent homicide, or sexual assault. Although many of them were as adept at manipulating their environment and exhibited the same capability for completing requirements, they were far less likely to be released from prison.

These youths' continued imprisonment, regardless of their behavior, reflected both the program's concern that violent offenders be held accountable *and* the prison system's political relationship with the larger society. Prison administrators were generally reluctant or unwilling to risk being criticized, even when youths had been highly successful in the model program. They were fearful of unfavorable media coverage and the threat to the model program and the prison system's reputation in the event one of these youths committed another violent crime after release. As a result, these youths averaged about fourteen and a half months in prison, more than two times longer than other youths categorized as high risks.

Younger, unsophisticated, less vocal, emotionally disturbed, or mentally challenged youths—referred to as "the cream puffs"—had the *greatest* difficulty in adapting to the environment and did poorly in completing the model program. They tended to "get lost" in the system or to become irritants to staff members because of their immaturity. They were generally unsuccessful in conforming to the program guidelines and in demonstrating "changed" behavior. These youths had been committed for relatively minor offenses, such as shoplifting, attempted theft, and simple assault (including fistfights over petty disagreements). However, they frequently served more time than initially recommended by prison guidelines, as well as *more time than the youths classified as high risks to the community*. On average, youths categorized as *low* risks to the community were imprisoned for over seven and a half months, compared to the average six and one-third-month stay for youths classified as *high* risks. This anomaly existed despite the system's guidelines recommending that youths in the low-risk category be assigned to treatment programs *in the community* immediately after a thirty-day diagnostic period.

Those youths who fell into a medium-risk classification exhibited a wide range of behaviors and abilities to adapt. Committed for such offenses as burglary, vehicle theft, sexual abuse, criminal damage, and criminal trespass, the amount of time they spent in the program approximated the system's recommendations: approximately seven and a half months compared to the recommended three to nine months.

The difficulties within the model program clearly included the failure of individual components, such as the school and group discussions, as well as the failure to create an integrated, unified system. It also reflected the individual inadequacies of administrators, staff members, and youths. But these alone do not capture the overriding difficulties and the insidious way in which the program deteriorated. Perhaps more than anything, it was the repeated and systematic violation of the program's fundamental principles and spirit that signaled the decline of the program within the prisons. Externally, the program's demise resulted from a profound lack of support and political will. We now turn to a discussion of those issues.

Four

Political Opposition, Bureaucratic Inertia, and Individual Inadequacies

▟ Unilateral Decision Making and Lack of Accountability

The program's decline began within three and a half months of its inception. By the time eight of the original twenty-four youths were moved to a second model living unit to provide its foundation, or "seed culture," the program's fundamental principles and code of ethics had been violated. The extent to which external pressures and organizational expediencies undermined the success of the program is demonstrated by the tremendous pressure on staff to establish an additional model unit immediately, despite the fragile, embryonic success of the first unit. The pressure sprang from administrators' dual needs to resolve the lawsuit and to demonstrate progress to the legislature and the governor's office.

The manner in which the eight youths were chosen to leave Unit Four exemplifies the process by which the program was ultimately destroyed. Essential principles, such as the importance of youths' participation, open discussion, and collective decision making, were violated because two perceived imperatives dominated. First, the program *had* to be expanded without delay. Second, precisely *eight* youths *had* to move to establish the new unit. The first imperative, the political necessity of expanding the program, was conceded universally, but "too much, too fast" was a common assessment of this expansion. Everyone was placed in the untenable position of diminishing the program's effectiveness because of the need to demonstrate its success. External pressures were formidable and irresistible.

The second imperative that dominated decision making, that is, that *eight* youths from Unit Four were essential to initiate the second unit, provides an example of the way in which program principles were violated because of organizational expediency and staff members' propensities. The number was decided upon by staff members and administrators based on the reasonable logic that the new unit's success would be enhanced by the ratio of eight youths experienced in the program to sixteen new youths. The violation of the program's principles resulted not from the establishment of this number but by the way in which it became ossified into an inflexible, needlessly destructive, insistence.

The spirit of the program held that youths were to share decision-making responsibilities; the importance of transplanting the program's culture to the new unit was discussed with Unit Four youths and volunteers were sought. A few youths were encouraged, even as a few were discouraged, and seven volunteers were approved. The selection of the eighth "volunteer," however, reflected the coercive power traditionally characteristic of juvenile prisons. The eighth youth, Bernardo, did not want to move, said so clearly and repeatedly, but was forced to go.

Undeniably, the concept of "volunteering" in a total institution such as a prison is highly suspect and problematic.[1] Whether an individual, especially a young person, can truly volunteer in such a controlled setting is questionable, but, in accordance with the program, initially the youths had been led to believe they were making decisions about their lives. Two youths, Bernardo and Manny, were called individually to attend a treatment team meeting in which staff members stated why they wanted one of them to move to the new unit. Staff members said each youth had done well in the program and would serve as a role model for the new youths.

In turn, Manny and Bernardo fervently pleaded their cases. Each insisted he did not want to move, refused to "volunteer," and pleaded to stay in Unit Four. Manny, lithe, attractive, and charming, humorously said he could not bear to leave the staff, he could not possibly leave. Bernardo, heavy bodied, less verbal, and less charming to the staff, stressed his fondness for his room and the other youths. When staff members asked why he had been drawing gang symbols in school, Bernardo murmured that he did not know. No one acknowledged that this began after he was told he must move. At the end of the session, Bernardo finally said, angrily, "I do not want to go. I will not go."

Manny was permitted to remain, while Bernardo, his strong protestations ignored and his objections trivialized, was forced to move. The importance of stability for Bernardo and the tenuous nature of his faith in the program were underestimated. This is Bernardo's private journal entry the night he was moved into the new unit:

How do I feel. Sad because I'm sitting here in this room by myself tears running down my cheeks and [I] start to draw what I see. . . . I see a calendar which I hate to look at because that's one more day of my life I lost to do nothing and as a day goes by I check them one by one and that's bad for me.

I see a little cartoon that represents how gang members do their crimes. They shoot first and ask you after they shoot you which set are you from.

I see two pictures which tell me what the fuck is happening to this world. We have so much money that we don't care about anybody but our self, and we forget about those who are starving.

I see a picture of a kitten. It says Desperately Seeking Someone which means its fucked up being locked up. TAKE ME HOME. (Sorry for all the cursing I did.)

Staff members' unilateral decision and their disregard for Bernardo's strong desires marked a turning point. This violation and reversal of the program was of major significance. Bernardo's forced move proved to be a decisive factor in reaffirming, in his mind, that his feelings and needs were negligible and that "nothing ever goes right for me." After he involuntarily moved to the new living unit, Bernardo never "demonstrated notable progress" in the program again. Other youths recognized both the injustice of Bernardo's situation and the success of Manny's approach.

The problem could have been avoided had the suggestion of another Unit Four youth, Larry, been taken seriously. He suggested that eight individuals be "loaned" for one to two weeks to the new unit, as "practice" for new staff members, and then returned to Unit Four when the new program youths arrived. Unit Four youths would contribute to the establishment of the new living unit and provide "on-the-job training" for the new staff, but the staff and new program youths would be permitted to form their own team, without criticism from Unit Four youths. It also would have permitted the new unit to create a unique culture stamped with their own personalities. Equally important, Unit Four could retain its integrity, and the youths' progress within that environment would not be disturbed. Larry's suggestion was ignored and the program's potential for success was damaged irrevocably.

▉ Perceptions of Inconsistency and Lack of Fairness

Widespread perceptions of inconsistency and capriciousness contributed to the decline of the program. Youths, staff working within the prison, and members of the central administration became alternately frustrated and angry at behavior they viewed as arbitrary. Participatory decision making and mutual respect and responsibility were touted as the essence of the program, but these crucial principles were often violated by all participants.

Many youths, like Daniel, were dissatisfied:

How are decisions made in the unit here?

The staff do it, and the supervisors. They make all the decisions. They said we was gonna make our decisions and our rules up, but they do it.

In the beginning what did they tell you?

They told us, they said, "Y'all gonna be—" They said juveniles gonna be makin' up our rules. We were gonna make up our own rules and stuff we'd like to do, but they the ones that's doin' it.

Did you ever get an opportunity to try to do that?

We tried to do some stuff, but they be sayin' no all the time. They'll say yes to the *little* things.

Larry also expressed strong disenchantment with the program:

We were told that we were always going to have a say-so in what happens and what goes on in our cottage, because it is our cottage. . . . You know, if we ever had a problem, we were supposed to talk to somebody about it, and let them know how you're feeling about whatever it is that's going on. Then they're supposed to come up with a solution. . . .

I felt uncomfortable talking to people I didn't know [two visiting psychology interns]. . . . They were asking me to talk about—it's a Limit and Lead group, so basically it's like asking you who you are and what kind of person you are and everything. I'm not just going to go up to anybody I don't know and start telling them my whole life story. So, you know, I brought it up to Miss Truro that I was feeling uncomfortable talking to them, and she didn't have any problems with that. . . . And then Mr. Martin [the staff psychologist conducting the group] came up and started like flying off the handle. And I was trying to explain to him that—because he kept saying that I "didn't want to program, didn't want to program!" And I kept trying to tell him that wasn't what I was trying to get to. I was just trying to tell him that there's a problem. We need to solve it. And he just kept yelling.

When I first got here, I probably would have started yelling and cussing, but I think I've gone past that. I don't really go off anymore, so I told him—you know, he started yelling, and I said, "Just calm down. There's no need to start yelling. We can talk about this." He started yelling, "If you're doing any talking, then you're talking to me, and you ain't talking to nobody else!" . . . So I told him, I said, "Well, I'll go [inside] and sit down, but if it comes to a question that I don't feel comfortable answering in front of the group, then, you know, I don't feel that I want to answer it." So he said, "Alright.". . .

The reason I took it outside is so I wouldn't make a big scene about it because there was a group going on. So we went back inside—and so he brought it inside, too, you know? "If you want to play your games, play them outside. Don't play them in here." I didn't say anything. The group got distracted, because he started saying stuff. So I sat down right next to him, and he was looking at the two psychs, and he started rolling his eyes. And I saw him do it, and I looked at him, and I said, "There's no need to roll your eyes at me, you know. There's no need for that." And he, "Get him out of here! I don't want to see his face! Get him out of here!"

Now the next day he apologized to you.

Yeah. The next day he apologized. . . . He learned, I guess, that I was doing what I was supposed to do.

Youths' potential for communal action and their support for the program were undermined by inconsistent implementation of the model. The energies of youths such as Larry and Mitch, who comprehended the basic treatment philosophy and methods inherent in the model program, could have formed the nucleus of the program and provided leadership. In many ways the program was genuinely attractive to them in terms of their strong self-concepts and the tremendous energies at their command. If the program had been implemented in a systematic, consistent fashion, these youths could have endorsed the model's ostensible commitment to respecting individual integrity and dignity. Some of the youths, such as Larry, were intellectually astute, and others, such as Marcos, exercised influence by virtue of their personalities and quick wits.

Mitch and Larry were among the youths who were frustrated but controlled. They were able to articulate their anger in a manner that conformed to the program's rules, although in the staff's opinion they often skated on the edge between "appropriate" and "disrespectful" behavior. Both were white, middle-class youths sentenced to prison for first-time violent offenses. Like an increasing number of youths, they had minimal delinquency histories, but were convicted of major violent offenses, including shooting friends with handguns.[2] Neither Mitch nor Larry believed he belonged in prison, and each reacted strongly to the irrationalities of institutional routines and to what he perceived as the incessant exercise of arbitrary and petty power.

Larry's experiences within the program were a combination of acceptance and support of the program's principles and endless frustration with the inconsistencies in the program. He was one of the few youths who did not receive level drops for violating program principles, yet he rarely was given the highest scores because of his constant challenges to staff. He was annoyed, angered, and, finally, dismayed by the widespread arbitrariness and the fact the program was "never done right."

Early in the program Larry was one of ten young men from Unit Four involved in an architectural project to revitalize the living unit's landscape and to construct ramadas (open outdoor shelters). He was committed to the project, but continually lost points in the level system for questioning staff members' failure to coordinate activities or permit time for the project.

> When I was doing all that architectural stuff, you know, I lost I don't know how many points because of that. Because when I first got on that, *I believed in it*, and . . . when they said, "You can't go in there and work." And then I'd argue for it, "I've got to go in there. I've got something due. You know I want to get it done." I'd lose all kinds of points in the arguments and that. But then I just started shutting my mouth, and things weren't getting done and this and that. And it's, now, we quit. Me and Jeremy just quit it.

The seeming inability of some staff members to grasp the fundamental components of the program became more irritating to these
youths than the unjust treatment they associated with the traditional punitive, rule-bound regime.

And she started, you know, gettin' all hyper like she usually
does, slammin' her arms around, you know, gettin' overex-
cited. And I said, "Calm down." And she said, "Don't intimidate me!" I said, "How am I intimidating? I'm just asking you
to calm down." I said, "Just calm down. It ain't that big of
a deal." Ms. Truro said, "You're intimidating me, Mr. Viner.
Don't intimidate me." And I'm trying, you know, it's like staff
who do like that, they feel you're intimidating them when
you're just doing what you're supposed to be doin'. And, you
know, they don't—she doesn't know how to control herself.
We have to control ourselves, otherwise this [punishment]
occurs and this [punishment] occurs. Then how can we possibly, when we're doin' what we're supposed to be doin', and
we're still losin' points for it?

Throughout the first three months of the program these youths
provided what could be viewed as spontaneous leadership. They
conferred legitimacy on the program and generally behaved in a
manner consistent with the prison system's new Code of Ethics and
Philosophy Statement. They had taken staff and administrators "at
their word," displayed high levels of responsibility and maturity, and
attempted to exercise their nascent rights.

When the staff members' and administrators' commitment to
the program appeared to wane, some youths began expressing their
frustration cleverly by using the rules and language of the program
to address their individual needs. These youths had the potential to
provide leadership and to enhance the program's success, but once
they believed the program was a sham, the opposite occurred. They
confined their behavior, which was often visibly irritating to staff, to
the minimum requirements of acceptable conduct.[3]

The model program was undermined significantly whenever

policies or procedures were communicated ineffectively to youths and whenever youths believed the rules had been changed to their disadvantage. A prime example was the question of whether youths would be released from prison once they completed the model program. Initially, the youths were told that it was possible to complete the program in a minimum of three months. Staff members failed to explain that they believed it would take youths longer than three months to be able to "consistently meet behavioral expectations" and be ready to leave. Although completion of the program was established as a *prerequisite* for release, it was never intended to be synonymous with release. Other criteria, such as the severity of the crime, protection of the community, and media attention to the case, entered into the final decision to allow an individual to return to the community. This was not made clear to the youths.

An analysis conducted seven months into the program confirmed that most youths would remain in the institution longer than three months after entering the program. Several completed the program but, in their eyes, their situations remained unchanged. Although the smaller of the two prisons had a graduation ceremony for youths being released, there was no provision for special recognition for youths who had completed the program but remained in the institution. The youths viewed release from prison as the only meaningful end to the program.

For staff members, bureaucratic expediencies and personal interests assumed major significance. Due to their own professional and personal concerns and insufficient administrative support to develop a cooperative environment, many gave priority to protecting their self-interests and job security. In so doing, they frequently took a rigid stance that undermined the basic philosophy of the model program.

The youths balked at staff behavior they viewed as arbitrary and needlessly authoritative. At first the youths insisted that staff adhere to the principles, but later they acquiesced to a cynicism that mocked the program, viewing promised changes as illusions and lies. Daniel's comments are telling:

At first they told us we could wear anything we want to. Right?

And then I had some blue shoestrings in my shoes, and then they said we couldn't wear blue shoestrings. They said we gonna be able to make our own dress code up, but we didn't get to make it up. They made it up for us.

What reason did they give for not allowing you to do that?

'Cause they say everything gonna be gang-related. They think everything's gang-related. They don't know nothin' about gangs, and when we try to tell 'em, they still don't listen. . . . They say—they say—well, [Mr.] Hill, he said that he don't care if I wore blue shoestrings 'cause they just shoestrings, but they say—they know I'm in a gang so they expect—they said we wasn't in the gang while we was in this cottage. So, I was like, alright, I ain't bein' in a gang, so why can't I wear my blue shoe-strings? And they just said I couldn't.

One meeting between youths and the chief of child care, the administrator most directly responsible for the prison programs, provides an apt example of both the model program's tremendous potential and the insidious ways in which that potential was under-mined. Staff members did not attend the meeting and youths were given an opportunity to discuss their concerns openly. During the session they demonstrated a great familiarity with the program's principles and language, even when they charged that some of the staff members' behavior was inappropriate. They maintained that some staff were disrespectful, interrupting youths and not permit-ting them to make their points fully in groups discussions, even when youths appropriately followed group rules and procedures.

Perhaps because of the youths' need for stability and fairness, the issues of rule making and consistency were of primary concern. Youths felt that staff members made up rules whenever they wanted and unjustly rationalized their actions, displaying an attitude of "I'm staff and I can do whatever I want to." One of the youths' strongest and most insightful complaints related to the staff's use of the con-cept "criminal thinking." They told the chief of child care that they resented being unfairly told they were displaying criminal thinking.

One youth explained:

> They wanted us to speak our mind, and what they want us to
> do is to tell 'em what is on our mind. And once we start doin'
> that, they start interruptin' us and sayin' "This is 'criminal
> thinking' and 'delinquent thinking.'"... That gets people's self-
> talk, self-conscious mind, thinkin' they're criminals, so after a
> while they start believin' they're really criminals. They'll start
> doin' what they don't want to do.... It's real harmful, 'cause I
> know a whole bunch of people out there who started thinkin'
> they're criminals. And they're starting to act—at first, they was
> actin' better than what they is now.

The chief of child care attempted to make certain the youths
understood the concept of "criminal thinking," and that a fundamental aspect of the program was to deal with illegal behavior and
rationalizations for it. They quickly assured him they understood
and that was not what they were talking about. What concerned
youths most was their perception that some staff members objected
when the youths questioned everyday decision making in the unit
or any aspect of the program. They accused staff of cutting them
off and saying, "That's criminal thinking," simply because they
disagreed with the youths. Their grievance was very clear: "'That's
criminal thinking' is used by staff when we disagree with them and
really believe we're right. And we're not talking about anything violent, we're not saying we're gonna' steal, we're not going to do anything criminal. What's 'criminal thinking' is that we disagree with
the staff."

They were also concerned about the staff's failure to respond to
their questions about the dress code. First, they said it was unrea-
sonable that they could not wear shorts when they left their unit,
even to the extent of having to wear long pants over gym shorts on
the way to and from the baseball field for recreation. The appeal was
punctuated by exclamations such as, "It's 110 degrees out there!"
and "Man, it's June in the desert!"

Second, they objected to being made to tuck in their shirts while
inside Unit Four. They maintained that the student rules specified

the prison system's needs during the upcoming budget review process.

Violating the Spirit of the Program

The program vowed to deal with the youths as individuals. However, there were many times when youths were treated as anonymous inmates, and frequently rule-bound approaches outweighed the commitment to dealing with each youth as a person. One example related to escorting program youths from the prison to attend doctor's appointments at a local hospital. Regardless of their positive behavior or progress in the program, youths were placed in handcuffs, attached to a belly chain, with shackles at the ankles, in accordance with old institutional rules that allowed no exceptions. In the first instance we observed, the youth met the criteria for supervised off-campus activity (without restraints) and was expected to be released from prison within the week. Because of his limited juvenile record he was also classified as a low risk to the community. Nevertheless, he was shackled and chained in transit and during the doctor's appointment.

Ironically, this practice had been singled out for criticism in the class-action lawsuit six years earlier. When we questioned the apparent conflict in philosophy, administrators agreed that the old rule and such treatment were inappropriate and unnecessary and stated that this "error in judgment" would be addressed. Nevertheless, eight months later the same situation was observed with another youth, a slightly built fourteen-year-old who was having radiation treatments after surgery for prostate cancer. The youth's previous offenses were classified as medium risk to the community and he was obviously in a weakened condition as he shuffled down the walk in chains. He had lost his hair and was visibly despondent.

Both youths said they were shamed and frustrated at having to walk through a public hospital cuffed and shackled "with everyone staring at them." They believed that, in good faith, they had worked within the program to achieve a measure of trust and respect that did not warrant the use of this level of physical restraint. They felt betrayed.

The problem of "stalled youths" also reflected the program's considerable difficulty in recognizing and responding to the needs of individual youths. "Stalled youths" referred to those who were not progressing in the program in a timely manner. On average, it required four and a half months for youths from the first two model units to complete the program (not to be confused with their total length of stay inside the prison). However, after seven months, four of the initial twenty-four participants had not "graduated." Ten of the forty-eight youths in the two model units—almost one-fifth of the youths in the program at that time—were still at the first level after more than three months of participation. Half of these youths had been in the program for more than *six* months, that is, twice as long as the projected minimum.[5] There had been no comprehensive review to determine why these youths had failed to progress. One of the model program's basic tenets, that each youth's individual needs would be addressed, was violated.

The spirit of the program was violated in other important ways. At the beginning, the program's principles mitigated several negative aspects of society in general, including overt racialized hostilities. Despite the prevalence and intensity of racism throughout society, staff and youths attempted to deal with the issue openly. As the program's effectiveness deteriorated, however, racialized behavior increased among staff members as well as among youths. This included youths' perceptions that some staff members showed favoritism toward youths of their race or ethnicity, or behaved in overtly racist ways.

This one staff called me a "taco bender." . . . They know they're wrong, but when you tell them that they're wrong, they tell you that's putting the blame on somebody [else]. "You're not doing what the prototype expects you to do." . . . Miss Hunter called a black youth who was here "a colored person." She called him a colored person! If she calls the black a colored person, I don't even know what she's gonna say about me. I don't hope to hear "a taco bender" again, 'cause I don't appreciate that. . . . 'Cause I don't show her disrespect, why should she come in here and show me disrespect? You know, if she says something like that, we *know* what she's teaching her children. . . . I was—that's one thing I always thought about myself—I have a sense of fairness. I don't care what color you are, you treat me fair, I'll treat you fair, too.

Several youths believed that at least two staff members, an African-American male and a white female, showed favoritism toward Daniel, an African American. Youths said that these staff members gave snacks exclusively to Daniel, allowed him special, unearned privileges, and had frequent conversations with him laced with profanities and gang references that were explicitly forbidden by the program. Larry observed:

Favoritism—whoa! . . . It seems that staff always has their favorites—some staff . . . Miss Donnelly [a white female staff member] would always be with Daniel's group talkin' to them, and then people over here playing chess and people over here playing chess or whatever. But *she'd* always be with their group, and they'd always be over there, "Fuck this," "I'm a Crip this," you know, or "West Side City this. . . ."

With her there?

With her there, and she wouldn't say a word about it. When I once used the word "fuck," Miss Donnelly went in there and gave me a zero for points—for my language. So then I said, "Sure, you give *me* a zero. I say one little thing and you give me a zero, but they're over there swearing all night long and you don't say nothing!"

And Mr. Jackson [a black male staff member] was, "Hey, Cuz! [gang greeting]" You know, he'll be like he's just one of the gang bangers, but then when you turn around, you know, Daniel'll "Fuck this," "Crip this," "Cuz this," and nothin'll ever happen. But if I [say] "Shit!" Bang! Zero [points]!

Gradually staff attention to program principles declined, as did the influence of their initial training. Some staff members appeared unaware of the impact of their actions, including the ways in which their behavior could trigger memories and generate strong reactions among the youths. These complex interactions were often precipitated by something as seemingly "simple" as addressing youths with inappropriate and obscene language. For example:

> Mr. Jackson makes me so mad I can't help it. I just go off! He's big, and when he stands close and stands over me and cusses at me or laughs at me or makes fun of me in front of other people, I can't help it, I just go off. He's just like my dad when he gets drunk!

Other examples of unprofessional and unethical behavior included a shouting match between two staff members in full view of the youths, exhibitions of hostility between teachers and living unit staff in the classroom, a team meeting in which a staff member was confronted with arriving for work intoxicated and falling asleep on the job, and allegations of intimacies between a female staff member and a youth, resulting in dismissal of the staff member. One youth care worker remarked that a significant number of her coworkers "barely tolerate each other."

The systemwide team concept was decimated by a serious lack of communication among team members, and by the authoritarian behavior of a few staff members and administrators. Supervisors of the residential units had not established a consistent presence among staff members to provide encouragement and appropriate guidance and training; rather, they spent most of their time in central planning meetings. The demands of running the bureaucracy required constant attention from the central administrators. There was a vast difference between the original program plan and efforts to meet the actual needs of the youths.

The central administration's failure to establish a supportive presence within the prison was especially damaging. Key administrators needed to dedicate more time to staff members and their problems, and this required being at the institution in order to fully understand staff members' problems with schedule disruptions, the exigencies of program delivery, and addressing the individual needs of the staff and youths. This was apparent to the youths.

> About this prototype program—it's easy for somebody to sit in an office somewhere downtown and write, "Well, this is what the kids are going to do at this time. This is what the kids are going to do at that time." You know, without being here, seeing how it runs.

The conspicuous decrease in attention and support from administrators, punctuated by staff feelings of abandonment, confusion, disappointment, and frustration, contributed to the tense atmosphere that undermined the successful implementation of this highly structured and integrated treatment program. In a survey conducted at the end of the first six months, 73 percent of the program staff members viewed the management style of the majority of administrators as "authoritarian" or "superior." Eighty-two percent of the respondents indicated that discussions with coworkers about upper-level managers reflected general fear and anger. In contrast to the enthusiastic reactions early in the program, 78 percent expressed frustrations with their jobs, and overall responses indicated that the staff felt uninformed, powerless, and generally ignored.

Staff members' demoralization and lack of unity was devastating to the effective delivery of treatment, and many youths were aware of the transformation taking place, including understanding when staff members' actions violated model program principles.

> Some of us don't usually cuss, but every now and then when we'll slip up and staff hears it, they make a big old issue out of it. . . . I had a big problem with this one staff named Beth Carter, because at night I was cleaning up the cottage, and her and the staff was sitting there having a conversation and they was cussing back and forth. And, you know, I heard it, but I kept on doing [my chore]. The next day, I said a cuss word playing softball on the softball field, and she told me don't cuss, and I told her, "You're no better than *me*, 'cause last night you were

sitting there and every other word was a cuss word. You're telling *me* not to cuss!" And she said, "I'm not on the point system. I go home every night." And I said, "Practice what you preach. If you're not going to practice not cussing, then don't try to make me not cuss." We had a big old argument, and I ended up losing all my points. . . .

- - - - -

They don't let you explain . . . like when you'd be talking to them and you'd be telling them about your problems and stuff, they'd interrupt you and stuff like that. I like to get all of it out, you know?

- - - - -

The staff are feeding into it. If you're interrupting, they'll get louder than you are. You get louder than they are, and they're going to get louder than you are.

The importance of *consistently* advocating and following the model program's principles was critical to the success of the program. The new director had emphasized repeatedly the importance of "walking the walk"—of modeling the program principles for the youths and for each other—and the directive was emphasized again in a memo to all employees from the associate director, approximately one year into the program. In furthering the goal of "improving our working environment and providing an atmosphere that contributes to learning and mutual respect for both staff and our youth," staff were asked to refamiliarize themselves with specific behaviors in the employee handbook that would "not be tolerated."

These included fifteen causes for disciplinary action, "up to and including dismissal. In some instances, a single violation will provide evidence of a breach of the employment contract between an employee and the Department, and result in termination." The examples cited included: physical or verbal abuse of youth; verbal abuse of staff; failure to report unethical behavior; discrimination; falsification of official documents; fraud; sexual harassment; breach of confidential documents or information; use of profanity directed at or in presence of youth; and failure to treat youth with dignity and respect. The memo further commended staff who demonstrated their commitment to the agency's philosophy and code of ethics and admonished others to do the same.[6]

Less than a month later, during a period of low morale, frustration, and increased distrust, an incident occurred in which many staff members and youths observed the director, the chief administrator of the prison system, violating both the program's philosophy and the code of ethics. On a Sunday afternoon approximately thirteen months into the program, he visited the recently opened fourth model unit. Both youths and staff who were present said the director singled out one particular youth, Michael, whom he believed was standing inappropriately, with his hands inside the front of his sweat pants. In the verbal confrontation that followed, inches from the youth's face, he yelled, "Get your hands out of your mother-fucking pants!"

Although Michael was new to the model program, he did not respond in a hostile or aggressive manner, but later the same day he wrote a letter to the governor to protest his treatment.

> Today we moved over to Cottage Frontier & the Director and his wife came to look over the new cottage. While [the Director] and his wife were here I started adjusting my pants. [The Director] told me to take my hands out of my pants. Then as me, my peers & some staff belive [the Director] began to intimadate me useing foul language and by getting in my face. Me and my fellow peers were greatly disapointed by his actions. We thought he would be a positive role model and a caring person toward the youth. We believe he is not fit for the job.

Staff members expressed dismay but appeared to deal with the incident in accordance with program principles. The youth said he viewed the director's actions as a human mistake, but felt the appropriate remedy would be the same as required of youths. He requested that the director apologize to him and the rest of the unit. Over a month later, when he had received no response, he filed an official grievance reiterating the incident [7] and added:

> After the insident accured, me and Brian wrote a letter to the

Govenour. We were recorded on tape [by a staff member] & talked to [a researcher from the university]. Twice now I have heard the Director was coming to talk to us. Both times he never showed. Once he sent the Asst. Director but my cottage supervisor felt it was inapporeate. It's been over a month now. We feel the Director has had more than enuff time to come and talk to us.

I have heard more than once of staff being fired for so much as yelling at youth. If this is true then why can the Director cuss at and intimade youth.

By verbally abusing and intimating me he not only shocked and disappointed me, other youth & staff. He also broke his own Code of Ethics.

The youth quoted specific principles from the code of ethics and concluded, "We want some feedback." The director was asked by several individuals to respond to this request, and two and a half months after the incident he returned to the unit to meet with youths and staff. Although he did not agree that he had been intentionally intimidating and stressed the inappropriateness of the youth's behavior, he also said, "If I offended you, I'm sorry." Subsequently, he wrote a letter of apology to the youth:

Your grievance is important to me. I reviewed it on the same day you gave it to me. Therefore, it concerns me that you state that this was your second letter to me about your grievance. I never received your first letter, if I had, you would have received a response.

It was not my intention to be "verbally abusive and physically intimidating" when I instructed you to take both of your hands out of the front of your pants. Instead, my intent was to firmly bring to your awareness the inappropriateness of this behavior.

Michael, sometimes people pick up a variety of behaviors in an institutional setting that are not appropriate to the community. The "hands in pants" behavior that you displayed when I toured the school is a behavior that is common for males in institutional settings. I emphatically responded to the behavior intentionally. I wanted you to remember that such a behavior, no matter how unconscious on your part, is inappropriate and reflects poorly on you.

The manner in which I confronted your behavior made you feel disrespected. When I met with you individually, and in the group setting, I apologized for this verbally. I apologize to you now in writing.

You have done an excellent job of using the proper procedures for handling your grievance. Keep working hard in your treatment program.[8]

The director's verbal and written apology were appropriate in that they reflected the program's spirit, and, indeed, a public admission of fault by a chief administrator is rare, but the fact the incident even occurred undermined the program. Equally important, the director's tremendous energy and visionary efforts on behalf of the program were overshadowed by such inconsistency. Perceptions of arbitrariness, unfairness, and insincerity were heightened among numerous youths and staff members within the institution. Also, the incident provided political currency for those who opposed the model program, as evidenced by the fact that the youth's first letter was hand delivered immediately to the governor's office by a member of the crisis management team, while the director stated he never received a copy of the letter.

Organizational Impediments, Bureaucratic Inertia

The working conditions for most staff members did not improve significantly during the two years. Their jobs within the prison bureaucracy included low salaries, demanding working conditions, menial tasks, and perceptions of a lack of support and respect from superiors. Although the staff members were older, wore different clothes, and went home daily, the parallels between their experiences and those of the youths' were striking.[9] The circumstances generated an impossible situation for many, in which staff members reported feeling unappreciated and abandoned, powerless in an ineffective and ever-changing environment. Most believed they would remain invisible and unheard unless they made a major mistake.

Originally, staff members had been uniformly pleased when they were selected for training in the new, highly visible program. Many suggested that this was the first time their opinions had been sought and they were treated as important contributors. But the stress due to the unrelenting scrutiny of the program soon became evident. Some reveled in newfound power and a sense of self-importance, some felt challenged to meet an important goal, but others were overwhelmed and uncertain of their ability to meet the task.

The central administration's support for the program was often inconsistent and inadequate, and many staff members working in the prison felt they received insufficient backing to pursue the model vigorously or to maximize its potential for success. One staff member declared:

> Now I would prefer that [the director] get out here and help us out. Of all the people that I have to deal with I have the most faith in him. He just, he impresses me. And he came in and told the kids the same thing, "We're going to make successes out of you. We're not going to see you back here, and we're not going to see you at [the adult jail]." I don't think we have enough contact with him, and I realize he's very, very busy, but it would be just so nice if he could be out here and give us the groundwork. . . . But we don't see enough of him.

While it remains a valid point that increased administrative attention and participation in the program was essential for its continued success, this also illustrates the tremendous demands on administrators and staff members and the difficulty of emphasizing treatment in a prison setting. Both institutional personnel and administrators were understaffed, overwhelmed with responsibilities, and unable to accomplish all that was needed, despite the concerted efforts of many. Several dedicated staff members in other living units attempted to follow the model philosophy and principles. One unit declared itself part of the new program, remodeled their physical environment as much as possible through donations, and attempted to run groups and follow the model, despite few resources and over-crowding. Alongside such dedicated efforts, prison life continued as usual within most nonprogram units, with fights, graffiti, hostilities, and lack of programming as the norm.

Although running the model program involved a major commit-ment and was key to the long-term transformation of the prison sys-tem, it was a relatively small part of the central administrators' responsibilities. The same administrators responsible for overseeing the new program were in charge of the entire juvenile prison sys-tem; inevitably, "damage control" frequently superseded attention to the model program. They were engaged in controlling a volatile environment, replete with angry, frequently aggressive youths, and disgruntled, overworked staff.

In the face of these competing demands, central administrators would violate important program principles regarding participatory decision making and procedural openness, clarity, and accountabil-ity. As a result, they were commonly perceived as failing to uphold the key commitment to mutual respect and responsibility. Despite early pledges of support and personal attention to the difficult jobs that institutional staff faced daily, the director was seen infrequently at the prison after the first month Unit Four was open. Although informed of deteriorating morale and the inevitable presence of a few staff members who threatened the integrity of the program, key administrators sometimes failed to take appropriate action. When no intervention occurred, managers within the institution responded with increased control, which contributed to an atmos-phere of defensiveness, polarization, cynicism, and insecurity. Administrators confirmed rumors of their furtive night searches of computer files, desks, and wastebaskets; tamperings with hiring decisions after final deliberations by a selection committee; and unwarranted verbal abuse of employees.

▟ Limited Sphere of Influence

Despite the fact that many staff members, especially those involved in the initial model unit, had a genuine commitment to provide meaningful treatment for youth, the incursion of bureaucratic and political realities resulted in marked frustration and cynicism. For many staff members, their primary desire was to find effective ways to influence the youths' behavior and lives positively, but they were aware that their sphere of influence was limited. One staff member stated:

> I think we have to build a rapport with the police department, and with the courts so that we can show them that we're willing to do something and give these kids an opportunity, but also to be there for guidance, to be there for the parents. One of the big things on parole, the parents feel that they're alone. . . . [The parents] are out there by themselves. The kids *know* they're out there by themselves.
>
> And to get people to understand that if we do not put money into the system, if we do not put money into the staff who are giving treatment to these kids, who are there for them—if we don't give raises, if we don't get good people, if we don't have good treatment, then the state will be paying dearly, because they'll be paying for these kids to be on parole and on welfare and in hospitals and their kids being taken care of by welfare while they're sitting in state prison. So it will cost us a lot more in the long run. And somehow we have to get that message out. And the fact that—yes, these kids have done crimes, but there's a chance they can turn it around. . . . We can't throw them away.

The tangible limits of the model program's influence were highlighted when some of the first twenty-four youths who had completed the model program returned to the prison. Even when youths returned for lesser offenses, staff members were disturbed, despite the fact this type of "positive recidivism" is viewed by many as "progress." Although they recognized the enormous impact of social forces beyond the prison walls, staff were clearly *not* prepared for the feelings they experienced when the first "model program" youth returned to the institution with new serious charges.

They were visibly angry at Marcos when he came back charged with vehicle theft, drug use, and second-degree homicide. Staff members initially refused to visit him in the security unit where he was held the first couple of weeks. Despite the program's original plan to reinstate returning youths in their original living units as quickly as possible in order to discover "what went wrong" and to reinforce the basic program principles, a substantial number of the staff members in Unit Four argued against Marcos rejoining the unit. They candidly revealed their unwillingness to work with him, expressing their disgust and anger at what had transpired since they last saw him. Staff lacked the professional training to deal with these issues, and some individuals' sense of personal failure exacerbated the dilemma.

After supervisors forced Unit Four staff to take him back, Marcos responded with a defensive cockiness that further alienated the staff. Although staff psychologists were informed of the problems erupting in Unit Four, no one met with Marcos or the staff members to help them through this difficult period. Staff were reminded in a graphic manner that all of their efforts inside the institution were diluted, at best, if they were not augmented with support for the youths in the community. They were also reminded that the program's ability to effect change was extremely limited. Carol, a staff member, brought this to the fore:

How do you feel about the support that is currently set up for these youths to make the transition back to the community?

It stinks. . . . We don't have anything out there. One of the things we *really* need is—when you've got kids that are depressed, have a problem at home, the parents kick them out for that night because they've been arguing, or something's going on—some place for them to go for that twenty-four hours, somebody to talk to. They don't need to be back in the institution, but what they're going to do is they're going to go back to the homeboys. And if they get in trouble—*when* they get in trouble—they're going to wind up back here.

Until Arizona gives us funding to do this and to have those

things out there—a lot of the parole officers are overburdened as it is, and it's hard going to other agencies and finding other funding and free programs so that our kids are kept busy when they're out there. The schools don't want to accept them. . . . First mistake they make, they get kicked out and suspended and they're out of school. So they're back on the streets again. . . . So the success we've built isn't [supported] in the community.

An emphasis on the youths' return to their communities was essential to the program's vision. Its true test was grounded in continued support of the youths and the relevance of its principles under fire in the outside world. But from the beginning, post-release services failed to receive sufficient resources and support. Parole officers were not among those trained in the new treatment modalities despite the requirement that they conduct follow-up groups. Their caseloads remained high, and until much later there were few resources for families and youths within the communities. A few dedicated individuals, staff members and volunteers, provided services and support, but these were not commensurate with the need.

From the beginning it was clear the program should focus attention on youths' needs when they were released from the prison and returned to their communities. Considerable energies and resources needed to be dedicated to this crucial aspect; someone must provide support for each youth and coordinate community services. At the end of the two years of research, this aspect of the program still received insufficient attention and resources.

▋ Political Imperatives and Impediments

We have discussed the punitive themes that permeate contemporary society, especially widespread images of delinquent youths as being increasingly predatory and dangerous. These images—of imprisoned youths as singularly and uniformly violent, beyond hope, and destined for a life of adult crime—all question the relevance of treatment efforts. Such portraits deny the considerable variation among imprisoned youths and lay the foundation for punitive policies. They belie the fact that many imprisoned youths are not violent and do not have extensive delinquency records.

The political support for the model program was qualified and limited, which greatly undermined its potential for success. Wide-ranging structural factors contributed to the program's decline, including erratic media portrayals, the lack of resolve at the legislative and executive levels, and unsupportive ideological themes within Arizona and U.S. culture in general.

Over the two-year period of the study, media responses to the consent decree and the "new" juvenile prison system were generally positive. Initially, the media characterized the consent decree as ending the "draconian" era of juvenile prisons and as providing a chance for imprisoned youths.[10] There was supportive television coverage, including several segments highlighting the model program's objectives and methods and some coverage providing human interest stories, such as a dermatologist volunteering his services in response to youths' desires to remove tattoos.[11] A few journalists evidenced concern with more encompassing societal issues and with placing the youths' lives in context:

> The face of juvenile crime we all fear belongs to a child with a complicated story. Nothing in that history, no matter how awful, can excuse the choice to break into the homes or break the bones of one's fellow citizens. But finding the common threads that weave in and out of the lives of many juvenile offenders is critical to finding solutions to juvenile crimes that go beyond "lock 'em up and throw away the key."
>
> Only by trying to understand their stories can we hope to turn them around before they become so dangerous that long prison sentences are the only available answer. Only by understanding what made them step off the path can we hope to keep their younger brothers and sisters from following in their wayward footsteps.[12]

However, throughout the two-year study, media portraits of a prison system undergoing reform were overshadowed by persistent and extensive coverage of adolescent violence and gang activities.[13]

Far less coverage was given to the restorative justice emphasis of the model program than to calls for increased punishment, including editorial support for increased transfer to adult courts and incarceration in the juvenile prisons.[14]

A primary reason the model program did not reach its full potential was the lack of political resolve at the state level. When the lawsuit was first filed in 1986 and negotiations and reform efforts had begun, the governor in office at that time expressed support for investigation and change and initiated the Commission on Juvenile Corrections and the subsequent task force. When a new governor took office in early 1991, he supported proposed legislation that renamed the Department of Juvenile Corrections the Department of Youth Treatment and Rehabilitation and mandated changes that reflected treatment and public safety concerns. This legislation was adopted and the consent decree signed during his first term.[15]

Initially, at least nominal support for the model program was assured by the need to avoid going to trial by negotiating the consent decree. This was a political necessity, and a major constraint forced by the lawsuit. But political, moral, and financial support for the treatment aspects of the program would prove to be underemphasized and seriously inadequate. The lawsuit cost the state approximately $3 million in settlements and attorney fees,[16] and an estimated $12 million would have been necessary to bring about changes agreed to in the consent decree, including additional staff, salary increases, improvement of facilities, specialized treatment programs, and provision of advocates for parole revocation hearings.[17] As the new governor predicted at the time of the consent decree, however, "there [was] no guarantee the full sum would be appropriated during tight fiscal times."[18] Indeed, the state legislature appropriated only $1 million of the $4–5 million needed in the first year to begin implementing the consent decree.[19] Full funding has never been provided.

The monumental conflict between the philosophy of the program and the political expediencies of the hour contributed greatly to the program's stagnation and ineffectual implementation. The program's main mandate was to imprison only those who absolutely required such confinement, and, once the number of incarcerated youths was reduced, to serve those imprisoned few more effectively through an intensive focus on accountability and treatment. In contrast, the primary political imperative of the state's "get tough" policy was to imprison greater numbers of youths for longer periods of time in the juvenile and adult prisons. The new governor did not applaud the model program's accomplishments publicly, nor did he or his representatives visit the prisons regularly or attend events for families and community supporters.

From the very beginning and throughout the two years of research, the new governor's political agenda appeared to be at cross-purposes with the objectives of the model program. The primary policy championed by the governor was automatic or presumptive transfer of youths to adult courts for prosecution, to the diminishment of all other concerns.[20] His "get tough" theme reigned, despite the explicit opposition of several professional associations and advocacy organizations, as well as the Arizona Juvenile Justice Advisory Council, the Governor's Task Force on Juvenile Corrections, and the Director of Juvenile Corrections. Significantly, all of the individuals serving on the council and task force, and the Director of Juvenile Corrections, were appointed and then ignored by the governor and his staff. For example, the chair of the Governor's Task Force on Juvenile Corrections wrote to the governor:

> Because of [the Task Force's] opposition to transfer [of juveniles to adult courts], we were in the difficult position of testifying against legislation proposed by your office. I spoke of this potential situation in my last letter, and tried to discuss it with you either in person or by phone. This situation might well have been avoided if you had brought to the table the very people who were thought to advise you on juvenile issues—[the Director of Juvenile Corrections] and members of the Task Force and Council. I was very disappointed that this did not interest you enough to warrant some response.[21]

When the state senate's judiciary committee unanimously voted against and thus killed the governor's automatic transfer bill, a local newspaper editorial writer commended them for their action and urged them to fund the juvenile system adequately.

> [A] growing number of . . . lawmakers are also admitting that a better answer would be to do what has never been done in Arizona: Adequately fund the juvenile system so it can treat and rehabilitate troubled kids rather than simply warehousing them before tossing them back onto the streets.
>
> The governor and Legislature have refused to provide the state's Department of Youth Treatment and Rehabilitation [DYTR] with enough money to make real rehabilitative efforts anything more than a pilot program. In fact, funding for DYTR has shrunk the past three years.[22]

It was politically unfeasible for the governor to simultaneously support excluding many youths from the juvenile system via transfer to adult courts, and to support a revitalized juvenile prison system that would provide a meaningful alternative to transfer for many youths. A year and a half after the model program began, following the governor's address to a statewide conference on violence, one headline proclaimed, "[Governor] Calls for War on State's Juvenile Crime."[23]

Although this conference focused on both adult and youth violence, the governor's remarks were directed almost exclusively toward youths. He announced that available bed space for juveniles transferred to the adult prisons would be doubled and more beds would be made available as necessary. He also stated that he would ask the legislature to appropriate $1.5 million for a "specialized gang unit" within the state police, and announced that he had asked the Adjutant General of the Arizona National Guard to "alert his troops and keep them prepared in the event they are needed" to combat street gangs.[24]

In outlining his proposals, the governor never mentioned the model program, not even acknowledging it as a secondary initiative or as a complement for youths who might prove themselves redeemable. Without specifying any amount, he did state that he would ask the legislature "to begin funding our existing juvenile justice programs in accordance with a federal consent decree." Additionally, he expressed his intention to request $930,000 to begin a "[shock incarceration, militaristic] boot camp for committed delinquents" in the juvenile prison system.[25]

Then, nineteen months after hiring the highly recommended director of juvenile prisons, the governor summarily fired him and his associate director. The firings came without warning. State police arrived at the agency's downtown offices and stood guard while the two cleaned out their desks of personal items and were escorted to the door. The governor then appointed an administrator from the adult prison system who had previously served as interim director of the youth prisons.

The firing came after a much publicized incident in which the "Victory Outreach" church theater group, with the prior approval of the prison authorities, brought weapons loaded with blanks into the prison's diagnostic unit for use in their dramatic presentation. The performance by former gang members was graphic and geared toward "realism," depicting rape, murder, suicide, and street warfare in an attempt to "show inmates the dangers of gang life."[26] An editorial in a major Arizona newspaper referred to "much unnecessary ado about the presentation" and reported that the governor's office said it was not linked with the firing of the director.[27]

The governor did not discuss publicly the reasons for the firings, but his spokesperson stated that the agency had "been in the news frequently of late" and that the governor had been concerned about the safety of employees and youths in the prisons. The media pointed to controversies regarding prison escapes, assaults on staff and youths, and sexual activity between an employee and an inmate. Those who opposed the governor's decision maintained that such problems were greater prior to this director's administration and that the "strictly political" firing occurred despite the director's "remarkable" accomplishments.[28]

Undoubtedly, there were numerous and diverse factors that may have contributed to the governor's action, including unfavorable reports from some staff and youths regarding the director's demeanor and behavior, discontent among some staff regarding the overall changes taking place within the prison system, and the crucial issue of whether the Director of Juvenile Corrections was perceived by the governor and his staff as furthering their political agenda.[29] Questions posed by one newspaper editorial included, "Is this a political move at a time when juvenile justice issues are hot topics?" and "Did the forces against change win out in a long-standing battle over whether juvenile incarceration was about reform or punishment?"[30]

The fired director's failure to endorse the governor's punitive agenda contributed to his fate. Unlike the head of adult prisons, he was not a vocal supporter of the governor's policies. At the very least, the concerns of the Director of Juvenile Corrections were less compatible with the governor's interests than were those of the head of adult prisons. One editorial characterized the Director of Juvenile Corrections as demonstrating a "serious and manifest failure to be a champion of public safety." It continued, "[his] failure should not diminish the real accomplishments of his tenure. But it does confirm the suspicion that the juvenile justice system in Arizona is so bad that even good men can be chewed up in the process."[31]

In a newspaper interview prior to his firing, the Director of Juvenile Corrections made statements characteristic of his approach and indicative of his differences with the governor:

> "People want a quick fix," he said in an interview before his resignation. "They want to put them (juvenile offenders) all behind bars. Well, why didn't that work for the 1.1 million Americans already behind bars?"
>
> [The director] said saving juveniles from the cycle of crime must be done with counseling, education and involvement of families and the community.
>
> "Eighty percent of our kids can be helped," he said. "People should have the right to be protected," [the director] said. "Their expectation is to get rehabilitation and protection at the same time. It's a balance. Not a matter of either/or."[32]

Perhaps most importantly, although the Director of Juvenile Corrections was appointed by the governor, he was chosen by and exemplified the restorative justice and treatment priorities of the Task Force on Juvenile Corrections and the vision of the consent decree. In response to the firing, the former chair of the task force responded, "There was something going on for a change [in juvenile corrections]. . . . [The director] did a remarkable job with limited funds."[33]

The Director of Juvenile Corrections, the deputy director, and their hand-picked central administrators, along with the majority of staff members working directly with youths in the prisons, behaved in ways that suggested they worked for youths, families, and the community. At the very least, they worked for the fulfillment of *their* vision of justice for juveniles. Their main concerns were transforming the prison system in accord with the consent decree's focus on individualized accountability and treatment as the true way to protect the public. Unfortunately, this did not coincide with the agenda of the state's top official who hired them and had the power to fire them.

The full trajectory of the governor's agenda was reasserted in his January, 1995, State of the State address following his reelection to a second term. He once again called for legislators to effectively abolish the juvenile court and handle youths such as those in juvenile prisons by transferring them to adult courts. Under the proposed plan, juveniles accused of a violent offense or a third offense of any type would be automatically transferred to adult courts regardless of age. Those accused of nonviolent crimes would be dealt with by neighborhood-action councils run by the county prosecutors' offices.[34] When a lack of legislative support for the proposal became evident, the governor began an initiative to place the proposal on a ballot to be voted upon directly by the public.[35]

The model program had little time to improve or prove itself. Despite the enormity of the task, that is, completely changing an entrenched bureaucracy and prison system, immediate signs of success were required, and the modest, but genuine, successes that were made were evaluated as inadequate within a political climate that wanted to see juveniles punished.

Five | **"Going Home"**

The true test of the model program came when the youths left prison. Their experiences revealed how the program had failed to deal with problems they brought with them, such as gangs and drug abuse. The youths' experiences also revealed how social and economic conditions undermined the model program. Their struggles when they returned to the community were not solely or primarily due to program deficiencies. The youths' many problems were inextricably bound up with society's problems. The prospects of aiding youths in their transformation attempts often seemed overwhelmingly difficult to staff members; changing society seemed inconceivable.

While the primary skill learned by most of the youths was how to survive within the institution, the program's initial intent and most important goal was to provide them with the skills necessary to survive—and succeed—within their families, neighborhoods, and society.[1] Nevertheless, for a variety of reasons, ranging from a lack of time and resources to a lack of emphasis on its urgency, the development of a comprehensive community program was consistently subordinated to other demands.

For most youths, going home meant a return to poverty and unemployment, troubled homes, the allure of alcohol and drugs, the dominance of gangs, and daily hardships. Even when the prison's model program was functioning at its best, youths' changed attitudes and emergent hopes often were not sufficient to sustain them in the community. Their support system had been nurtured in a closed environment, but unresolved problems awaited the youths when they were released from prison. Outside the prison, fundamental social conditions remained unchanged. When they were paroled, within a few days or a few hours youths confronted the same old pressures and many reverted to familiar responses and solutions.

The Ubiquitous Influence of Drugs

Substance use and abuse dominated many youths' lives before they were incarcerated, yet these problems were virtually unaddressed by the prison experience. The model program forced the youths to be "straight," because they had little or no access to drugs. This was important, but in light of their eventual return to a drug-ridden society, the lack of effective drug and alcohol treatment was far more consequential. For the first six months after Unit Four was opened, no licensed psychologist supervised the treatment program, and for the first two years no specialized treatment for substance abuse existed.[2] In the interim, community volunteers from twelve-step alcohol and drug abuse programs conducted weekly groups inside the institution.

Some youths did not view drug use as a problem nor were they concerned about related dangers. Two such individuals had been in the program for approximately five months and they planned to resume drug use as soon as they were released:

> Jeff: I've already been here five months for what should have been a three-month charge, and now they're talking about sending me to a [residential facility] for drug counseling. That doesn't have anything to do with my charges!

Christopher: Yeah, but you're always talking about what you're going to do when you get out. You're always talking about drugs. That's why they're sending you to placement.

Jeff: But it's not going to change anything. I'm still going to do the same thing when I get out!

You plan to continue using drugs when you get out?

Jeff: Of course!

Could you help me understand? You're straight now. Don't you think this is healthier?

Christopher: If you ever used crystal once, you'd know—and you'd do it again, too.

Describe to me how it makes you feel.

Christopher: You just feel kind of mellow and hyper at the same time. You think faster. You just can't describe it.

So you plan to continue using drugs when you get out, too?

Christopher: Sure!

Do you worry about your health?

Christopher: You think I'm thin now—I've put on forty pounds since I've been in here!

Jeff: I've put on at least twenty pounds.

Don't you want to live to a ripe old age?

Christopher: I won't live beyond thirty anyway, and living to thirty is good enough.

Jeff: I don't care. It's worth it.

Why don't you care?

Christopher: My mother went to prison when I was two years old. I've been bounced around from foster home to foster home all my life. I don't care if I live.

In contrast to those who were casual about alcohol and drugs, many youths expressed grave concerns about drug problems and what would happen once they were released from prison.

> I have a drug problem. And I said, "If you guys can't help me, then what's the use of me being here?" They said, "Well, yeah, that's what KIVs [Keys to Innervisions] are for." I said, "Hey, there's one section on drugs. . . . [The KIV workbook] only has one section on drugs, and that's not gonna help me." I said, "If you guys keep me until I'm eighteen, I'm just gonna go out those gates, and you guys ain't gonna help me." I'll be on my own. Yeah, I'll try, but it's just like in here I *know* I can't do drugs, 'cause there ain't no drugs. . . . But when I get out there, it's like I have friends that are into that.

> *So the pressure is going to be back on you when you get out.*

> Yeah. It's like right here I know, you know, I can laugh at it, but when I get out there, it's gonna be like bad. . . . I guess that's the addiction.

Some youths planned to live with relatives outside their old neighborhoods so peer pressures to return to drugs would not be as intense. Jacob had been incarcerated on three previous occasions, twice for using and selling drugs. Although he had not seen his father for five years, arrangements were made for him to move out of state to live with him. Jacob hoped that because he would not be going back to the same friends, he might have a chance to stay off drugs. He said the other times he was released he felt like he was "being sucked into a swirling pool." Intellectually, he knew that he needed to "avoid drugs or die," but he also knew how "good it felt" when he used drugs and how much money he could make by selling them. Jacob was certain that he would resume old patterns if he stayed in the area, but he was not sure if he would be able to avoid drugs even in a new environment.

Despite the widespread need for treatment, a substance abuse program was the last of three specialized, intensive programs to be developed by the prison system during the program's third and fourth years.[3] A treatment program for sexualized (aggressive) behavior was the first specialized unit to open, even though less than 10 percent of the youths in the model program were charged with some type of sexual misconduct. The second specialized unit to be developed was the violent behavior treatment program, although less than 40 percent of the youths in the model program were involved in violent crimes. In contrast, the prison's chief of counseling estimated that at least 85 to 90 percent of the youths had used drugs.[4] Almost all the imprisoned youths were involved with drugs, but these needs were not prioritized.

The model program's failure to confront the youths' extensive drug and alcohol problems mirrored society's failure. The "war on drugs" has been lost, the casualties of drug abuse and addiction are widespread, and the projections for change are nonexistent. Media attention and political rhetoric have shifted to other issues. Violence is now the surrogate for deep-seated social problems, and the war has been reconfigured as a war on youth.[5]

▌ Make New Friends, But . . .

Most youths doubted they could follow staff members' admonitions to find new friends who were not involved in drugs and gangs. The youths knew that when they were released from prison they were unlikely to meet an entirely new set of friends to provide "positive influences and companionship." At best, the youths considered the possibilities of continuing old friendships with new guidelines.

> I've figured out a game for when I get out. When I get out, I'll still have the same friends, because I live right next door to the same neighborhood as all of them. . . . I'll just probably— maybe I'll drink with them, but if they're going to go do a crime, I'd just as soon say not. Because I've got some friends that all they do is have a good time and kick back and drink or do whatever we're doing. But when it comes time to go do a crime, maybe like hold up a Circle K or whatever the crime is,

they'll just say, "No, I don't want to go," stuff like that. And they stay out of jail!

Imprisoned youths are placed in an untenable position when they are encouraged to change their behavior and to develop high aspirations, only to return to their virtually unchanged communities.[6] The prison system's chief of counseling candidly suggested that, in many ways, it is *irrational* for these youths to change their approach to life on the streets. He described the situation: "It's currently working for them, and there's some safety in numbers. To ask them to disavow their loyalty to the gang and to walk away—alone—can bring danger upon themselves and their families." One youth expressed this sentiment precisely:

> You try to get out, you know, and you're dead, man. . . . They say, "Hey, man," you know, "I remember when you used to be down," or something like that. And they want to get him, you know? He's not around them no more, and they don't like it. Maybe you pick new friends, and you just don't want to be around them anymore, and they don't like it, you know? They feel left out, and they say, "Well, go get him, man!"

Prior to his release from prison, Larry discussed the improbability that youths, especially gang members, could return home and sustain program goals.

> I think the program's a good idea because, you know, it is calming people down a bit. It's teaching them not to go off on every little thing, you know, when a person looks at them wrong. But still, once people get on the outs, they're still gonna slowly revert to their old ways. . . . I think the only thing they could do to keep them out of trouble is to make them move. Ninety percent of the people—

Make them move to another community, you mean?

Yeah. Ninety percent of the people in here are gang-related. Okay. So you teach them all this stuff in here, once he gets out, where's the first place he's going to go? Right back to his neighborhood, right back to his hood, his gang. And they're just going to suck him back in.

Many of the youths *wanted* to do well on the outside. They *wanted* their lives to be different. They did not want to waste their lives locked inside an institution. However, they had seen nothing to indicate that their prospects "on the outs" would be any different. Several youths, like Elias, viewed the model treatment program as unable to negate their fates: "Deep inside you really want to change, and then when the time comes to change, you've already adapted to being with [your homeboys] and doing the same things again. And then you just end up doing bad things and come back here."

Elias completed the model program two months before his sixteenth birthday, but within three months he had returned to the institution on charges of burglary and reentered the model program. Seven months later he was released again. Soon after his seventeenth birthday, he ran away from home. Elias became television news a year and a half later, seven months after his eighteenth birthday, when he was arrested in a stabbing incident. He was charged with attacking a stranger who intervened in an argument among Elias, his mother, and his older brother, all of whom have histories of substance abuse. The argument reportedly was over change from the purchase of a six-pack of beer.

Although they were eager to be released, many youths also expressed frustration that they were unprepared for what awaited them. Richard's comments were representative: "I don't want my life to be messed up—like I don't want to end up in [adult] prison. I want to change my life. I was hoping this place would help me, but it hasn't helped me much. It just makes me angry—and frustrated."

Youths' frustrations were tinged with fear. Carlos commented, "I feel happy I'm getting out. And I also feel scared." Several staff members remarked on this fear, as illustrated by a teacher's comments:

> You can tell the ones who are scared. They'll play the big game, "I want to go home," because that's what every kid is supposed to say. And when it comes time for someone to be released, they will behave in a manner so that they don't get released.

Those kids are obvious. Some of them are real quiet and don't say anything, but you know they are scared to death to go home. . . . Carlos has a lot of problems to face before he can really be ready. I'm not sure about Carlos. And I've brought that up before—that he bothers me a little bit. Carlos isn't playing a game. . . . I think [leaving prison] scares him, too. What he's in here for is scary, and I don't know if he feels he has enough confidence to go back out there and stay away from it. At least he's open enough to admit it.

Few youths openly acknowledged their fear. It was more acceptable for them to express frustration, hostility, or indifference. It was more difficult to express the deep fears they experienced, but they were afraid—of the possibilities of going to adult prison, of violence, and of death.[7]

Why are some people having such a tough time getting through the program? You're getting out, and there are a lot of other people who aren't. Why is that?

Terrence: Because I think they don't want to go.

You think they don't want to go home?!

Terrence: Yeah. They make me think they don't want to go home, maybe.

Maybe this is easier in here than it is at home.

Terrence: For some people, yeah.

Ricky reflected on the violence that occurred when he was released from prison the previous time.

Why did you get jumped when you were out the last time?

Because I'm from a different gang, that's why.

And that's the only real reason?

Yeah.

When you got jumped—what happened?

There were a whole bunch of them. They jumped me. They hit me with a crowbar. They broke my jaw. And I had to go to the hospital, and I had to stay there for about a week. I got stitches and stuff . . .

They're still trying to pay you back for things you've done before?

Yeah.

Within three months of his release, Ricky ran away.[8] After two months on the streets, he was taken into custody and returned to the juvenile prison for technical violation of his parole. Faced with familiar circumstances back in the community, 54 of the 254 youths who graduated from the program (21 percent) ran away—some more than once during the two-year period, a few as many as four times. Neither their families nor the justice system persisted in trying to find several of these youths, and their fates are unknown.[9]

Daniel was also very mindful of the violence on the streets: "It's getting wicked out there." When asked to explain, he replied, "Like a couple weeks ago, this Blood, he just got out of jail 'cause his brother got killed. . . . He seen the Crip who shot [his brother] at a liquor store and ran up and shot him in the face. Everybody gettin' shot. Another Crip died from the same dude."

Terrence expressed similar thoughts:

I understand there was a kid who was killed this weekend in a drive-by while you were on furlough.

That was my friend. . . . We was really close friends. . . . [My sister and me] were just getting something to eat, and I heard some shots on the next street. We just heard some shots, and I told my sister, "Let's go." And we went back to our house, and the next thing I know my girlfriend, she called and said it was Bird. We called him Bird. He just got shot in a drive-by.

Why?

It's just somebody come by and shoot at us. . . . If somebody else had been with him, he probably would have got shot, too. . . .

Does that happen very often in your neighborhood? Do you hear shots a lot?

Yeah, 'cause last Sunday my uncle got shot in my neighborhood—and he died, too.

Oh, my God. Was it somebody—do they know who did it?

They'll probably find out, 'cause his girlfriend, she was standing right there. She saw who did it, but she don't want to snitch, because they'd probably come back and try to do something to her. She don't want to snitch. . . . I'd snitch.

The dreams and ambitions the youths discussed when they were in prison were often insufficient to withstand the forces that had been set in motion long before their incarceration.[10] In a violence-permeated environment, old enemies are not likely to forget, and several youths released from the model program were killed.

Before he was released, Charles said he believed there was little that could be done to change the violence: "[Staff members] can't do nothing for me. . . . I'm just gonna go—you know, I'm gonna go with the flow, do what needs to be done, and stay out of trouble. It's as simple as that." Charles said he believed he could avoid trouble with the law, as well as control his drinking. Despite his intentions, Charles was drinking heavily within three weeks after leaving prison. He said that, because alcohol leaves your bloodstream within twenty-four hours, "you can produce clean UAs [urinalyses] for your P.O. [parole officer]" even while drinking heavily. Four months after his release, Charles was arrested for the murder of two men in separate armed robberies. He was transferred to the adult court to stand trial on two counts of first-degree murder.

When he was in adult jail awaiting trial, Charles said that when he left the juvenile prison he really didn't think he would be back again, but he had bad dreams about what "being locked up" in adult jail would be like. "I really thought that I was rehabilitated, but no one understands how hard it is out there." He said he was "disappointed and sad" when they took him back to the juvenile prison after he was arrested. He said, "It would have broken me down to see all those staff who believed in me. It kinda broke me down when I first saw you [the researcher]."

Readily available weapons played a major role in Charles's fate. Guns seemed to represent both a solution to some youths' fear and a key to identity and power. Charles talked about his inability to resist the attraction of guns after he was released from prison.[11] He said that he had access to a gun for some time before he actually touched it. "But once you touch it . . . the bigger the gun, the bigger you feel. . . . It's like nobody else out there has a gun."

Charles said that when he first went to adult jail he was scared, but "eventually the fear turns into anger." He likened his anger to a ball inside him, a ball that is always bouncing, sometimes higher than other times. He said "things just set me off," including "when someone you trust turns on you." Charles also said he felt like he was at the bottom of a dark stairway, "hollering for help." He believed that "people are convinced that I'm further down than I am."

Charles was convicted of two counts of first-degree homicide. Currently he is waiting to be sentenced. Two possibilities exist: a life sentence without parole, or death.

▌ "You Can't Take It Back"

Many of the youths originally joined gangs for security and belonging. Only later did fear and violence replace the sense of safety they first experienced.[12] Still later they discovered that once you make enemies on the street, "you can't take it back." As one youth explained: "There are a lot of people out here who want to kill me. I don't go to concerts or anything, because somebody'll kill me. I can only stay home at night."

Mark did not expect to avoid becoming involved in violence. He was accustomed to living in such an environment, and he was resigned to the idea that change was unlikely.

When I went on furlough, I got shot in my leg. I wasn't gang banging or nothin'. I was just in front of my house, and they just came by and I got shot. I don't know, it's just [that] everybody out there now's just killing everybody. That's all it is out there. They don't fight one-on-one or nothin'. . . . Gangs ain't never gonna stop. You can't get jumped out or nothin'. . . . They're just gettin' back at the neighborhood.

Mark returned to his small, rundown house in the barrio to live with his mother and seven of his nine brothers and sisters. Dealing drugs was the only way he knew to get "quick money." An aborted drug deal was probably the cause of his death. Less than three months after Mark's release from prison, the local newspaper reported that an unidentified body had been discovered with "trauma to the upper body." The body was Mark's.

Manny's story provides a graphic reminder that even when prison programs appear to be effective for specific youths, structural forces within society have great potential to negate those modest successes. Manny had done well in the program, and said he was determined to change. Upon his release, he enrolled in a community college, but was not able to escape old gang animosities.

Manny quickly became aware of the challenges he faced when former gang rivals jumped him in broad daylight at a local market. They held a 12-gauge shotgun to his chest and pointedly reminded him of his past. Manny said he was concerned that it was unsafe to spend any time with his girlfriend and their baby, since his very presence could place them in danger. At his home, which was riddled with bullet holes from previous drive-bys, he feared that his younger siblings might become victims. He said that he "would be able to ignore just about anything but that." His fear was ominous and his haunting words were prophetic: "I don't want to be the next victim. I just don't want to be the next victim."

Despite the threats from those on the streets, Manny visited his former prison unit and expressed interest in becoming a peer counselor. Manny's dreams went unfulfilled, but his fears were realized. Ten months after his release, he and his stepfather were shot down at their front door. Manny's stepfather died at the scene; Manny was taken to a local hospital where he remained in critical condition until his death three weeks later.

A neighbor in the home at the time of the shooting said that two young men came to the door and asked for Manny by name. "He walked up to the door, and they blasted him," the neighbor said. Within four hours, a fifteen-year-old male suspect from another barrio was arrested; ten days later, an eighteen-year-old male was also arrested. Both were charged with first-degree murder. Witnesses and neighbors said the shooting was motivated by "gang hatred."[13] The realities were grim for youths released from prison after completing the model program: within two years at least four youths were killed,[14] and one committed suicide.[15]

■ Social and Economic Realities: Poverty, Unemployment, Dead Ends

When the youths returned to the community, they were confronted with the social and economic realities of their existence. Almost without exception, life was extremely difficult for them, and opportunities to lead new lives were severely limited. Most were unsupported in their attempts to obtain the further education and employment necessary to achieve their goals. Youths' successes generally came only after extensive frustrations and prolonged struggles.

Few youths were able to find employment, even those who were determined to apply for jobs, traveling on foot in a wide radius around their homes. One employer was candid about his reluctance to hire "a kid on parole, fresh out of prison" when he also had applications from honor students who apparently had never been in trouble. After facing a series of disappointing rejections, many youths were disillusioned about their inability to "earn money the honest way."

Educational dreams and aspirations, at an all-time high upon release, often were deflated by tedious, demanding requirements and persistent failure. Darnell's experiences after five months in prison reflected these complexities. A soft-spoken and gentle person of average intelligence and exceptional leadership qualities, he had the lowest risk assessment score among the 385 youths who participated in the program during its first two years. His imprisonment five months earlier for simple (misdemeanor) assault had undermined his self-concept greatly, but when he left the treatment program he was reassured of his abilities and the promise of a better future. Having earned his GED, he was encouraged to enroll in a community college when he was released four months before his eighteenth birthday. He eagerly signed up for a full-time class schedule, full of confidence that he would succeed.

No one advised Darnell to sign up for only one or two classes the first semester to allow himself time to adjust. No one worked with him or his grandparents to structure his environment or his daily schedule. No one provided him with the one-on-one support essential for surviving in an unfamiliar, demanding setting. After a few pressure-filled weeks in which he was unable to keep up with the work, Darnell dropped out of the community college and disappeared for four days. When he came home he was unwilling to return to school. Within two months of leaving prison, he was discouraged and depressed. Darnell said that when he was sentenced to prison he had questioned his value as a human being. After he "failed" at the community college he was *certain* he would "never amount to anything."

For many youths, forces outside the prison seemed insurmountable. This was true for those who returned directly to their neighborhoods and families, as well as those released to residential placement facilities within the community. The irony of residential placement was that, after an extensive wait in prison for an opening at a community facility, youths often experienced disappointment, frustration, and failure in their placements. Among the 385 youths who participated in the model program during this two-year study, twenty-eight were released from prison to residential placements. Ten of those ran away within two weeks, and five others were reimprisoned due to problems they had in placement. Half of the youths sent to residential facilities were unsuccessful, due to conflicting philosophies and methods between the prison and placement facilities as well as a grave lack of coordination between prison and placement staff members. Youths' reactions to the personnel and programs in these facilities ranged from disappointment to intense anger, and several prison administrators and staff members agreed with the youths' negative assessments.

Services in the community for the first twenty-four youths included family orientation to the juvenile system and the model program, home contacts, and family groups. Ninety-minute groups met weekly for three months and combined group discussion with communication and parenting skills, networking, and peer counseling. A primary objective was to acquaint families with the problem-solving and conflict-management skills used within the model program and to encourage parents and youths to use them at home. At one of the sessions, a mother remarked that the parents needed to "catch up" with what their sons were learning in the treatment program. Other parents commented on youths' helpfulness in familiarizing them with the new ideas and concepts.

Youths imprisoned for relatively minor offenses were most successful in their transition back to the community, although a strong argument can be made that, had adequate community resources been available to address their needs, they might never have been imprisoned. Several of the youths with minor records learned skills from others inside the prison that undermined the model program's intentions. Many of the younger, less sophisticated prisoners were introduced to gangs, tattooing, drugs, weaponry, and illegal behavior. Because prison administrators rejected recommendations to separate these youths from the general population, for some the institution became an education in delinquency.

The new program raised staff members' hopes and expectations for youths. They were frequently disappointed and frustrated when youths returned. Although it was not accurate, from inside the prison, the perception was that "they're all coming back." Staff members knew little about youths' success stories, but they were acutely aware of those who either were returned for violation of parole or transferred to the adult system for new charges after completing the program.

Of the 254 youths who completed the program, 28 percent were recommitted to the prison. On average they had been in the community 150 days, or less than one-half year, before being recommitted. Youths' time in the community prior to recommitment ranged from seven days to 502 days. Assuming that the recommitment rate was stable over time, an estimated 68 percent of those who completed the program would have been recommitted if each youth had been tracked for a full year. This estimate is an annualized rate of recommitment that takes into consideration the actual number of days each youth was in the community and could have been recommitted to the prison, and has been calculated based on the 254 youths who completed the program. It excluded those who did not complete the program and were still in prison when this research ended and those transferred to the adult system directly from the juvenile prison and thus not returned to the community.

The experiences of program youths who were reimprisoned underscored the importance of providing them with intense support and supervision in the community for at least six months following release. Six percent of those who completed the program were recommitted within thirty days of their release, 18 percent were recommitted within three months, and 35 percent within the first six months.[16] The reasons for their return ranged from technical violations of parole, such as curfew violation or failure to report to a parole officer, to new criminal charges.

▌ Ever After

It is too soon to know how many youths who completed the model program will be able to succeed in the community—even if "success" is conceptualized narrowly as not being charged with new crimes. In the few years that have passed since the end of the research and the youths' release from prison, several youths, including some who have been highlighted in this book, have met this standard of success.

Larry was imprisoned for over seven months, four of which were spent in the model program. His time in the program was filled with conflict about the rules and their enforcement, and his departure was similarly controversial. Other youths as well as a staff member presented obstacles. The day before Larry was scheduled to leave, several youths goaded him and tried to make him "mess up" so he would not be released.

> The subject came up that I was leaving tomorrow, or that I was supposed to leave tomorrow. Earl said, "So if I throw this chair at you, you can't do nothin' about it. Right?" And I didn't say nothin'. . . .
>
> So then Marcos started punching me, started saying "What?" Like [he'd] hit me in the leg [and then say], "What?" "What?" . . . I said, "Don't fuck around with me like that. You know I can't do nothin'. Why do you have to go and do that? Why do you try to piss me off?" He said, "Well, go ahead and hit me back. Go see if you can leave tomorrow. Go ahead. Hit me."

Larry resisted other youths' taunting, but he was less prepared to meet a staff supervisor's objection to his release. The date of his release had been determined and his plan had been approved to spend a few days with his aunt and uncle before leaving the state to live with his parents. Nevertheless, the day before his scheduled release, a supervisor threatened to veto the plan because he questioned whether Larry should return to the neighborhood in which his victim and his victim's family remained.

The last-minute opposition dismayed Larry and the staff members who had supported his release. Larry was extremely upset: "I feel that I've worked their program the way they wanted me to, and I've made very good progress the way I'm supposed to be doing. And I felt I *have* earned [my release]. . . . It's a very, very big disappointment to have [the release plan rejected], especially to come down to that moment."

The disagreements were resolved and Larry was released as scheduled. The visit with his relatives was brief but uneventful and he left the state to join his parents. Two years later he was still living with his parents, was employed, and had remained law abiding.

Tomás was released from prison after serving six months, five of them in the model program. Of the first twenty-four youths to participate in the program, Tomás was the twelfth released despite his excellent record in the program. During the next year and a half, staff members mentioned Tomás infrequently, except on one occasion when he was returned to the prison after disappearing for several weeks and failing to report to his parole officer. He was brought to the institution for a hearing to determine whether his parole would be revoked. Two days later, his parole was reinstated and he was returned to the community.

By the time Tomás reached his eighteenth birthday, he was married and employed. He worked as a dietician's aide, his wife worked in physical therapy, and they appeared to be settled and doing well. Tomás was successful in achieving his goals of becoming a productive member of the community and living in a stable home environment.

Kevin completed the model program, but his mother was unwilling for him to return home. He remained imprisoned until sufficient funds and an opening in a residential facility in the community became available. When he ran away from the facility twice, he was returned to the prison.

Staff members were stymied in developing plans for Kevin's transition back to the community. He emphasized the importance of finding a viable place to go.

> I don't have any place to go. . . . I can't go home. Me and my mom don't get along, and that would just be like setting me up for failure. . . . What I'm looking for is a place that I could live and get a job, save up some money, but also not be in a jail-type setting like I am now [and like a number of the residential placement facilities]. Save up some of my money so I could get my own place and have people to support me and make sure I stay on track. . . . They've gotta work with you.

Although shoplifting a carton of cigarettes—a misdemeanor—was the only offense for which Kevin had been found guilty, he had spent an inconceivable twenty-six of thirty-six months in prison. During the three-year period between his first imprisonment and the end of this research, he spent only two and a half months at home with his mother, was committed to two different juvenile prisons on four separate occasions, and lived in four residential placement facilities—from which he ran away a total of nine times.

At the end of three years, Kevin had spent a total of eighteen months over three stays in the model program. When he was released from prison the last time, he and a female staff member at the prison became sexually involved. The staff member was fired and Kevin's mother took him into her home, where he remained for two months until he turned eighteen and moved to another state. In the next two years, Kevin was married, employed, and had not been charged with any illegalities.

Kevin wanted to and eventually did succeed in the model program. One of his poems conveys his sentiments:

My
life
is
as
a
nightmare
but
the
dream
is
never
ending.

Nick was similar to Kevin in that he was imprisoned for a prolonged period of time and was inexperienced in making decisions due to that confinement. Both are youths of whom the prison staff said, "We failed—we institutionalized them." When Nick discussed his eventual release from prison and his future possibilities, he stressed the necessity of remaining in prison until he was fully prepared to leave. He believed that staff members in the model program would make certain this happened.

Do you have any idea when you leave this time what it is you want to do with your life?

I don't know. I want to be a lot of things, you know, but it's like there's nothin' in particular. Sometimes I want to be like a preacher or somethin', you know, in some foreign countries. Other times I want to join the Army and get more of an education through the Army or, you know, the Air Force or the Navy or somethin'. Then there's other times it's just like I don't want to be nothin'.

So you don't have any plans yet for when you leave?

No, I don't even think I'm leavin' . . .

Do you think the staff are going to help you at all when you get out? What do you think they can do for you?

I think they'll help me. I think they'll help me more in here, you know. I don't think they're gonna let me go like they did last time before I was done, you know. I was just like, they were ready to kick me out, you know? They looked at how much time I was here and it was like. . . . They're gonna make sure, you know, I'm ready to leave and get out this time—what I'm gonna do, what I'm supposed to do.

Nick stayed in prison until his mandatory release on his eighteenth birthday, when the prison's jurisdiction ended. Prison personnel drove him to the local YMCA and gave him a check for $334, the money he had earned working in prison for 10 to 20 cents per hour. After almost four years inside the juvenile prison, Nick was on his own.

Following a series of temporary jobs, Nick answered a newspaper ad for door-to-door sales. On the spur of the moment, he accepted the company's free ticket to California on a plane leaving the next day. He was attracted by the security of low-cost housing and meals in exchange for his commitment to work on a sales crew that would be dropped off in a different affluent neighborhood every day to sell an all-purpose cleaning product. After a few weeks on the job, Nick was unable to sell enough to reimburse the crew chief for his expenses, and the company put him on a bus back to Phoenix. Nick returned to the YMCA.

With the help of people he had met while inside the institution, he was able to land a steady factory job making $6.50 an hour. Coached by friends, he opened a checking account for the first time and got his driver's license. However, assuming full responsibility for his well-being, coupled with the loneliness of life in a metropolitan business district, proved to be untenable for Nick.

After he received his first sizable paycheck, Nick left the YMCA in the middle of the night, owing several weeks' rent. He took a bus to his mother's home in California, and this time, when he arrived unannounced, she let him move in. It proved impossible for Nick and his mother to establish a good relationship after four years of separation. His mother said that she preferred her former lifestyle and felt her home was being invaded by "a near stranger."

Nick continued to look for something or someone to provide him with the structure he had experienced inside the juvenile institution. He joined the Army, where he found structure, housing, and food. He finished basic training, and qualified for advanced training. Just before his eighteenth birthday, he wrote on Army letterhead to a staff member at the prison:

> Surprise! I bet you never thought you would get a letter from me. I thought I would write a letter to let you know how I am doing in the Army. Well, I am fine but there's lots of hard work they make me do. . . . The Army is not a place to play my games at. They got a set of rules here that change at the drill sergeant's wish, and I can't stand that. I can't win. Maybe one of these days I'll be around and would like to speak in one of the cottages to let them know how hard it is. Because this is what I would think [adult] jail to be. . . . Thank you all.

Despite Nick's frustrations with Army life, everything appeared to be going well. He said he intended to stay in the Army "until they kick me out." As Nick put it, "I never thought I'd get in the Army and now they pay me to be here." But within his first few weeks in the Army, he was injured and had emergency surgery. He returned to his mother's home for a thirty-day convalescence, and he decided that he was no longer "willing to tolerate the mind games" played in the Army; he did not return for several months, and was discharged after a court-martial.

Nick subsequently found a job with a carnival, staffing a game of chance on the midway. Although his income vacillates with the carnival season, he makes a living on a commission basis. He is uncertain regarding the long-term viability of his job, but expresses pleasure that it provides him opportunities "to con people legally." In the two and a half years since his release from prison, Nick has had no problems with the law.

After twenty-five months in prison, the last five of them in the model program, Mitch was released after completing the program. He lived with his mother and stepfather for nine months, but when conflicts intensified he left home and stayed with friends. A month later Mitch was arrested and charged with burglary after he and another youth entered a friend's unoccupied apartment through a window. They ate food in the refrigerator and settled in to stay the night. Mitch said that his friend had offered to let him stay at her place, but when her mother discovered the two youths in the apartment she called the police.

Mitch was not taken to court on the burglary charge, but his parole was revoked and he was reimprisoned for an additional nine and a half months. At the end of that time, Mitch was sent to a residential facility. He ran away from the facility two months later and was returned to the prison for a week while placement in a new residential facility was arranged. Mitch did well at the second residential facility and returned to school. Later he worked with a program for other youths released from prison until he reached his eighteenth birthday and became a legal adult. Almost five turbulent years had passed since Mitch entered the juvenile prison. In the year and a half since Mitch became an adult, he has moved to another state, been employed regularly, and not been arrested.

Although their transitions from youthful prisoner to law-abiding young adult varied, Larry, Mitch, Tomás, Kevin, and Nick have not become enmeshed in the legal system since achieving adulthood. In contrast, other youths have become involved in new crimes and several have been jailed or imprisoned in the adult criminal justice system.

Daniel's strong identification with a gang lifestyle did not prevent him from considering other aspects of his future, including living with his family or girlfriend and getting a legitimate job. When asked about his future, he made comments such as, "I might be a fireman" and "[I'll] probably go to [tech school] or do something to stay out of trouble, stay with my girlfriend or something." But, at the same time, he acknowledged the primacy of his gang. When asked what was really important in his life he responded, "Just our hood. Just the blue rag. Just . . . loyalty to your color." He also expressed uncertainty about his ability "to go straight."

If you decided that you didn't want to do anything illegal anymore, would that be possible?

I don't know. . . . Your homeboys, they'll think you punked out.

What would they do?

They'd probably just say, "You little punk, 'Cuz! There's no need to be from *this* hood."

Unfinished tasks also awaited Daniel on the outside, including the need to retaliate against a rival gang for a recent drive-by shooting: "Now my homeboy, he told me that if I don't get the dude when I get out, he's gonna kill him."

Daniel described life on the streets as war and expressed disbelief that anything could be changed.

Nowadays we got high-tech weapons, and if you're going to be on the streets, you've got to go for yours. You gotta look out for yours and your homeboys. . . .

If you could change your neighborhood—

Well, I couldn't change nothing, because when my homeboys gonna have kids, their kids gonna grow up to be gang bangers, so the hood is just gonna stay the same or get worse.

There's no way to stop it?

You can't stop anything. It's gonna always be there.

But the point is it wasn't always there, back when.

It was there, but it was—

It wasn't as violent?

Yeah.

You think it's just because they didn't have the weapons?

Yeah. They didn't have the weapons. . . .

Besides the weapons, is there anything that's a lot different now?

It's just kids. They know more about the streets and drugs and stuff. The fact is, you didn't have all this kind of stuff where, "You step on my feet, I'll beat you up. You got a beef with my homeboys, I got a beef with you, too." Back then, it wasn't like that. It was just like—he's my friend and he's my friend and everybody was just friends. Nowadays you got enemies . . .

It's just inevitable that it keeps getting worse? What's going to happen eventually?

Everybody's gonna die.

Do you know anybody who's gotten out of the gang or moved away or started over?

Well, he got tired of seeing his homeboys dying and his little cousins dying, so he just moved to a different state, and he grew up, and he started working with kids and stuff.

What do you think of that?

That's good. . . . He probably didn't want to get, probably didn't want to die, didn't want to go to no more funerals and stuff.

After six months Daniel successfully completed the model program and was released on parole. Eighteen days later he returned for a technical violation of parole when he failed to contact his parole officer or follow his prescribed parole plan. He was released from this second stay in the juvenile prison two and a half months later on his eighteenth birthday. Within his first year as an adult, he was arrested for selling crack cocaine.

Bernardo was one of several youths from the model program who served time in adult jails and prisons while still a juvenile. Despite his lack of enthusiasm and progress in the program after he was forced to move from Unit Four, Bernardo was released from prison after seven months, with six of them spent in the model program. Prior to his release Bernardo described his plans for the future: "I'm going to move in with my sister and go to [the community college] when I get out. . . . Get me a job."

Bernardo did as he had planned and enrolled in GED preparation classes at the community college. He said he was determined to be successful: "For the first time in my life, I really like going to school." But within three months he became frustrated and depressed by his inability to find a job. He felt like his old self, like a failure. Then, three months after he was released from juvenile prison, Bernardo joined a friend in stealing an automobile. Later Bernardo tried unsuccessfully to reach the prison staff for support, and he went along with the car theft because he "just wanted to go for a ride."

For the second time in his life Bernardo was arrested and, again, the arrest was for auto theft. He was subsequently transferred at age sixteen to be tried as an adult. At his adult court sentencing the judge asked if he had anything to say, but Bernardo remained silent. Later, he said he was convinced he deserved whatever the system chose to do with him. He was sentenced to a year in county jail, then returned to his old neighborhood. He was placed on probation for eighteen months and ordered to pay $7,000 in restitution at the rate of $60 a month for close to a decade. His desperate job search was rendered unsuccessful by his lack of education and his adult criminal record.

Marcos had been in the model program almost nine months when he was finally scheduled to be released. His grandmother died less than two weeks before his projected release, and he was permitted to attend her funeral on an unescorted furlough. Within a matter of hours after his mother picked him up, Marcos was using cocaine. He didn't return to the institution at the appointed time and was placed on escape status. For three weeks, he continued to evade officials, although it appeared they were not searching seriously for him.

One morning a police officer spotted a stolen car with Marcos behind the wheel. A high-speed chase ensued during which Marcos lost control of the vehicle, crossed the center line, and struck three cars, including the car in which a ten-year-old boy was riding. The youngster's seat belt failed, and he was killed in the collision. Our fieldnotes describe Marcos's condition when police brought him back to prison.

> My first impression, and I'm not certain why, was that they brought me the wrong kid. After a split second, I realize that thought is ridiculous; the youth obviously has to be Marcos. He is very changed—he has lost a noticeable amount of weight, he has a small mustache, he is in stained white coveralls, and none of his usual demeanor is evident. There is no smile, no crisp and cocky Marcos walk, and no sparkle in his eyes. His eyes are indescribable. They seem flat, with no life behind them. . . .
>
> I ask Marcos where he got the drugs and he responds, "They were just there." He knows "a lot of people out there." I ask if his family was taking care of him. Not really, he was taking care of himself. How? He would just sell some drugs now and then. . . . When we talk about his problems he always returns to the drugs. "That stuff can mess you up!"

Like many other youths, Marcos's substance abuse was never addressed directly during his stay in the juvenile prison, despite his nine months inside and countless hours in discussion groups. Staff members claimed they had not read his file thoroughly and were not aware of a problem.

During the high-speed chase with police did you ever once think of stopping the car and giving yourself up?

By that time, I had been so high for so long—I wasn't thinking, period.

Marcos was tried as an adult and convicted of second-degree homicide, four counts of aggravated assault for injuries to other people involved in the accident, two counts of theft, leaving the scene of a fatal accident, possession and use of a narcotic drug, criminal damage, and unlawful flight from a law-enforcement officer. He was sentenced to sixty-two years in adult prison, with no hope of parole until the year 2052. Marcos will be seventy-six years old at that time.

During Marcos's adult court trial, local newspapers carried the prosecutor's declaration that "the defendant is heartless and basically a sociopath. The only thing the court can do is put him away as long as possible."[17] This seemed an exaggerated and inappropriate condemnation of a youth whose acts prior to this tragedy had been vehicle theft and drug abuse.

From the model program's inception, its foremost goal was ostensibly to prepare youths to return to the community. All of the program's components and activities were supposed to facilitate this and provide the participants with the skills necessary to survive and succeed. Youths' difficulties once they were released from prison accentuated the program's ineffective treatment of major problems such as drug abuse. Youths' struggles outside prison could be attributed to the magnitude of the problems awaiting them. The program should have been more effective in preparing them, but the poverty, unemployment, danger, and despair that welcomed youths home were more powerful than any model prison program.

Six | # Conclusion

◼ The Power and Futility of Prison Fences

The imprisonment of youths represents the explicit rejection of two
fundamental American principles: the sanctity of individual freedom and the innocence of childhood. Traditional U.S. ideology pro-
claims a *presumption against incarceration,* a presumption in which
freedom of movement and freedom in decision making are portrayed as inalienable rights. Despite this, the United States has one of
the highest incarceration rates in the world[1]—a use of state power
that extends to adolescents as well as adults. In contrast to images of
childhood as a protected, nurtured status, those young people who
are classified as dangerous or repeat offenders are portrayed as meriting both imprisonment within juvenile prisons and transfer to
adult courts for prosecution and punishment.[2] Traditional images of
youths as unsophisticated and as needing and deserving benevolent
guidance are suspended when "hard-core delinquents" are under
consideration.

Imprisoned youths are depicted as violent and irredeemable. The
increase in violent acts among youths fuels public fear, but the crime
statistics and "the facts" do not justify monolithic images of youths

in prison.[3] Closer examination of who is incarcerated and why does not confirm popular notions, for incarcerated youths are not universally, uniformly, or singularly violent. Nor are they all repeat offenders or youths charged with or convicted of major felonies. Imprisoned young people represent a wide range of backgrounds, behaviors, attitudes, and potentials, and it is important to ask why exaggerated caricatures of them are so prevalent.

In many ways, the imprisonment of youths has more to do with the concerns and objectives of adults within contemporary society than with the delinquent acts or case histories of those youths. The characterization of imprisoned youths as predatory and beyond hope serves symbolic and political ends, especially in reassuring the public that the cause of social unrest has been identified and that politicians and government have taken action to provide safety and maintain social control.[4] The most telling criticisms of imprisonment policies are not only that they are politicized, but also that they do not combat juvenile crime.

This research examined a model prison program initiated in response to a class-action lawsuit against Arizona's juvenile prison system. The promise of the model program was a new vision of delinquent youths and society's potential response to them. Originally, the model program insisted on taking great care to ensure that only youths who present a threat to public safety, or those for whom alternative programs had failed, should be imprisoned. Equally important, the program emphasized accountability and guidance for young people, including providing them with essential skills for their survival in society.

To critics of traditional prison structures and to those who understand the urgency of finding more effective ways to influence youthful behavior and lives, the appeal of the model program is evident. The program maintained that punishment and isolation alone are ineffective responses to youth crime. It prioritized rehabilitative change and successful reintegration into society. Accordingly, exclusively coercive methods were to be replaced by an atmosphere in which youths were afforded respect and dignity. Calls for accountability and change were viewed as viable only in a situation where youths could have meaningful experiences in prison and were provided alternative models for living life in the larger society.

The model program was not about just "doing something for" the youths, as many treatment efforts are. Nor was it just about "doing something to" them in the name of punishment. Primarily, the model program was intended to provide opportunities and skills so that the youths could do something for themselves and the community. The program honored youths' humanity even as it held them accountable for their behaviors. It offered much to youths—respect, skills, new chances. It also required much of them—respect for others, genuine efforts to understand themselves and others, and a commitment to change. Despite its limitations, the program represented a model of potential hope for both young people and the public. Clearly, full realization of the model's potential would be possible only within a wider social and political context of commitment and support.

The model program's limitations, its "failure" to live up to its ideal, mirrored the reasons that many genuine attempts at change fall short: structural and political impediments, bureaucratic logistics, and individual limitations. This experiment attempted to effect monumental changes. On an institutional level, it sought to transform a hierarchical, punitive prison into a respectful, therapeutic community. On an individual level, it sought to change interpersonal relationships from those of hostility and suspicion to ones based on mutual trust and support. Politically, it sought to end the abandonment of imprisoned youth and to supplant it with an imaginative, profound commitment to youth and society. The program was to engender mature individuals, self-confident in their ability to return to a harsh world and survive with dignity and self-respect.

Ironically, our critical examination occurred during what was the best period in youth prisons in this state. Despite the difficulties in implementing the model program, life within the prison was far improved over the situation before the lawsuit. Some of the changes have remained and further progress has been made in limited areas, such as the initiation of specialized programs for violence and substance abuse. The state still has not lived up to all of the agreements it negotiated in the consent decree. For example, it has failed to reduce the prison population sufficiently to enhance treatment opportunities for those who remain.[5]

There are other signs of further erosion of both the philosophy and structure of the program. The agency name is again the Department of Juvenile Corrections; gone is the Department of Youth Treatment and Rehabilitation. Perhaps most symbolic, the internal security forces within the prisons once more resemble those in the adult prisons: they are uniformed personnel referred to as "security officers," not crisis management team members. There is reason to believe that, once the federal court monitoring of juvenile corrections ends, some of the conditions that eventuated the lawsuit may re-emerge.

Nationwide, departments of corrections represent one item on a dwindling list of resources for young people. Most juvenile systems face reduced resources and limited funding of community-based programs, such as substance abuse programs and counseling, that could give them alternatives to incarceration.[6] Because the state correctional system cannot refuse to accept youths who have been sentenced to it, in many situations the only available "treatment service" is prison.[7] Importantly, when state monies are allocated for youths, they are frequently designated for the end of the system— the prisons. They are also most likely to be allocated for construction of more prisons, not for treatment services within prisons.

Even in more bountiful economic times, youths who are hard to place in private treatment facilities are committed to state correctional systems, and those whose families do not have insurance or personal wealth sufficient to afford private treatment efforts are more likely to end up in prison.[8] There is an acute lack of alternatives for young people and those charged with the responsibility of dealing with delinquency. Overcrowding, low staff salaries, aging physical plants, and an overall lack of resources have combined to create a system that often perpetuates the worst possible consequences of incarceration and mocks the lofty ideals that justify such a response to youths.

The model program was conceived and initiated within a larger political context that emphasizes the need for punishment. The program's structure and fate reflected contemporary struggles regarding social problems and debates about appropriate responses to youths, especially the debate between the treatment and guidance implicit in traditional images of youths and the punitive responses advocated by those who regard such images as inapplicable to today's delinquents.

Society appears mired in fierce contests over the sources of and solutions to our problems. In extreme instances it has become a stalled, senseless, and polarized debate between rigid notions of individual responsibility and societal responsibility. Such polemics suggest that either individuals are exclusively to blame or, conversely, society is to blame. Currently, those who cast individuals as the villains seem to be winning or, at least, have the loudest voices and greatest resources. Perhaps what is most important is how grossly oversimplified demands for punishment frequently become, how devoid of dialogue or exchange. They are dominated by sensationalism, demagoguery, and self-righteous proclamations. Much of the political process, its dramatic verbiage as well as tangible policy, is directed toward responding to these sentiments even while it magnifies them.

Aided and encouraged by a national sentiment that focuses on individual accomplishment as virtue and individual failure as a lack of character, proponents of punishment have come to focus on individuals (millions of them) as being the source of the problem.[9] But, clearly, the lives and fates of imprisoned youths are greatly influenced by forces they do not understand and do not control. Neither youths' behavior nor their problems can be addressed effectively without changes in the economic, political, educational, and legal institutions. "Big-picture changes" are necessary to really make "the situation" better.

Our society has come to rely more and more upon the criminal and juvenile justice systems to resolve social conflicts and to exact payment and promise protection. Alternative action and policies are said to cost too much,[10] but currently we are paying—at all costs—for increased punishment, especially imprisonment. At the end of our study in 1994, juvenile prisons in Arizona cost about $128 dollars per day for each youth, approximately $46,700 per year for each youth.[11] Nationwide, prisons are a major growth industry, and the incarceration of young people figures prominently in the rise of the prison industrial complex.

Within this state, as well as nationwide, we need to critically examine if youths who are behind bars really need to be there. Indeed, adults should "wear mourning as a sign of civilization"[12] if *they* are most responsible for youths being imprisoned. This may be because prisons are the only alternative offered to them, or because imprisoned youths' greatest importance is not as human beings, but as currency for political purposes. Imprisonment, especially of a culture's future, will bring only disastrous consequences for youth and for all of us.

For those few for whom confinement is essential—and that number is far fewer than those now imprisoned—changes of short- and long-term value must be instituted. Considering the principles and approaches advocated by the model program would be a wise place to begin, a good place to seek hope. The program principles would provide avenues for strengthening families and communities, rather than blaming them. They would provide avenues for rehabilitating society, rather than generating deeper divides.

"Youth in prison" is a shameful banner for a society. It signals a great collective loss as well as individual destruction. Change is essential to nurture youthful hopes and to rekindle our own.

Notes

Notes to Preface

1. *Johnson v Upchurch*, CIV-86-195-TUC-RMB (D. Ariz., filed April 6, 1986). This became the class-action lawsuit. See Note 3.
2. At the time of the lawsuit, Arizona had the third-highest rate of youth incarceration in the United States. According to the Arizona State Juvenile Justice Advisory Council's *State Plan for Juvenile Justice and Delinquency Prevention,* on May 13, 1985, 654 youths were incarcerated in Arizona's correctional facilities and an additional 719 were under the supervision of the Department of Corrections (cited in National Center for Youth Law, "CMJI Proof of Facts" [submitted to the United States District Court on behalf of plaintiffs in *Johnson v Upchurch* case, San Francisco, Calif., 1988], pp. 9, 12).

   During the two years this research was conducted in two of the juvenile prisons for males, the average number of prisoners in the two facilities was approximately 420 youths—about 275 at the larger institution and 145 at the smaller. Approximately 150 additional youths were incarcerated at a third facility for diagnostic evaluation of youths imprisoned for the first time and for youths with special mental health needs.
3. *Johnson v Upchurch*, CIV-86-195-TUC-RMB, "Fifth Amended Complaint" (D. Ariz., filed April 11, 1988).
4. James Alan Fox, *Trends in Juvenile Violence: A Report to the United States Attorney General on Current and Future Rates of Juvenile Offending* (Washington, DC: Bureau of Justice Statistics, U.S. Department of Justice, 1996), pp. i, 2.
5. Thomas J. Bernard, *The Cycle of Juvenile Justice* (New York: Oxford University Press, 1992); Richard L. Schuster, "Violent Juveniles and Proposed Changes in Juvenile Justice: A Case of Overkill?" *Juvenile and Family Court Journal* 33 (4) (1982): 37–42.
6. Until recently, the rate of incarceration remained relatively constant, with less than 10 percent of the youths officially tried and found guilty being imprisoned. Nationally, less than 30 percent of youths found

guilty of delinquency are placed outside their homes, the majority in nonprison residential settings. See Timothy Flanagan and Kathleen Maguire, eds., *Sourcebook of Criminal Justice Statistics 1991* (Washington, DC: U.S. Government Printing Office, 1992), p. 598; Timothy Flanagan, Ann L. Pastore, and Kathleen Maguire, eds., *Sourcebook of Criminal Justice Statistics 1992* (Washington, DC: U.S. Government Printing Office, 1993), p. 582.

In 1994 in Maricopa County, the largest county in Arizona and the one that accounts for 80 percent of the youths imprisoned annually, 11 percent of youths found guilty of delinquency were sentenced to prison. See Superior Court of Arizona, *Maricopa County Juvenile Court Center: 1994 Annual Report* (Phoenix, AZ: 1995), p. 44, published by Juvenile Court.

7. Flanagan and Maguire, *Sourcebook 1991*, p. 598; Flanagan, Pastore, and Maguire, *Sourcebook 1992*, p. 582.

8. See Ira M. Schwartz, Gideon Fishman, Radene Rawson Hatfield, Barry A. Krisberg, and Zvi Eisikovits, "Juvenile Detention: The Hidden Closets Revisited," *Justice Quarterly* 4 (2) (June 1987): 219–35.

In most states, youths' sentences are open ended, and the length and conditions of their imprisonment remain the province of prison administrators and personnel in charge of those systems. Members of the public, as well as the politicians who enact punitive policies, are far removed from the actual prison situation, and there is minimal review of what occurs there (Michel Foucault, *Discipline and Punish: The Birth of the Prison,* trans. Alan Sheridan [New York: Vintage, 1979], pp. 7–9). Even when legislative policies specify conditions or programs, as is becoming more common, putting those policies into practice is literally out of the hands of those who legislate them (Barry C. Feld, "The Transformation of the Juvenile Court," *Minnesota Law Review* 75 [3] [1991]: 691–725).

9. *John L. v Adams*, 969 F. 2d 228 (6th Cir. 1992); *People v Hana*, 443 Mich. 202 (1993). Although appellate courts have reinforced youths' rights to access to the courts, implementation of that right varies.

10. Foucault, *Discipline and Punish*, p. 7; Zillah R. Eisenstein, *The Color of Gender: Reimaging Democracy* (Berkeley: University of California Press, 1994), pp. 158–61, 181.

11. See M. A. Bortner, *Delinquency and Justice: An Age of Crisis* (New York: McGraw-Hill, 1988); and Anne Schneider and Helen Ingram, "Social Construction of Target Populations: Implications for Politics and Pol-

icy," *American Political Science Review* 87 (2) (1993): 334–47.

12. Such images are perpetuated by published research such as "The Exploitation Matrix in a Juvenile Institution," by Clemens Bartollas, Stuart J. Miller, and Simon Dinitz (*Juvenile Victimization: The Institutional Paradox* [Beverly Hills, CA: Sage, 1976], p. 202), that depicts incarcerated youths as predatory, antisocial nonchildren who victimize one another as a way of life in prison. Bartollas et al. state that "there are no innocents here" (p. 202).

13. Robert E. De Como, Sandra Tunis, Barry Krisberg, Norma C. Herrara, Sonya Rudenstine, and Dominic Del Rosario, *Juveniles Taken into Custody Research Program: FY 1992 Annual Report* (Washington, DC: Office of Juvenile Justice and Delinquency Prevention, U.S. Department of Justice, 1995); Howard N. Snyder, Terrence A. Finnegan, Ellen H. Nimick, Melissa H. Sickmund, Dennis P. Sullivan, and Nancy J. Tierney, *Juvenile Court Statistics 1986* (Pittsburgh: National Center for Juvenile Justice, 1990).

14. See Gregg J. Halemba, *Profile Study of Juveniles Committed to the Arizona DOC During 1989* (Mesa, AZ: Research and Information Specialists, 1990).

    Violent offenses are defined as "felonies against person(s)." Included within this category are aggravated assault or robbery, aggravated assault with a deadly weapon, arson of an occupied structure, assault as the result of a riot, attempted murder, child molestation or abuse, custodial interference, drive-by shootings, endangerment, gang intimidation, homicide, kidnapping, leaving the scene of an accident in which death or injury occurred, manslaughter, first- and second-degree murder, negligent homicide, poisoning of food, strong arm robbery or robbery with a weapon, setting explosives, sexual abuse or assault, sex with a minor, sodomy with a minor, threatening intimidation (gang-related), and unlawful imprisonment (Superior Court of Arizona, *1994 Annual Report*).

15. See Jonathan Simon, *Poor Discipline: Parole and the Social Control of the Underclass, 1890–1990* (Chicago: University of Chicago Press, 1993); Thomas J. Bamonte and Thomas M. Peters, "The Parole Revocation Process in Illinois," *Loyola University of Chicago Law Journal* 24 (1993): 211–58; A. Verne McArthur, *Coming Out Cold: Community Reentry from a State Reformatory* (Lexington, MA: Lexington Books, 1974); Ted Palmer, *A Profile of Correctional Effectiveness and New Directions for Research* (Albany: State University of New York Press, 1994).

16. All names within the book are pseudonyms.
17. See Mitchell Duneier's discussion of attempts to conceal the specific location of research in *Slim's Table: Race, Respectability, and Masculinity* (Chicago: University of Chicago Press, 1992), pp. 177–78 n. 6.
18. The Youth Law Center in San Francisco, California, maintains records on lawsuits and consent decrees related to the incarceration of youths.
19. Youths experienced restrictions equal to or greater than adult prisoners in areas such as decision making and freedom of movement, as well as access to families, attorneys, and the community. For an astute analysis of the similarities between juvenile institutions and adult prisons in Arizona immediately prior to the model program, see Kelly E. Spencer, "Juvenile Incarceration: Translating Policy to Practice" (master's thesis, Tempe, AZ: Arizona State University,1991).

    The lawsuit (*Johnson v Upchurch*) alleged that the juvenile prison "was indistinguishable in appearance from an adult closed security penitentiary" (National Center for Youth Law, "CMJI Proof of Facts," pp. 95–96). Indeed, during his statement in response to the lawsuit, the director of corrections acknowledged he was unable to identify significant differences between the youth prison's isolation unit and the adult prison's death row (p. 96). The lawsuit went on to say:

    Rather than provide funds for staffing and equipment necessary to maintain [the prison] in accordance with accepted standards, the defendants have funded expensive and unnecessary security hardware. During the period when [the prison] has failed to meet state fire and safety codes and regulations, [it] has constructed guard towers, erected a twenty-foot high security fence topped with razor wire, instituted 24-hour vehicular perimeter patrol, has placed security staff in uniforms and provided them uniform allowances, has increased uniformed security staff, has installed a pedestrian sallyport into which all persons entering or leaving the institution are locked; and has installed a TV camera to monitor the pedestrian entrance. (pp. 95–6)

Notes to Chapter One

1. Erving Goffman, *Asylums: Essays on the Social Situation of Mental Patients and Other Inmates* (Chicago: Aldine, 1961).
2. *Morales v Turman*, 364 F. Supp. 166 (E.D. Tex 1973).
3. *Morgan v Sproat*, 432 F. Supp. 1130 (S.D. Miss. 1977).
4. *State v Werner*, 242 S.E. 2d 907 (W.Va. 1978).

5. For discussions of suicide among incarcerated youths, see Howard N. Snyder and Melissa Sickmund, *Juvenile Offenders and Victims: A National Report* (Washington, DC: Office of Juvenile Justice and Delinquency Prevention, 1995); Michael G. Flaherty, *An Assessment of National Incidence of Juvenile Suicide in Adult Jails, Lockups, and Juvenile Detention Centers* (Washington, DC: Office of Juvenile Justice and Delinquency Prevention, U.S. Department of Justice, 1980); and Howard James, *Children in Trouble: A National Scandal* (New York: McKay, 1970).

6. *Johnson v Upchurch*, CIV-86-195-TUC-RMB, "Fifth Amended Complaint" (D. Ariz., filed April 11, 1988), pp. 2–3.

7. Victoria Harker, "Young Department's Future Unclear: Debate on Role Fuels Confusion Among Officials Saving Arizona's Children," *Arizona Republic*, 31 January 1994, p. A7.

8. David Lambert, "*Johnson v Upchurch* Victory Brings Big Reforms in Arizona Juvenile Institutions," *Youth Law News* 14 (2) (March–April 1993): 2.

9. Lambert, "*Johnson v Upchurch* Victory."

10. Within two and a half months of the filing of his case, Johnson had been removed from the disciplinary unit and provided additional services. In October 1990, he settled out of court for damages from Upchurch.

11. Lambert, "*Johnson v Upchurch* Victory."

12. These included the chief administrator of the institution at the time of Matthew Johnson's confinement, the chief administrator of the institution at the time of the lawsuit, the director of the state department of corrections, the director of the juvenile services division of that state agency, the state's superintendent of public instruction, and the state's board of education. Johnson sought damages from James Upchurch, superintendent of the prison at the time of Johnson's incarceration, who was sued in his personal capacity. All other defendants were sued in their official capacities as public officials. The other plaintiffs (youths) sought "declaratory, injunctive, and other equitable relief on behalf of themselves and all other juveniles similarly situated who are, or who will be confined at [the institution] and thereby subjected to the cruel, unconscionable, and illegal practices of defendants" (Lambert, "*Johnson v Upchurch* Victory").

13. National Center for Youth Law, "CMJI Proof of Facts" (submitted to the U.S. District Court on behalf of plaintiffs in *Johnson v Upchurch*, San Francisco, CA [1988]), pp. 133–35.

14. "Cutting" is the terminology used by institutional staff members and youths to refer to the wounds that youths inflict upon themselves. These are not viewed as suicide attempts but, rather, acts of depression and desperation or pleas for help. The lawsuit stated:

    There is a widespread acceptance among [youths at the prison] that the only way to get attention or to escape the boredom and hopelessness of [disciplinary] confinement is to cut on one's self or inflict other self injury. The high incidence of repeated acts of self-mutilation, some of which are life threatening, and the fact that psychology staff respond to such actions, offers support to this widely held belief among [youths]. (National Center for Youth Law, "CMJI Proof of Facts," p. 120)

    See also James Gilligan, *Violence: Our Deadly Epidemic and Its Causes* (New York: G. P. Putnam's, 1996), pp. 39–43.
15. National Center for Youth Law, "CMJI Proof of Facts," pp. 118–20.
16. National Center for Youth Law, "CMJI Proof of Facts," pp. 117–18.
17. National Center for Youth Law, "CMJI Proof of Facts," p. 121.
18. Similar programs later replaced "motivational hold," including "structured management" or "administrative hold." All permitted indefinite solitary confinement (National Center for Youth Law, "CMJI Proof of Facts," pp. 164–66).
19. *Johnson v Upchurch*, p. 13.
20. National Center for Youth Law, "CMJI Proof of Facts," p. 151.
21. National Center for Youth Law, "CMJI Proof of Facts," pp. 221–24.

    [The prison has] a policy that all juveniles transported from the institution are to be handcuffed and shackled. There have been instances in which juveniles have required emergency medical attention which has been delayed while staff applied handcuffs and shackles to the juvenile. For example, on September 24, 1988, in a suicide attempt [one youth] seriously cut his left arm with a piece of metal. . . . Civilian emergency personnel were called. Before they could transport [him] to the hospital, [prison] security personnel had to put [the youth] in leg irons and shackles and cuff his arm (in which there were two IV needles) to the waist of the belly chain. . . .

    Juveniles from [the prison] who leave the institution on "medical runs" are required to remain in handcuffs and shackles the entire time, including while they are administered medical or dental care or treatment. (pp. 221–22)

22. National Center for Youth Law, "CMJI Proof of Facts," p. 175.
23. *Johnson v Upchurch*, p. 12.
24. National Center for Youth Law, "CMJI Proof of Facts," p. 176.
25. National Center for Youth Law, "CMJI Proof of Facts," p. 177.
26. National Center for Youth Law, "CMJI Proof of Facts," p. 178.
27. National Center for Youth Law, "CMJI Proof of Facts," pp. 178–79.
28. National Center for Youth Law, "CMJI Proof of Facts," p. 175.
29. *Johnson v Upchurch*, p. 13.
30. *Johnson v Upchurch*, p. 13.
31. *Johnson v Upchurch*, p. 22.
32. At the time of the lawsuit and this research, the state operated three high-security institutions for juvenile males, one of which was a diagnostic unit.
33. This included "tours of the facility by expert witnesses retained by plaintiffs, the deposition of over forty prison employees, the review of thousands of pages of logs and journals at [the Tucson institution], and the review of over 15,000 pages of other documents" (Governor's Task Force on Juvenile Corrections, *Arizona's Troubled Youth: A New Direction* [Phoenix: Governor's Task Force on Juvenile Corrections, June 1993], p. 2).
34. National Center for Youth Law, "CMJI Proof of Facts," pp. 1, 132.
35. This major issue was emphasized in the lawsuit and confirmed by the Arizona Department of Corrections' "Twenty-Year Plan" (National Center for Youth Law, "CMJI Proof of Facts," pp. 1–2). See also Governor's Task Force, *Arizona's Troubled Youth*, pp. 4–5.
36. National Center for Youth Law, "CMJI Proof of Facts," p. 132.
37. National Center for Youth Law, "CMJI Proof of Facts," p. 133.
38. National Center for Youth Law, "CMJI Proof of Facts," p. 135.
39. National Center for Youth Law, "CMJI Proof of Facts," p. 118.
40. These details are taken from *Johnson v Upchurch*, CIV-86-195-TUC-RMB (D. Ariz., consent decree entered May 5, 1993).
41. The reform process included numerous stages and extensive involvement of private citizens and juvenile justice personnel. In June 1988, the appeals court appointed a "special master of education" who conducted an investigation and, within five months, filed a report specify-

ing deficiencies in the educational programs. In May 1989, the governor advised the court that Arizona would undertake "a comprehensive reform of its juvenile justice system," and she signed an executive order "recognizing a right to treatment in the least restrictive environment consistent with public safety for all youth in juvenile institutions." In September 1989, the governor established a Commission on Juvenile Corrections to conduct an extensive study, hold public hearings, consult with juvenile justice professionals, and issue specific recommendations for reforms. Within seven and a half months, in May 1990, the commission's recommendations were issued, including the appointment of a task force to implement the recommendations. The court continued (delayed) the trial to provide an opportunity for the recommendations to be implemented. The subsequent Task Force on Juvenile Corrections played a primary role in changing juvenile corrections and in making the consent decree possible.

42. *Johnson v Upchurch,* consent decree, pp. 7–8.

43. The decree specified that the Tucson prison could not average more than 110 youths per month and the Phoenix prison not more than 240 youths per month. During the two years of our study, the Tucson prison averaged about 145 youths and the Phoenix prison 275. By January 1996, the Phoenix prison's official population limit had been amended to 312 by opening three additional units of 24 beds each. Nonetheless, the population exceeded this number and was reported to be 364. In February 1997, the population remained at 363. The official population limit for the Tucson prison had been increased to 124, but in January 1996, this population was reported at 132. By February 1997, the Tucson population was reported at the prescribed number. On February 14, 1997, an order issued by federal judge Richard Bilby levied fines against the state and barred it from accepting any more juvenile inmates until the population at the Phoenix prison dropped below the cap. Fines levied for overcrowding amounted to $300 per day per youth.

44. For a discussion of the classic Massachusetts experiment in community-based corrections see Robert B. Coates, Alden D. Miller, and Lloyd E. Ohlin, *Diversity in a Youth Correctional System: Handling Delinquents in Massachusetts* (Cambridge, MA: Ballinger, 1978). Also see Paul Lerman, *Community Treatment and Social Control: A Critical Analysis of Juvenile Correctional Policy* (Chicago: University of Chicago Press, 1975).

45. In reporting the aggregated results from thirty-two meta-analyses and literature reviews, Ted Palmer suggests that cognitive-behavioral or cognitive approaches have been evaluated as the most "positive and promising" (*A Profile of Correctional Effectiveness and New Directions for Research* [Albany: State University of New York Press, 1994], p. 29). This was clearly the approach emphasized by the model program examined in this study.

46. These phrases are those of Cornel West, but they aptly capture the focus of the program. *Race Matters* (Boston: Beacon, 1993), pp. 22–23.

47. Staff, teachers, and administrators held authority over the youths because of the youths' incarcerated status, and as a result of the power differential based on age and experience throughout society. Likewise, central administrators held authority over those staff working directly with youths due to their status in the agency's hierarchy and their responsibilities to and relationships with external authorities—specifically, the governor and the legislature.

48. See Arizona Department of Youth Treatment and Rehabilitation, "Prototype Treatment Program: Adobe Mountain Juvenile Institution" (Phoenix, 22 June 1992, photocopy).

49. The model program incorporated the work of Matthew L. Ferrara, especially *Group Counseling with Juvenile Delinquents: The Limit and Lead Approach* (Newbury Park, CA: Sage, 1992); Ronald Kuhn and Phyllis R. Antonelli, *Keys to Innervisions* (Scottsdale, AZ: Keys to Excellence, 1990); the work of the Family Life Development Center, *Therapeutic Crisis Intervention* (Ithaca, NY: Cornell University Press, 1991); and Peter M. Senge, *The Fifth Discipline: The Art and Practice of the Learning Organization* (New York: Doubleday / Currency, 1990).

50. See Linda M. Williams, "Ethics Policy and Society: Responsibility, Repression, or Rhetoric?" (Ph.D. diss., Tempe, AZ: Arizona State University, 1994) for a discussion of the value of this approach.

51. Terry Williams and William Kornblum, *The Uptown Kids: Struggle and Hope in the Projects* (New York: G. P. Putnam, 1994); and Williams, "Ethics Policy and Society."

52. Ferrara, *Group Counseling.*

53. Arizona Department of Youth Treatment and Rehabilitation, "Daily Groups" memorandum (Phoenix, 15 September 1993, photocopy), pp. 1–3.

54. Arizona Department of Youth Treatment and Rehabilitation,

"Overview: Critical Components of Treatment" (Phoenix, n.d., photocopy), p. B.

55. Arizona Department of Youth Treatment and Rehabilitation, "[Chief of Counseling's] Talk Highlights New Directions: Excerpts from a Speech at the First Annual Community Contractor Forum by [the] Chief of Counseling," *DYTR Notes* 3 (7) (1993): 2. See also Ferrara, *Group Counseling*.

56. Arizona Department of Youth Treatment and Rehabilitation, "[Chief of Counseling's] Talk," p. 2. See also Kuhn and Antonelli, *Keys to Innervisions*.

57. Arizona Department of Youth Treatment and Rehabilitation, "Overview," p. A. See also Family Life Development Center, *Therapeutic Crisis Intervention*.

58. These groups were outlined by Matthew L. Ferrara, creator of the Limit and Lead program.

59. Arizona Department of Youth Treatment and Rehabilitation, "Success School: Program Description Overview" (Phoenix, n.d., photocopy), pp. 12–16.

60. Arizona Department of Youth Treatment and Rehabilitation, "Success School," p. 2.

61. Sources for the discussion of the Level System include two Arizona Department of Youth Treatment and Rehabilitation publications: *Youth Handbook* (Phoenix, October 1992, photocopy), pp. 11–15, and *Fact Pack 1992* (Phoenix, October 1992, photocopy), p. 4.

62. Arizona Department of Youth Treatment and Rehabilitation, "Overview," p. B.

63. For alternative perspectives, see Diane C. Dwyer and Roger B. McNally, "Juvenile Justice Reform, Retain, and Reaffirm," *Federal Probation* 51 (September 1987): 47–51; Alfred S. Regnery, "Getting Away with Murder: Why the Juvenile Justice System Needs an Overhaul," *Policy Review* 34 (Fall 1985): 65–68; Stephen J. Brodt and J. Steven Smith, "Public Policy and the Serious Juvenile Offender," *Criminal Justice Policy Review* 2 (1) (March 1987): 70–79; and Peter W. Greenwood and Franklin E. Zimring, *One More Change: The Pursuit of Promising Intervention: Strategies for Chronic Juvenile Offenders* (Santa Monica, CA: Rand Corporation, 1985).

64. See Anne L. Schneider, *Deterrence and Juvenile Crime: Results from a National Policy Experiment* (New York: Springer-Verlag, 1990); and the

Balanced and Restorative Justice Project, *Balanced and Restorative Justice for Juveniles: A National Strategy for Juvenile Justice in the 21st Century* (Fort Lauderdale: Florida Atlantic University, 1994).

65. The entire organizational structure of the juvenile justice system, originally much different from the adult criminal justice system, was based on two key premises. The first was the belief that because youths were not hardened or serious criminals, they were worthy of and deserved treatment. The second premise was the belief that, through the juvenile justice system, the state should exercise wide-ranging power in order to act as a "super parent" to protect and guide young people. See Robert M. Emerson, *Judging Delinquents: Context and Process in Juvenile Court* (Chicago: Aldine, 1969); Ellen Ryerson, *The Best-laid Plans: America's Juvenile Court Experiment* (New York: Hill and Wang, 1978); David J. Rothman, *Conscience and Convenience: The Asylum and Its Alternatives in Progressive America* (Boston: Little, Brown & Co., 1980).

66. Vaughan Stapelton, David P. Aday Jr., and Jeanne A. Ito, "An Empirical Typology of American Metropolitan Juvenile Courts," *American Journal of Sociology* 88 (1982): 549–64; Thomas J. Bernard, *The Cycle of Juvenile Justice* (New York: Oxford University Press, 1992), p. 141. Terminology used within the system reflected this orientation: juvenile prisons were commonly referred to as "training schools," or "rehabilitation centers." When we began the research for this book in 1992, Arizona authorities referred to the juvenile prisons as "three secure schools" (Arizona Department of Youth Treatment and Rehabilitation, *Fact Pack 1992*, p. 4).

67. Assessments of rehabilitative interventions have varied greatly. For a thorough overview and original assessment, see Palmer, *Profile of Correctional Effectiveness*.

68. Questions about the efficacy of the juvenile system's treatment efforts, as well as challenges to the ethics and legality of state intervention in the name of treatment, greatly influenced the first major reforms to take place in juvenile justice resulting from a series of U.S. Supreme Court decisions during the 1960s and 1970s. See *Kent v United States*, 383 U.S. 541 (1966); *In re Gault*, 387 U.S. 1 (1967); *Breed v Jones*, 421 U.S. 519 (1975); and *A. Schall, Commissioner of New York City Department of Juvenile Justice v Martin et al.*, 467 U.S. 253 (1984). These cases challenged the juvenile justice system's discretionary powers and pro-

cedural laxity, both of which were ostensibly necessary to accommodate the expansive reviews of juveniles' lives essential to individualize and expedite justice.

The landmark cases questioned juvenile courts' relaxed rules of evidence, less demanding level of proof for establishing "guilt," and minimal procedural rules. They questioned whether the system's inattention to and inconsistency regarding constitutional protections were justified by the unproven, and perhaps erroneous, assumption that the state was acting "in the best interests of the child." Not all youths were denied basic procedural rights prior to these U.S. Supreme Court rulings, but it was a matter decided by each court. The importance of the rulings lies not in the fact that all juveniles were previously denied any rights but, rather, that these rulings mandated that particular constitutional rights be extended uniformly to all youths throughout the United States. Of course, the mandate could not ensure uniform or universal implementation of rights.

These challenges involved treatment issues because they questioned whether the juvenile system had the ability to diagnose and treat youths' behavioral problems and whether youths were actually being punished in the name of treatment. Critics were particularly concerned about the violation of youths' rights in the rush to treatment, but the vast majority did not challenge the fundamental assumption that the juvenile system *should* provide treatment.

Rights established for youths in jeopardy of being institutionalized include: timely notice of specific charges, access to counsel, right against self-incrimination, confrontation and cross-examination of witnesses, sworn testimony, basis for appeal (recorded proceedings), and proof beyond a reasonable doubt. Rights established for youths being considered for transfer to adult courts include: access to counsel, counsel's access to all records considered by the court, required procedure on the juvenile court level, judicial statement of reason for transfer, and decision to transfer made prior to guilt-finding to avoid double jeopardy.

The Supreme Court rulings reinforced the system's emphasis on rehabilitation, for although they provided increased due process and protections in the guilt-finding stages, they did not challenge or alter the fundamental mandate of juvenile justice. And although these decisions granted certain rights to juveniles for whom incarceration was a possibility, Supreme Court rulings did not extend to youths all the rights afforded adults. The primary rationale for not doing so was that the mission of the juvenile system was viewed as treatment, not punishment. In *McKeiver v Pennsylvania*, 403 U.S. 528 (1971), the Court ruled that juveniles do not have a right to jury trial and, in *Schall v Martin*, they upheld the constitutionality of preventive detention of juveniles. The expansion of procedural rights was opposed because it was viewed as having the potential to slow down the process and prevent the delivery of treatment services to youths because of legal technicalities.

Although the U.S. Supreme Court has emphasized rights during the guilt-finding process rather than sentencing, appellate courts have focused on the right to treatment and the right to be free from cruel and unusual punishment. The appellate courts have also found specific institutional conditions and abuses to be unconstitutional. Nevertheless, once young people are imprisoned, their rights are engulfed in uncertainty, neglect, and silence. See Thomas J. Bamonte and Thomas M. Peters, "The Parole Revocation Process in Illinois," *Loyola University of Chicago Law Journal* 24 (1993): 211–58; Gray Cavender and Paul Knepper, "Strange Interlude: An Analysis of Juvenile Parole Revocation Decision Making," *Social Problems* 39 (4) (November 1992): 387–99. The exceptions to the lack of rights have been appellate court rulings focusing on the right to treatment and the right to be free from cruel and unusual punishment. These rulings reaffirmed the rehabilitative purpose of the juvenile system and maintained that youths could not be imprisoned if treatment services were not provided. See *Inmates of the Boy's Training School v Affeck*, 346 F. Supp. 1354 (D.R.I. 1972); *Nelson v Heyne*, 355 F. Supp. 451 (N.D. Ind. 1973); and *Morales v Turman*.

Court rulings have also found specific institutional conditions to be unconstitutional and in violation of a youth's right not to be subjected to cruel and unusual punishment. Excessive use of tranquilizing drugs, solitary confinement, strip-cells, and hand restraints have been ruled antitherapeutic and unconstitutional. See *Pena v New York State Division for Youth*, 419 F. Supp. 203 (S.D.N.Y. 1976); *Inmates of the Boy's Training School v Affeck*. In addition to prohibiting specific practices, courts have specified essential, mandatory elements of treatment, such as adequate and appropriate clothing, bedding, hygienic supplies, medical treatment, and educational programs (*Inmates of the Boy's Training School v Affeck*).

69. Critics argue that belief in the relative innocence of youth and their rehabilitative potential is misguided; and, increasingly, selected youths are depicted as hardened criminals, equally as "depraved and unworthy" as their adult counterparts. See Anne Schneider and Helen Ingram, "Social Construction of Target Populations: Implications for Politics and Policy," *American Political Science Review* 87 (2) (1993): 334–47; M. A. Bortner, *Delinquency and Justice: An Age of Crisis* (New York: McGraw-Hill, 1988), pp. 364–72. Positive images of the juvenile justice system are also under siege, with critics alternately and simultaneously indicting the system for failing to protect, guide, and treat youth; failing to inflict needed punishment; or failing to protect the public. See Barry C. Feld, "Juvenile (In)Justice and the Criminal Court Alternative," *Crime and Delinquency* 39 (4) (1993): 403–24; Mark D. Jacobs, *Screwing the System and Making It Work: Juvenile Justice in the No-fault Society* (Chicago: University of Chicago Press, 1990); Ira M. Schwartz, *(In)Justice for Juveniles: Rethinking the Best Interests of the Child* (Lexington, MA: Lexington Books, 1989); and Bernard, *The Cycle of Juvenile Justice*.

70. See Peter W. Greenwood, Joan Petersilia, and Franklin E. Zimring, *Age, Crime, and Sanctions: The Transition from Juvenile to Adult Court* (Santa Monica, CA: Rand Corporation, 1980); Joel P. Eigen, "The Determinants and Impact of Jurisdictional Transfer in Philadelphia," in *Major Issues in Juvenile Justice Information and Training: Readings in Public Policy*, eds. John C. Hall, Donna Martin Hamparian, John M. Pettibone, and Joseph L. White (Columbus, OH: Academy for Contemporary Problems, 1981), pp. 333–50; Donna M. Hamparian et al., *Major Issues in Juvenile Justice Information and Training/Youth in Adult Courts: Between Two Worlds* (Columbus, OH: Academy for Contemporary Problems, 1982); M. A. Bortner, "Traditional Rhetoric, Organizational Reality: Remand of Juveniles to Adult Court," *Crime and Delinquency* 32 (1986): 53–73; Cary Rudman et al., "Violent Youth in Adult Court: Process and Punishment," *Crime and Delinquency* 32 (1986): 75–96.

For recent and methodologically sophisticated analyses of decisions to transfer juveniles to adult court and adult court sentencing of transferred juveniles see, respectively, Marcy Rasmussen Podkopacz and Barry C. Feld, "Judicial Waiver Policy and Practice: Persistence, Seriousness, and Race," *Law & Inequality: A Journal of Theory and Practice* 14 (1) (December 1995): 73–178; and Elizabeth W. McNulty, "Transfer of Juvenile Offenders to Adult Court: Panacea or Problem?"

(Phoenix, AZ: Arizona Supreme Court, Administrative Office of the Courts, 1995, photocopy).

71. For alternative perspectives, see Regnery, "Getting Away with Murder"; Brodt and Smith, "Public Policy"; and Greenwood and Zimring, *One More Change.*

72. A wide range of perspectives and policies may be grouped under the banner of "punishment" or "treatment," despite significant nuances and differences within each camp. Advocates from "one side" may address primary concerns and use terminology associated with "the other side." For example, individuals advocating punishment may also speak of changing youths' behavior or "helping" them to become productive members of society. Their disagreement with treatment proponents hinges upon the crucial question of what generates change in behavior. Advocates of punishment may view their proposed policies as addressing the past failures of treatment programs and as "getting youths' attention." They may view imprisonment as a way to provide an effective incentive for youths to change their behavior, that is, to avoid further punishment, and to benefit youth and society in the long run.

The image of punishment policies as "antiyouth" springs primarily from their frequent portrayal of youths as hardened criminals, as unlikely to change, unworthy of society's resources, and, sometimes, unworthy of its concern. The antiyouth image also reflects the fact that advocates of punishment do not focus on or emphasize the needs or futures of youths, except to expect the worst. They are more likely to focus on public fear, youths as victimizing innocent members of society, and the need to remove such young people from the community as expediently and for as long as possible. "Protection of the public" is heralded as the pivotal concern, and the issues are often posed as delinquent youths versus decent citizens. Damning images of unlawful and imprisoned youths sustain this perspective, including portraits of imprisoned youths as uniformly violent, committed to criminal lifestyles, and intractable and irredeemable.

73. Zillah R. Eisenstein has provided a poignant critique of such oppositional politics: "Oppositional politics are not conducive to real democracy. Oppositional politics often lead those in power to use oppressive strategies to hold the oppositions in place" (*The Color of Gender: Reimaging Democracy* [Berkeley: University of California Press, 1994], p. 10).

74. Retribution and just deserts are frequently cited as the justifications for punishment, and arguments regarding responsibility are central to these positions. Accordingly, youths are viewed as fully responsible for their actions, as morally and legally blamable, and as deserving punishment. Some punishment proponents focus on youths fourteen years of age or older as mature minors and fully responsible, while others would extend full responsibility to all those over ten or to all children regardless of age. Especially when younger individuals are involved and it is difficult to attribute full responsibility, punishment advocates may shift their focus from individual responsibility to issues of retribution and the need to deter others by providing negative examples. Likewise, when protection of the public is heralded, punishment is portrayed as essential to accomplishing this goal.

75. See Gilligan, *Violence*, pp. 184–85.

76. In the juvenile prison system under study, the official philosophy and rejection of punitive approaches was expressed by the chief of counseling, a Ph.D. in psychology:

The punitive juvenile justice model is a function of reactive anger and retaliation toward youth that are perceived as already possessing adult knowledge and maturity. These youth are subsequently seen as making willful destructive choices over positive options. This focus on short-term retaliation . . . plays into juvenile thinking, leaving the youth with a perceived justification for continued delinquent behavior in order to "get even." Punitive models are implemented for the convenience of secure care personnel, not for public safety. A controlling environment reduces involvement of staff while a therapeutic environment requires effort, involvement with youth, risk, and a willingness to deal with mistakes as youth gain increasing freedom and responsibilities. Punitive systems are a proven failure. Theory, research, and practical applications clearly indicate that success is contingent on youth learning new skills and having the opportunity to practice and develop these skills within the context of healthy and encouraging relationships with staff. The most effective public safety is not a youth temporarily detained behind the walls of a prison, but a youth permanently changed from within. (Arizona Department of Youth Treatment and Rehabilitation, "[Chief of Counseling's] Talk," p. 5).

77. Jack Henry Abbot, *In the Belly of the Beast: Letters from Prison* (New York: Random House, 1981).

78. Avery Gordon suggests that "power relations are never as transparently clear as the names we give to them imply. Power can be invisible, it can be fantastic, it can be dull and routine. It can be obvious, it can reach you by the baton of the police, it can speak the language of your thoughts and desires. It can feel like remote control, it can exhilarate like liberation, it can travel through time, and it can drown you in the present. It is dense and superficial, it can cause bodily injury, and it can harm you without ever seeming to touch you. It is systematic, and it is particularistic and often both at the same time. It causes dreams to live and dreams to die" (*Ghostly Matters* [Minneapolis: University of Minnesota Press, 1997], p. 1).

79. Michel Foucault, *The History of Sexuality: An Introduction*, trans. Robert Hurley (New York: Penguin, 1978); see also Barry Smart, *Foucault, Marxism, and Critique* (London: Routledge and Kegan Paul, 1983), pp. 82–90.

80. Foucault, *The History of Sexuality*, pp. 92–93.

81. See Foucault, *Discipline and Punish* and *History of Sexuality*; and Stephen Pfohl, *Death at the Parasite Cafe: Social Science (Fictions) and the Postmodern* (New York: St. Martin's Press, 1992), pp. 12, 271–73.

Notes to Chapter Two

1. In Arizona, as in much of the U.S. Southwest, white or Caucasian youths who are not Latinos (Hispanics) are referred to as "Anglos." Both white youths and others commonly refer to themselves in this manner. Latino youths rarely use the terms "Latino" or "Hispanic"; rather, they identify themselves as "Mexican Americans" or "Mexicans."

2. In Arizona and nationwide, youths legally cannot be imprisoned for "status" offenses—those acts that are uniquely inappropriate or illegal for youths due to their *status* of being a juvenile within society, offenses such as possession of alcohol, running away, curfew violation, truancy, and incorrigibility. But Kevin's shoplifting offense provided the legal justification needed for his commitment to the juvenile prison at age fourteen.

3. The quotes about this case are from local newspaper articles, but the references are not provided in order to protect the youth's identity.

4. Tomás was among the five thousand runaway and homeless youths *reported* annually in Arizona. Phoenix South Community Mental Health Center, *Arizona's Alarming Trends 1994* (Phoenix: Arizona Association of Behavioral Health Programs, 1994), p. 39. Current national estimates for the number of children who run away each year exceeds one million. For a review of the literature and further discussion of runaway and homeless youths, see William H. Burke and E. Jane Burkhead, "Runaway Children in America: A Review of the Literature," *Education and Treatment of Children* 12 (1) (February 1989): 73–81; Stuart W. Fors and Dean G. Rojek, "A Comparison of Drug Involvement Between Runaways and School Youths," *Journal of Drug Education* 21 (1) (1991): 13–25; A. Therese Miller, Colleen Eggertson-Tacon, and Brian Quigg, "Patterns of Runaway Behavior Within a Larger Systems Context: The Road to Empowerment," *Adolescence* 25 (98) (1990): 271–89; Arlene Rubin Stiffman, "Physical and Sexual Abuse in Runaway Youths," *Child Abuse and Neglect* 13 (3) (1989): 417–26; Les B. Whitbeck and Ronald L. Simons, "Life on the Streets: The Victimization of Runaway and Homeless Adolescents," *Youth and Society* 22 (1) (1990): 108–25; Michael Windle, "Substance Use and Abuse Among Adolescent Runaways: A Four-year Follow-up Study," *Journal of Youth and Adolescence* 18 (4) (1989): 331–44; Marilyn R. Zide and Andrew L. Cherry, "A Typology of Runaway Youths: An Empirically Based Definition," *Child and Adolescent Social Work Journal* 9 (2) (April 1992): 155–68.
5. For a discussion of the relationship between drug and alcohol abuse by the youths and the patterns of behavior exhibited by older family members, see Ansley Hamid, "Drugs and Patterns of Opportunity in the Inner City: The Case of Middle-aged, Middle-income Cocaine Smokers," in *Drugs, Crime, and Social Isolation: Barriers to Urban Opportunity*, eds. Adele V. Harrell and George E. Peterson (Washington, DC: Urban Institute Press, 1992), pp. 209–39. Also Daniel J. Monti, "The Culture of Gangs in the Culture of School," *Qualitative Sociology* 16 (4) (1993): 383–404.
6. M. A. Bortner et al., *Equitable Treatment of Minority Youth: A Report on the Over Representation of Minority Youth in Arizona's Juvenile Justice System* (Phoenix: Governor's Office for Children, 1993), pp. 33–34.
7. These estimates are based on the 668 youths committed to prison in Arizona between January 1991 and August 1992. See Bortner et al., *Equitable Treatment of Minority Youth*, p. 35B.

8. At the time of our research, 44 percent of the youths in the program were Mexican Americans, as were 44 percent of the juvenile prison population; 35 percent of both the program participants and prison population were Anglos (non-Latino Caucasians); and approximately 3 percent of the model program and prison youths were American Indians. There was a slightly greater percentage of African-American youths in the program than in the overall prison population, 16 percent compared to 15 percent. The racial identities of 1 percent of both the prison and program populations were recorded as "Other."

9. Howard N. Snyder and Melissa Sickmund, *Juvenile Offenders and Victims: A National Report* (Washington, DC: Office of Juvenile Justice and Delinquency Prevention, 1995), p. 175.

10. At the time of the research, approximately thirty young women were in secure care in a locked residential facility in the community. The identities of the young women in the youth prison system are clearly gendered. Their experiences within the juvenile justice system, including incarceration, are influenced by their social status and self-concepts as girls or young women. This research dealt exclusively with youths in the secure prisons, all of whom were males during this period. Currently, females are incarcerated in these institutions as well.

11. There was a slightly smaller percentage of thirteen-year-olds in the model program than in the overall prison population, 2 percent compared to 3 percent. Slightly greater percentages of fifteen- and sixteen-year-olds participated in the program (22 and 35 percent, respectively) than were in the general prison population (21 and 32 percent, respectively). Thirty-two percent of the youths participating in the program were seventeen years old, compared to 34 percent within the overall prison population.

12. See Holly Sklar, *Chaos or Community? Seeking Solutions, Not Scapegoats for Bad Economics* (Boston: South End, 1995), and Henry A. Giroux, *Fugitive Cultures: Race, Violence and Youth* (New York: Routledge, 1996), p. 119.

13. Iris Marion Young, *Justice and the Politics of Difference* (Princeton, NJ: Princeton University, 1990). See also Monti, "The Culture of Gangs"; and Joan W. Moore, *Going Down to the Barrio: Homeboys and Homegirls in Change* (Philadelphia: Temple University Press, 1991), and *Homeboys: Gangs, Drugs, and Prison in the Barrios of Los Angeles* (Philadelphia: Temple University Press, 1978).

14. For discussions of delinquency and masculinity, see William E. Thornton, "Gender Traits and Delinquency Involvement of Boys and Girls," *Adolescence* 17 (68) (1982): 749–68; Karen Wilkinson, "An Investigation of the Contribution of Masculinity to Delinquent Behavior," *Sociological Focus* 18 (3) (1985): 249–63; Stephen Norland, Randall C. Wessel, and Neal Shover, "Masculinity and Delinquency," *Criminology* 19 (3) (1981): 421–33.

15. See Elijah Anderson, *Streetwise: Race, Class, and Change in an Urban Community* (Chicago: University of Chicago Press, 1990).

16. For examples of research on factors related to juvenile justice decisions that found no relationship between legal variables and outcomes, see Charles E. Frazier and John C. Cochran, "Detention of Juveniles: Its Effects on Subsequent Juvenile Court Processing Decisions," *Youth and Society* 17 (3) (1986): 286–305; Belinda R. McCarthy and Brent L. Smith, "The Conceptualization of Discrimination in the Juvenile Justice Process: The Impact of Administrative Factors and Screening Decisions on Juvenile Court Dispositions," *Criminology* 24 (1) (1986): 41–64; and Edward J. Pawlak, "Differential Selection of Juveniles for Detention," *Journal of Research in Crime and Delinquency* 14 (2) (1977): 152–65.

17. See Jonathan Simon, *Poor Discipline: Parole and the Social Control of the Underclass, 1890–1990* (Chicago: University of Chicago Press, 1993); and Young, *Justice and the Politics of Difference.*

18. See Robert M. Emerson, *Judging Delinquents: Context and Process in Juvenile Court* (Chicago: Aldine, 1969); and M. A. Bortner, *Inside a Juvenile Court: The Tarnished Ideal of Individualized Justice* (New York: New York University Press, 1982).

19. Bortner et al., *Equitable Treatment of Minority Youth.*

20. Bortner et al., *Equitable Treatment of Minority Youth.*

21. See Bortner et al., *Equitable Treatment of Minority Youth*, pp. 73–4. Analysis of the 185 interviews was conducted by Andy Hall of the Urban Studies Institute at Arizona State University.

The 1991 report of the New York State Judicial Commission on Minorities reached a similar conclusion. It stated that minorities have unequal access to the courts, and receive disparate treatment and fewer opportunities. Zillah R. Eisenstein states that "the report documents two justice systems at work in New York: one for whites and a harsher one for minorities and the poor" (*The Color of Gender: Reimaging Democracy* [Berkeley: University of California Press, 1994], p. 43).

22. Bortner et al., *Equitable Treatment of Minority Youth*, p. 74.

23. Youths' experiences of being mistrusted and, in their eyes, mistreated extend far beyond their interactions with unprofessional police officers. While some youths appear to savor the ability to intimidate, others privately report being "hurt" and "humiliated" when someone crosses the street to avoid meeting them, presumably out of fear and images of violence associated with their age, appearance, or racial and ethnic identity.

24. Some community leaders criticize police officers' bias toward minorities and their use of excessive force. One critic, a former state legislator, accuses the police of "looking for scapegoats for the problems they themselves created. . . . They want to deviate the attention from the real issue" of police harassment and brutality. However, other community members believe that a show of strength from the police eventually will be able to contain the presence of guns and drugs in their neighborhood (William Hermann, "Gangs Fight Police for Neighborhoods," *Arizona Republic*, 11 March 1995, p. A1). See also Catherine H. Conly, *Street Gangs: Current Knowledge and Strategies* (Washington, DC: National Institute of Justice, 1993); and C. Ronald Huff, "Denial, Overreaction, and Misidentification: A Postscript to Public Policy," in *Gangs in America*, ed. C. Ronald Huff (Newbury Park, CA: Sage, 1981), pp. 312–13.

25. For a discussion of the victimization of runaway and homeless youths, see Whitbeck and Simons, "Life on the Streets."

26. Innovation is elevated to an art form for those who, for a variety of reasons, live on the streets. For youths without the support system provided by gang membership, it is essential to develop transitory friendships and identify creative options that offer acceptable alternatives to homelessness. These superficial relationships, or loose associations (not gangs), are what these youthful prisoners refer to in their discussions about groups of friends. And they bear little resemblance to the relationships that other young men have with their "homeboys," long-time friends who grew up in the same neighborhood, sharing similar experiences and hardships.

27. See David G. Curry and Irving A. Spergel, "Gang Involvement and Delinquency Among Hispanic and African-American Adolescent Males," *Journal of Research in Crime and Delinquency* 29 (3) (1992): 273–91; Marjorie S. Zatz, "Los Cholos: Legal Processing of Chicano Gang Members," *Social Problems* 33 (1) (1985): 13–30.

28. This broad definition of respect and lack of respect for young people is referenced in the literature in terms of the scarcity of available support when difficulties arise in the home, the neighborhood, or the schools (frequently embedded in the research on runaways); the high incidence of physical, sexual, psychological, and emotional abuse among incarcerated youth; the hardships experienced in relationship to a lack of supervision, difficult family situations, neglect, and parents who do not want to be bothered with the problems of their children; and the willingness for gangs to fill the void. See also Irving A. Spergel, "Youth Gangs: Continuity and Change," in *Crime and Justice: A Review of Research 12*, eds. Michael Tonry and Norval Morris (Chicago: University of Chicago Press, 1990).

29. For further discussion of the social reasons for joining a gang, see Conly, *Street Gangs*, pp. 18–19; Susan R. Takata and Richard G. Zevitz, "Divergent Perceptions of Group Delinquency in a Midwestern Community: Racine's Gang Problem," *Youth and Society* 21 (3) (March 1990): 282–305.

30. Gangs in these neighborhoods are not always associated with crime and violence. They are comprised of close family and friends who grew up together and are an integral part of social lives that revolved around their immediate neighborhoods. For further discussion of the relationships between gang members, their families, their schools, and their neighborhoods, see Monti, "The Culture of Gangs"; Moore, *Going Down to the Barrio* and *Homeboys*; Luis J. Rodriguez, *Always Running: La Vida Loca, Gang Days in L.A.* (Willimantic, CT: Curbstone Press, 1993); and Martin Sanchez Jankowski, *Islands in the Streets: Gangs and American Urban Society* (Berkeley: University of California Press, 1991).

31. See also Ruth Horowitz, "Sociological Perspectives on Gangs: Conflicting Definitions and Concepts," in *Gangs in America*, ed. C. Ronald Huff (Newbury Park, CA: Sage, 1990), pp. 37–54.

32. The youths described a process quite similar to the one described by Monti:

The term "recruitment" was too strong and formal a term to describe how young persons became gang members. . . . They became active members in a fairly natural and nonthreatening way, youngsters said. They were introduced to it during the course of their everyday life and, having found it a source of fellowship and self-identity, simply slid into gang membership as easily as adults might slide into the local church. Children avoided becoming active gang members in much the same way. . . . The municipally-based gangs provided most youngsters with their first exposure to a real "voluntary organization" intended only for them. As such, the gangs introduced children to a type of organization that their elders count on for fellowship and mutual support. ("The Culture of Gangs," p. 390)

See also Jankowski, *Islands in the Street.*
33. Monti, "The Culture of Gangs."
34. The importance of family relationships to individual gang members is further addressed by Sanyika Shakur, *Monster: The Autobiography of an L.A. Gang Member* (New York: Penguin, 1993).
35. One juvenile court judge commented that some of these kids come from neighborhoods that are "analogous to Beirut or Belfast." A large percentage who come into his court are abused and neglected. He continued by saying that a significant number join gangs for the protection they offer. See Paul J. Schatt, "A Picture of Delinquency," *Arizona Republic*, 24 March 1994, p. B4.
36. See Jankowski, *Islands in the Street.*
37. For a discussion of the fear and misunderstanding attached to a perception of tagging as a "sign of social collapse," see Anne Winter, "More Than Scrawls: Tagging, Graffiti, Different Forms of Language," *Arizona Republic*, 19 March 1995, p. F1.
38. Conly, *Street Gangs*, pp. 5–7; Finn-Aage Esbensen and David Huizinga, "Gangs, Drugs, and Delinquency in a Survey of Urban Youth," *Criminology* 31 (4) (1993): 565–89; and Snyder and Sickmund, *Juvenile Offenders and Victims*, p. 54. See also G. Larry Mays, ed., *Gangs and Gang Behavior* (Chicago: Nelson-Hall, 1997).
39. For a discussion of this pervasive problem from the perspective of the youths who are involved, see Elliott Currie, *Dope and Trouble: Portraits of Delinquent Youth* (New York: Pantheon, 1991).

A national survey conducted by the Bureau of Justice Statistics among prison inmates found that 82.7 percent of youths in long-term public juvenile facilities had used drugs at some point in their lives, and 38 percent reported their first use before the age of twelve. See U.S. Department of Justice, *Profile of Jail Inmates, 1989* (BJS Special Report) (Rockville, MD: U.S. Department of Justice, 1991). For further discussion of the linkages between inner-city isolation, drugs, and crime see

Adele V. Harrell and George E. Peterson, eds., *Drugs, Crime, and Social Isolation: Barriers to Urban Opportunity* (Washington, DC: Urban Institute Press, 1992).

40. Snyder and Sickmund, *Juvenile Offenders and Victims*, p. 63; Phoenix South Community Mental Health Center, *Arizona's Alarming Trends 1994*, pp. 66–70; Eliot Hartstone and Karen V. Hansen, "The Violent Juvenile Offender: An Empirical Portrait," in *Violent Juvenile Offenders: An Anthology*, eds. Robert A. Mathias, Paul DeMuro, and Richard S. Allison (San Francisco: National Council on Crime and Delinquency, 1984), pp. 83–112; James A. Inciardi, "Drug Use Can Cause Youth Violence," in *Youth Violence*, eds. Michael D. Biskup and Charles P. Cozic (San Diego: Greenhaven, 1992), pp. 97–102; David H. Huizinga, Scott Menard, and Delbert S. Elliott, "Delinquency and Drug Use: Temporal and Developmental Patterns," *Justice Quarterly* 6 (3) (1989): 419–55; John K. Watters, Craig Reinarman, and Jeffrey Fagan, "Causality, Context, and Contingency: Relationships Between Drug Abuse and Delinquency," *Contemporary Drug Problems* 12 (Fall 1985): 351–73; and Martha A. Myers, "Symbolic Policy and the Sentencing of Drug Offenders," *Law and Society Review* 23 (2) (1989): 295–315.

41. In 1995, 367 of the 609 youths in Arizona's youth prisons were first timers.

42. Youths on parole are still under the control of the prison system. Decisions to revoke their parole, as well as additional time to be served, are internal administrative decisions.

43. *Johnson v Upchurch*, CIV-86-195-TUC-RMB, "Fifth Amended Complaint" (D. Ariz., consent decree entered May 5, 1993), p. 8. The Governor's Task Force on Juvenile Corrections developed the risk assessment instrument used during the two years of this study.

44. For discussions of recidivism, see Pamela K. Lattimore, Christy A. Visher, and Richard L. Linster, "Predicting Rearrest for Violence among Serious Youthful Offenders," *Journal of Research in Crime and Delinquency* 32 (1) (1995): 54–84; Renae D. Duncan, Wallace A. Kennedy, and Christopher J. Patrick, "Four Factor Model of Recidivism in Male Juvenile Offenders," *Journal of Clinical Child Psychology* 24 (3) (1995): 250–57; Brent B. Benda, "Predicting Return to Prison Among Adolescent Males: A Comparison of Three Statistics," *Journal of Criminal Justice* 17 (6) (1989): 487–500.

45. To avoid underestimating those who presented high risks to public

safety, we are including the 10 percent of program youths for whom secure care risk scores were unavailable. Many of these were transferred to adult courts and, although transfer is common for property offenders, it is possible a significant number were involved in violent offenses.

46. Linda Reyes and Nicolas Carrasco, "Special Training in Treating Youth Who Exhibit Violent Behavior" (presentation to Arizona Department of Youth Treatment and Rehabilitation clinical staff, Phoenix, AZ, 23 May and 7 July 1994); Matthew L. Ferrara, "The Journey Program: A Juvenile Sex Offender Treatment Program" (unpublished, 1994, photocopy), and *Group Counseling with Juvenile Delinquents: The Limit and Lead Approach* (Newbury Park, CA: Sage, 1992); Gail D. Ryan and Sandy L. Lane, eds., *Juvenile Sexual Offending: Causes, Consequences, Correction* (Lexington, MA: Lexington Books, 1991); Arnold P. Goldstein and Barry Glick, *Aggression Replacement Training: A Comprehensive Intervention for Aggressive Youth* (Champaign, IL: Research Press, 1987).

47. See Terry Williams and William Kornblum, *The Uptown Kids: Struggle and Hope in the Projects* (New York: G. P. Putnam's, 1994); Rodriguez, *Always Running*; Shakur, *Monster*; Alex Kotlowitz, *There Are No Children Here: The Story of Two Boys Growing Up in the Other America* (New York: Bantam Doubleday Dell, 1991); Currie, *Dope and Trouble*; Piri Thomas, *Down These Mean Streets* (New York: Vintage, 1991); and Fritz Redl and David Wineman, *Children Who Hate: A Sensitive Analysis of the Anti-Social Behavior of Children in Their Response to the Adult World* (New York: Free Press, 1951).

48. See Bortner, *Inside a Juvenile Court.*

49. See Jonathan Kozol, *Savage Inequalities: Children in America's Schools* (New York: Crown, 1991).

50. Giroux (1996) describes the processes through which education creates spaces of inequality and subordination (p. 17). See also Larry Van Sickle, *The American Dream and the Impact of Class: Teaching Poor Kids to Labor* (New York: Irvington, 1985).

51. See Phoenix South Community Mental Health Center, *Arizona's Alarming Trends 1994*; Morrison Institute for Public Policy, *Kids Count Factbook: Arizona's Children 1994* (Tempe: Arizona State University, 1994), pp. 2, 5.

52. See Williams and Kornblum, *The Uptown Kids*; Shakur, *Monster*; Kotlowitz, *There Are No Children Here*; Thomas, *Down These Mean Streets*;

and Jonathan Kozol, *Amazing Grace: The Lives of Children and the Conscience of a Nation* (New York: Crown, 1995).

53. See Susan Goodwillie, ed., *Voices from the Future: Our Children Tell Us About Violence in America* (New York: Crown, 1993); and Currie, *Dope and Trouble*.

54. See Kelly E. Spencer, "Juvenile Incarceration: Translating Policy to Practice" (master's thesis, Tempe, AZ: Arizona State University, 1991), p. 4.

55. See Kozol, *Amazing Grace*; and Kotlowitz, *There Are No Children Here*. An example of children being cast as nonchildren is provided by the "CNN [Television] Reports" with Judy Woodruff on 26 November 1995. Youths ten and thirteen years old were described as "adults in children's bodies" who should be incarcerated as adults.

56. Bortner, *Delinquency and Justice*.

57. See Neil Postman, *The Disappearance of Childhood* (New York: Vintage, 1994).

58. Stephanie Coontz, *The Way We Never Were: American Families and the Nostalgia Trap* (New York: Basic Books, 1992).

59. Michael Eric Dyson, *Making Malcolm: The Myth and Meaning of Malcolm X* (New York: Oxford University Press, 1995), p. 116.

60. Novelist Caleb Carr's imagery is appropriate: "Set out on the trail of a murderous monster and ended up coming face to face with a frightened child." Caleb Carr, *The Alienist* (New York: Random House, 1994), p. 5.

61. Dick Hebdige, *Subculture: The Meaning of Style* (London: Methuen, 1979); Stephen Pfohl, *Death at the Parasite Cafe: Social Science (Fictions) and the Postmodern* (New York: St. Martin's Press, 1992), pp. 272–73.

■ Notes to Chapter Three

1. For a discussion of lawsuits as potential agents for change, see Michael J. Dale and Carl Sanniti, "Litigation as an Instrument for Change in Juvenile Detention: A Case Study," *Crime and Delinquency* 39 (1) (1993): 49–67; Mark Soler, "Litigation on Behalf of Children in Adult Jails," *Crime and Delinquency* 34 (2) (1988): 190–208.

2. For a discussion of prison gangs, see Geoffrey Hunt, Stephanie Riegel, Tomas Morales, and Dan Waldorf, "Changes in Prison Culture: Prison Gangs and the Case of the 'Pepsi Generation,'" *Social Problems* 40 (3)

(1993): 398–409; John Irwin, *Prisons in Turmoil* (Boston: Little, Brown, 1980); James B. Jacobs, *Stateville: The Penitentiary in Mass Society* (Chicago: University of Chicago Press, 1977).

3. The teachers in the model program were selected from those already teaching at the prison. No new positions were authorized at the beginning of the program.

4. At the program's beginning, youths qualifying for special education services had limited opportunities; there was just one classroom, which was limited to fewer than ten program and nonprogram youths and one teacher.

5. The teacher inside the prison suggested that similarities in the youths' work might exist because *she* made common wording suggestions to different youths. She was concerned that preconceived notions about imprisoned youths played a role in the ultimate decision by the community college to discontinue the class.

6. The pay scale also reflected their twelve-month responsibilities, as opposed to other teachers' nine-month responsibilities.

7. On at least one occasion, members of the psychology staff attempted to address conflicts between the teachers and other staff members, but without success. Teachers were generally unreceptive, suggesting that "we've got real problems in the classroom, and we don't want to meet with psychologists to talk about philosophy."

8. Matthew L. Ferrara, *Group Counseling with Juvenile Delinquents: The Limit and Lead Approach* (Newbury Park, CA: Sage, 1992).

9. Arizona Department of Youth Treatment and Rehabilitation, "Level System" (Phoenix, 12 May 1992, photocopy), p. 25.

10. For a discussion of treatment-security conflicts, see Harald K.-H. Klingemann, "Goal Conflicts in Correction Institutions for Juvenile Delinquents," *British Journal of Criminology* 22 (2) (1982): 140–64.

11. Arizona Department of Youth Treatment and Rehabilitation, "Proper Terminology," memorandum from CMT manager to all staff (Phoenix, 25 September 1993, photocopy).

12. For both years, the average number of security calls from units in the model program was less than in the other prison units. During the first year there was an average of 9.6 calls per month in program units, compared to 21.7 in other units. During the second year it was 14.1 calls per month for program units, compared to 23.7 calls for other units.

13. Although vehicle theft is not a violent offense, repeated offenses were

cumulative in calculating risk scores under the secure care guidelines, resulting in high scores associated with serious offenses.

◾ Notes to Chapter Four

1. Total institutions are characterized by the complete ordering of and control of life by the keepers of the institution and an extreme lack of decision-making power for those who are kept. See Erving Goffman's *Asylums: Essays on the Social Situation of Mental Patients and Other Inmates* (Chicago: Aldine, 1961).
2. Between 1985 and 1994, the number of adolescents killing with guns quadrupled. James Alan Fox, *Trends in Juvenile Violence: A Report to the United States Attorney General on Current and Future Rates of Juvenile Offending* (Washington, DC: Bureau of Justice Statistics, U.S. Department of Justice, 1996), pp. i, 2.
3. In subtle but effective ways these youths were able to encourage others in Unit Four to join them in protest of what they perceived to be demonstrations of injustice and hypocrisy. Sometimes they sat back and appeared entertained by less perceptive youths' conflicts with staff members, which they had instigated. As the controversy escalated and other youths were removed to the disciplinary unit for threatening or assaultive behavior that resulted when frustrations and tempers flared, these youths could be observed enjoying the rewards of being among those who did not become "involved" in the conflict.
4. Linda M. Williams, "Ethics Policy and Society: Responsibility, Repression, or Rhetoric?" (Ph.D. diss., Tempe, AZ.: Arizona State University, 1994).
5. Only three of the ten were classified in the high-risk category, and it was agreed that the lack of progress for medium- and low-risk youths was unexpected.
6. Arizona Department of Youth Treatment and Rehabilitation, "Personal Conduct," memorandum from deputy director and assistant director to all employees (Phoenix, 19 April 1993, photocopy).
7. Youths' written grievances were routinely ignored by staff members within the institution. For example, after his altercation with the staff member Mr. Carpenter, Larry filed several grievances that did not receive a response. "So then a month later, I wrote another one, asking why my first two were never solved, and I had talked to Ms. Walsh

[unit supervisor], and she said that she would talk to him about it. And that was the last time I heard of it, and I just let it go."

8. Arizona Department of Youth Treatment and Rehabilitation, letter from director to youth (Phoenix, 23 July 1993, photocopy).

9. See Sanyika Shakur, *Monster: The Autobiography of an L.A. Gang Member* (New York: Penguin, 1993).

10. Victoria Harker, "'These Kids Want to Succeed': A New Education System for State's Juvenile Offenders," *Arizona Republic*, 7 December 1992, p. A1; Stephanie Robertson, "Boys at [the Phoenix Prison] Leave Lasting, Haunting Impression," *Arizona Republic*, 25 June 1993, p. A20.

11. Channel 3 News report with Marty Vellasco Hames, 3 December 1992; "Horizon" on KAET-TV, "Changes in the Juvenile Justice System," Camille Kimball, 2 June 1993; and Kevin Sheh, "Tattoos Scar Future for Ex-Gang Members: Removal Could Aid in Break with Past," *Arizona Republic*, 18 June 1993, p. B1.

12. Paul J. Schatt, "A Picture of Delinquency," *Arizona Republic*, 24 March 1994, p. B4.

13. For further discussion on the cultivation of linkages by the media between gang membership and violence, crime and drug involvement, see Douglas W. Pryor and Edmund F. McGarrell, "Public Perceptions of Youth Gang Crime: An Exploratory Analysis," *Youth and Society* 24 (4) (1993): 399–418; and James F. Quinn and William Downs, "Police Perceptions of the Severity of Local Gang Problems: An Analysis of Noncriminal Predictors," *Sociological Spectrum* 13 (2) (1993): 209–26.

14. Christopher Johns, "Arizona Is Part of a Juvenile-Justice Crisis: It's Not Just About Crimes, It's About Kids Who Are Abused, Neglected and in Need of Help," *Arizona Republic*, 28 November 1993, p. C1.

15. Governor's Task Force on Juvenile Corrections, *Arizona's Troubled Youth: A New Direction* (Phoenix: Governor's Task Force, 1993), pp. 6, 11, 13–15.

16. Abraham Kwok, "New Era Dawns for Juvenile-Justice System," *Arizona Republic*, 9 February 1993, p. B5.

17. Abraham Kwok, "State Near New Juvenile-Detention Era; Decree Forcing Upgraded Treatment," *Arizona Republic*, 4 April 1993, p. B1.

18. Kwok, "State Near New Juvenile-Detention Era."

19. Ben Winton, "Justice for Juveniles: Director Pushes for Overhaul of Youth Treatment," *Phoenix Gazette*, 14 May 1993, p. A1.

20. In "automatic" or "presumptive" transfer, juveniles are transferred to

adult courts based on the specific offenses with which they are charged. The legislature exercises decision-making power in designating which offenses will result in transfer, and prosecutors exercise extensive power in their decisions regarding what charges to file. Judges are not involved in the transfer decision, unlike "judicial" transfer in which, aided by review and recommendations of juvenile court personnel, judges make the final decisions.

21. Chair, Governor's Task Force on Juvenile Corrections, memorandum to Governor Fife Symington (Phoenix, 5 April 1993, photocopy).

22. Bob Schuster, "Glimmer of Hope: State May Give Juvenile Rehab a Chance," *Tribune Newspapers*, 3 April 1993, p. A14.

23. David Fritze, "Symington Calls for War on State's Juvenile Crime: Offers $31.7 Million Crackdown, Might Call Out Guard," *Arizona Republic*, 3 November 1993, p. A1.

24. J. Fife Symington III, "Address by Gov. Fife Symington to Arizona Town Hall" (Grand Canyon, 2 November 1993, photocopy), pp. 9–10, 12, 16.

25. Symington, "Address."

26. Carol Sowers and Victoria Harker, "Shake-up at Youth Correction: Director, Chief Deputy Forced Out by Governor," *Arizona Republic*, 6 January 1994, p. A1; Carol Sowers, "Minister Defends Violent Play: Says Ugly Truths of Gang Life Exposed," *Arizona Republic*, 3 January 1994, p. A1.

27. "Youth Corrections Shake-up Raises Questions," *Arizona Republic*, 7 January 1994, p. B6.

28. Sowers and Harker, "Shake-up at Youth Correction."

29. Administrators and staff members were uncertain regarding the implication of this action for the program. Some felt it would continue under new leadership from the adult prison, others felt this signaled a dramatic shift in course, and some considered it an essential move and a gesture of support for the program.

In July 1994, shortly after our evaluation ended, David Lambert of the National Center for Youth Law and cocounsel for youths in the Arizona lawsuit was quoted as expressing concern regarding the Arizona situation:

He said he doubted Arizona was truly dedicated to reform. As evidence, Lambert cited the Legislature's unbending "get tough on crime" stance and Symington's dismissal of [the director] as youth treatment director in January. Lambert, along with other juvenile justice experts, felt [the director] had done much to fix an ailing system.

But Arizona still has the potential to be a model for other states, Lambert said, if it fully follows its court order.

"I'm hopeful that Arizona will not let this opportunity pass and revert to the type of system it had in the past, and it will see this as a chance to chart a new course," Lambert said.

Peter Leone, chair of the oversight committee for the consent decree, expressed similar concerns:

But studies indicate bigger, more punitive situations do little to reform youthful offenders and actually do more harm than good, Leone said.

"Warehousing kids in large facilities—research doesn't show that helps," he said. "A lot of time they become more skillful in doing things the rest of us don't like to see them do."

Kristen Cook, "Arizona a Reluctant Player in Overdue Youth Corrections Reforms," *Arizona Daily Star*, 6 July 1994, pp. A1, A7.
30. "Youth Corrections Shake-up."
31. "Challenge for DYTR: Protect the Public," *Phoenix Gazette*, 7 January 1994, p. B14.
32. J. W. Brown, "Easy Answers Elude Struggle to Fix System," *Phoenix Gazette*, 9 January 1994, p. G3.
33. Sowers and Harker, "Shake-up at Youth Correction."
34. Frank Turco and Bill Muller, "Juvenile Justice in Limbo: Overhaul Idea Met by Lawmaker Static," and "Democrat May Be Hired to Revamp Juvenile Justice," *Arizona Republic*, 10 January 1995, p. A4.
35. The tenor of state politics, especially those related to youths, is further revealed by the July 1995 departure of the former chair of the Commission on Juvenile Corrections, which had initiated the hopeful era of response to the lawsuit and reform of the system. Under the headline, "Frustration Drives Activist Out of State," a political columnist analyzed the self-imposed exile of Bill Jamieson, an archdeacon in the Episcopal Church and former Director of the State Department of Administration and State Department of Economic Security.

Although Jamieson was credited with attempting to inform and educate the governor about children's issues during the 1990 campaign, he called this involvement "the biggest political mistake of my life." He further accused the governor and legislative leaders of promoting a narrow agenda, "one that creates everything in their own image, a very white-male-patrician image—no other discussion allowed."

▮ Notes for Chapter Five

1. For further discussion of youths' adaptation to the institution, see Ted Palmer, *A Profile of Correctional Effectiveness and New Directions for Research* (Albany: State University of New York Press, 1994); Clemens Bartollas, Stuart Miller, and Simon Dinitz, *Juvenile Victimization: The Institutional Paradox* (New York: Sage, 1976); Thomas J. Cottle, *Children in Jail: Seven Lessons in American Justice* (Boston: Beacon, 1977); David Street, Robert D. Vinter, and Charles Perrow, *Organization for Treatment: A Comparative Study of Institutions* (New York: Free Press, 1966).

2. The importance and effectiveness of family-focused drug intervention was unaddressed by the model program (see Robert A. Lewis et al., "Family-based Interventions for Helping Drug-Abusing Adolescents," *Journal of Adolescent Research* 5 [1] [January 1990]: 82–95). Additional references to this lack of substance abuse treatment in the prisons can be found in A. Verne McArthur, *Coming Out Cold: Community Reentry from a State Reformatory* (Lexington, MA: Lexington Books, 1974); Sanyika Shakur, *Monster: The Autobiography of an L.A. Gang Member* (New York: Penguin, 1993); and Henry Sontheimer and Lynne Goodstein, "An Evaluation of Juvenile Intensive Aftercare Probation: Aftercare versus System Response Effects," *Justice Quarterly* 10 (1993): 197–227.

3. This program was intended to provide residential treatment for twenty-four of the youths with the most serious problems and group therapy for youths with less serious substance abuse issues.

4. A precise figure is impossible to track, because drug charges are often dismissed or adjusted, and they are frequently viewed as "incidental" to other offenses that are reported.

5. The much-acclaimed "war" used drugs as a stand-in and a "political surrogate for the problems of the urban poor, racial ghettoes, and unemployment." See Zillah R. Eisenstein, *The Color of Gender: Reimaging Democracy* (Berkeley: University of California Press, 1994), p. 157.

6. Some youths underestimated the realities awaiting them on the outside, especially the magnitude of the support necessary to do well. These youths demonstrated a significant lack of understanding regarding what they could accomplish on their own.

You've got to *want* it to be successful. You know what I mean? Not just because you live at home with so-and-so means that you're going to be successful—because I live at home with my mom and my brothers and my uncle and stuff, and I choose to do what I do. But if I didn't have no one and I wanted to be someone, I could still be someone. . . . There's all kinds of orphans that you see on TV that are millionaires and stuff like that—that didn't have no one. *They* made it, because they *chose* to make it.

7. A significant number of these children anticipate violent death at an early age; they do not expect to live to be adults. The founder of Phoenix's Mothers Against Gangs commented that gang members "plan their funeral because it's the only thing they can think of." A campus police officer at a local junior high school, who routinely overhears twelve- and thirteen-year-old pupils talking about the possibility of dying, suggests there is a lack of hope and "a morbid acceptance of what in their perception would be reality, dying before they're in their 20s." (RuthAnn Hogue, "Gang Teenager Saw Death Coming," *Phoenix Gazette*, 5 December 1993, p. G1.) These youths repeat the perspective voiced in the critically acclaimed documentary *Hoop Dreams*: "To live, to see eighteen—that's good!" For a similar discussion, see Alex Kotlowitz, *There Are No Children Here: The Story of Two Boys Growing Up in the Other America* (New York: Bantam Doubleday Dell, 1991).

8. For a discussion of alternatives to runaway behavior, see William H. Burke and E. Jane Burkhead, "Runaway Children in America: A Review of the Literature," *Education and Treatment of Children* 12 (1) (February 1989): 73–81; and A. Thercse Miller, Colleen Eggertson-Tacon, and Brian Quigg, "Patterns of Runaway Behavior Within a Larger Systems Context: The Road to Empowerment," *Adolescence* 25 (98) (1990): 271–89.

9. For further data on the fate of young people who ran away in Arizona, see Phoenix South Community Mental Health Center, *Arizona's Alarming Trends 1994* (Phoenix: Arizona Association of Behavioral Health Programs, 1994).

10. For others among the first twenty-four youths, this resolve to be suc-

cessful likewise was insufficient to overcome the problems they encountered. Some, like Luke, needed specialized help with serious drug and alcohol problems. Despite a notation in his file indicating that his offenses were "committed while he was under the influence," Luke's problem would not be dealt with in the model program. On his eighteenth birthday, he was arraigned as an adult for aggravated assault while intoxicated.

11. The increased number of more sophisticated weapons is reflected in youths' responses to a variety of situations. The Phoenix Police Department's community services director suggests, "We're dealing more now with blatant violence. . . . Kids today have access to a whole different technology of guns. . . . Even some good kids carry guns to protect themselves. . . . Kids used to use their fists to settle their differences. These days, because of easy access to various automatic weapons, they can use a 9-millimeter." Christopher Johns, "Arizona Is Part of a Juvenile-Justice Crisis: It's Not Just About Crimes—It's About Kids Who Are Abused, Neglected and in Need of Help," *Arizona Republic*, 28 November 1993, p. C1.

12. For a discussion of the increase in delinquent behavior *after* joining the gang, see Terence P. Thornberry, Marvin D. Krohn, Alan J. Lizotte, and Deborah Chard-Wierschem, "The Role of Juvenile Gangs in Facilitating Delinquent Behavior," *Journal of Research in Crime and Delinquency* 30 (1) (1993): 55–87.

13. The newspaper citations are omitted to protect the confidentiality of the youths involved.

14. Arizona reported a 52.5 percent increase in firearm-related fatalities for youths under and nineteen years of age and a 45.2 percent increase in child homicide victims (under eighteen years) between 1990 and 1994. See Morrison Institute for Public Policy, *Kids Count Factbook: Arizona's Children 1994* (Tempe, AZ: Arizona State University, 1994). During 1991, Arizona had the country's seventh-highest rate of violent death rates for teens. See Phoenix South Community Mental Health Center, *Arizona's Alarming Trends 1994*.

15. Among youth aged fifteen to nineteen in Arizona, the suicide rate rose from 16.1 per 100,000 teens in 1990 to 18.3 during 1991. As of 1991, the teen suicide rate was well over twice the national objective (no more than 8.2 per 100,000) established for the year 2000. See Phoenix South Community Health Center, *Arizona's Alarming Trends 1994*.

16. These figures are based on youths released from prison who were in

the community for the specified time period (30, 90, or 180 days) prior to the end of our two-year research. For discussions of recidivism among incarcerated youths, see Steven P. Lab and John T. Whitehead, "Juvenile Correctional Treatment," *Crime and Delinquency* 34 (1) (January 1988): 60–83; and Snyder and Sickmund, *Juvenile Offenders and Victims*.

17. The newspaper citation is omitted to protect the confidentiality of the youth involved.

Notes to Chapter Six

1. Michael J. Sniffen, "Record Numbers in Prison," *Arizona Republic*, 2 June 1994, pp. A1, A12; "Prison Population at Record 1.5 Million in U.S.," *Arizona Republic*, 10 August 1995, p. A4; "Prison Population Tops 1 Million: Arizona Houses 18,809 Inmates," *Mesa* (Arizona) *Tribune*, 28 October 1994, p. B1; and Marc Mauer, *Americans Behind Bars: A Comparison of International Rates of Incarceration* (Washington, DC: Sentencing Project, 1991.)

2. Anne L. Schneider and Helen Ingram, "Social Construction of Target Populations: Implications for Politics and Policy," *American Political Science Review* 87 (2) (1993): 334–347; M. A. Bortner, *Delinquency and Justice: An Age of Crisis* (New York: McGraw-Hill, 1988), Chap. 13.

3. Ray Surette, "Predator Criminals as Media Icons," in *Media Process and the Social Construction of Crime*, ed. Gregg Barak (New York: Garland, 1994), pp. 131–58.

4. Bortner, *Delinquency and Justice*; Schneider and Ingram, "Social Construction of Target Populations."

5. See Karina Bland, "Cost of Crowding May Have Gone Up: Juvenile Corrections Officials Face Fine," *Arizona Republic*, 8 February 1997; "Juvenile Jail: State Defies Court, Logic," *Arizona Republic*, 15 February 1997. Failure to reduce the prison population reflects insufficient improvements in the prison system, as well as legislative changes that give judges power to sentence youth to specific prison terms. In these cases the prison system's discretion is curtailed.

6. Thomas J. Bernard, *The Cycle of Juvenile Justice* (New York: Oxford University Press, 1992).

7. Unlike when they send youth to private treatment facilities, county courts do not pay for the costs of juvenile prisons.

8. Robert M. Emerson, *Judging Delinquents: Context and Process in Juvenile*

Court (Chicago: Aldine, 1969); M. A. Bortner, *Inside a Juvenile Court: The Tarnished Ideal of Individualized Justice* (New York: New York University Press, 1982).

9. For discussions of the atomization of responsibility, see: Lillian Rubin, *Families on the Fault Line: America's Working Class Speaks About the Family, the Economy, Race, and Ethnicity* (New York: HarperCollins, 1994), and *Worlds of Pain: Life in the Working Class Family* (New York: Basic Books, 1976); Harold Kerbo, *Social Stratification and Inequality: Class Conflict in Historical and Comparative Perspective*, 2nd ed. (New York: McGraw-Hill, 1991), pp. 314–17; Richard Sennett and Jonathan Cobb, *Hidden Injuries of Class* (New York: Alfred A. Knopf, 1972); and Larry Van Sickle, *The American Dream and the Impact of Class: Teaching Poor Kids to Labor* (New York: Irvington, 1985).

10. Zillah Eisenstein, *The Color of Gender: Reimaging Democracy* (Berkeley: University of California Press, 1994) pp. 63, 157. See also Theodore Ferdinand, "History Overtakes the Juvenile Justice System," *Crime and Delinquency* 37 (2) (April 1991): 204–24.

11. Joel Nilsson, "Juveniles 'Follow the Dollar' in Treatment," *Arizona Republic*, 10 April 1994, p. E1.

12. Marguerite Duras, *Yann Andrea Steiner: A Memoir*, trans. Barbara Bray (New York: Charles Scribner's, 1993).

References

Abbot, Jack Henry. *In the Belly of the Beast: Letters from Prison*. New York: Random House, 1981.

Anderson, Elijah. *Streetwise: Race, Class, and Change in an Urban Community*. Chicago: University of Chicago Press, 1990.

Arizona Department of Youth Treatment and Rehabilitation. "[Chief of Counseling's] Talk Highlights New Directions: Excerpts from a Speech at the First Annual Community Contractor Forum by [the] Chief of Counseling." *DYTR Notes* 3 (7) (1993): 2, 5.

———. "Daily Groups." Memorandum. Phoenix, 15 September 1993. Photocopy.

———. *Fact Pack 1992*. Phoenix, October 1992. Photocopy.

———. "Level System." Phoenix, 12 May 1992. Photocopy.

———. "Overview: Critical Components of Treatment." Phoenix, n.d. Photocopy.

———. "Personal Conduct." Memorandum from deputy director and assistant director to all employees. Phoenix, 19 April 1993. Photocopy.

———. "Proper Terminology." Memorandum from CMT manager to all staff. Phoenix, 25 September 1993. Photocopy.

———. "Prototype Treatment Program: Adobe Mountain Juvenile Institution." Phoenix, 22 June 1992. Photocopy.

———. "Success School: Program Description Overview." Phoenix, n.d. Photocopy.

———. *Youth Handbook*. Phoenix, October 1992. Photocopy.

Balanced and Restorative Justice Project. *Balanced and Restorative Justice for Juveniles: A National Strategy for Juvenile Justice in the 21st Century*. Fort Lauderdale: Florida Atlantic University Press, 1994.

Bamonte, Thomas J., and Thomas M. Peters. "The Parole Revocation Process in Illinois." *Loyola University of Chicago Law Journal* 24 (1993): 211–58.

Bartollas, Clemens, Stuart J. Miller, and Simon Dinitz. *Juvenile Victimization: The Institutional Paradox*. Beverly Hills, CA: Sage, 1976.

Benda, Brent B. "Predicting Return to Prison among Adolescent Males: A Comparison of Three Statistics." *Journal of Criminal Justice* 17 (6) (1989): 487–500.

Bernard, Thomas J. *The Cycle of Juvenile Justice.* New York: Oxford University Press, 1992.

Bland, Karina. "Cost of Crowding May Have Gone Up." *Arizona Republic*, 8 February 1997.

Bortner, M. A. *Delinquency and Justice: An Age of Crisis.* New York: McGraw-Hill, 1988.

———. *Inside a Juvenile Court: The Tarnished Ideal of Individualized Justice.* New York: New York University Press, 1982.

———. "Traditional Rhetoric, Organizational Reality: Remand of Juveniles to Adult Court." *Crime and Delinquency* 32 (January 1986): 53–73.

Bortner, M. A., Carol Burgess, Anne Schneider, and Andy Hall. *Equitable Treatment of Minority Youth: A Report on the Over Representation of Minority Youth in Arizona's Juvenile Justice System.* Phoenix: Governor's Office for Children, 1993.

Breed v Jones. 421 U.S. 519 (1975).

Brodt, Stephen J., and J. Steven Smith. "Public Policy and the Serious Juvenile Offender." *Criminal Justice Policy Review* 2 (1) (March 1987): 70–79.

Brown, J. W. "Easy Answers Elude Struggle to Fix System." *Phoenix Gazette*, 9 January 1994.

Burke, William H., and E. Jane Burkhead. "Runaway Children in America: A Review of the Literature." *Education and Treatment of Children* 12 (1) (February 1989): 73–81.

Carr, Caleb. *The Alienist.* New York: Random House, 1994.

Cavender, Gray, and Paul Knepper. "Strange Interlude: An Analysis of Juvenile Parole Revocation Decision Making." *Social Problems* 39 (4) (1992): 387–99.

"Challenge for DYTR: Protect the Public," *Phoenix Gazette*, 7 January 1994.

Coates, Robert B., Alden D. Miller, and Lloyd E. Ohlin. *Diversity in a Youth Correctional System: Handling Delinquents in Massachusetts.* Cambridge, MA: Ballinger, 1978.

Conly, Catherine H. *Street Gangs: Current Knowledge and Strategies.* Washington, DC: National Institute of Justice, 1993.

Cook, Kristen. "Arizona a Reluctant Player in Overdue Youth Corrections Reforms." *Arizona Daily Star*, 6 July 1994.

Coontz, Stephanie. *The Way We Never Were: American Families and the Nostalgia Trap.* New York: Basic Books, 1992.

Cottle, Thomas J. *Children in Jail: Seven Lessons in American Justice*. Boston: Beacon, 1977.

Currie, Elliott. *Dope and Trouble: Portraits of Delinquent Youth*. New York: Pantheon, 1991.

Curry, David G., and Irving A. Spergel. "Gang Involvement and Delinquency Among Hispanic and African-American Adolescent Males." *Journal of Research in Crime and Delinquency* 29 (3) (1992): 273–91.

Dale, Michael J., and Carl Sanniti. "Litigation as an Instrument for Change in Juvenile Detention: A Case Study." *Crime and Delinquency* 39 (1) (1993): 49–67.

De Como, Robert E., Sandra Tunis, Barry Krisberg, Norma C. Herrara, Sonya Rudenstine, and Dominic Del Rosario. *Juveniles Taken into Custody Research Program: FY 1992 Annual Report*. Washington, DC: Office of Juvenile Justice and Delinquency Prevention, U.S. Department of Justice, 1995.

Duncan, Renae D., Wallace A. Kennedy, and Christopher J. Patrick. "Four Factor Model of Recidivism in Male Juvenile Offenders." *Journal of Clinical Child Psychology* 24 (3) (1995): 250–57.

Duneier, Mitchell. *Slim's Table: Race, Respectability, and Masculinity*. Chicago: University of Chicago Press, 1992.

Duras, Marguerite. *Yann Andrea Steiner: A Memoir*. Translated by Barbara Bray. New York: Charles Scribner's, 1993.

Dwyer, Diane C., and Roger B. McNally. "Juvenile Justice Reform, Retain, and Reaffirm." *Federal Probation* 51 (September 1987): 47–51.

Dyson, Michael Eric. *Making Malcolm: The Myth and Meaning of Malcolm X*. New York: Oxford University Press, 1995.

Eigen, Joel P. "The Determinants and Impact of Jurisdictional Transfer in Philadelphia." In *Major Issues in Juvenile Justice Information and Training: Readings in Public Policy*, eds. John C. Hall, Donna Martin Hamparian, John M. Pettibone, and Joseph L. White, 333–50. Columbus, OH: Academy for Contemporary Problems, 1981.

Eisenstein, Zillah R. *The Color of Gender: Reimaging Democracy*. Berkeley: University of California Press, 1994.

Emerson, Robert M. *Judging Delinquents: Context and Process in Juvenile Court*. Chicago: Aldine, 1969.

Esbensen, Finn-Aage, and David Huizinga. "Gangs, Drugs, and Delinquency in a Survey of Urban Youth." *Criminology* 31 (4) (1993): 565–89.

Family Life Development Center. *Therapeutic Crisis Intervention*. Ithaca, NY: Cornell University, 1991.

Feld, Barry C. "Juvenile (In)Justice and the Criminal Court Alternative." *Crime and Delinquency* 39 (4) (1993): 403–24.

———. "The Transformation of the Juvenile Court." *Minnesota Law Review* 75 (3) (1991): 691–725.

Ferdinand, Theodore N. "History Overtakes the Juvenile Justice System." *Crime and Delinquency* 37 (2) (1991): 204–24.

Ferrara, Matthew L. *Group Counseling with Juvenile Delinquents: The Limit and Lead Approach.* Newbury Park, CA: Sage, 1992.

———. "The Journey Program: A Juvenile Sex Offender Treatment Program." Unpublished, 1994. Photocopy.

Flaherty, Michael G. *An Assessment of National Incidence of Juvenile Suicide in Adult Jails, Lockups, and Juvenile Detention Centers.* Washington, DC: Office of Juvenile Justice and Delinquency Prevention, U.S. Department of Justice, 1980.

Flanagan, Timothy, and Kathleen Maguire, eds. *Sourcebook of Criminal Justice Statistics 1991.* Washington, DC: U.S. Government Printing Office, 1992.

Flanagan, Timothy, Ann L. Pastore, and Kathleen Maguire, eds. *Sourcebook of Criminal Justice Statistics 1992.* Washington, DC: U.S. Government Printing Office, 1993.

Fors, Stuart W., and Dean G. Rojek. "A Comparison of Drug Involvement Between Runaways and School Youths." *Journal of Drug Education* 21 (1) (1991): 13–25.

Foucault, Michel. *Discipline and Punish: The Birth of the Prison.* Translated by Alan Sheridan. New York: Vintage, 1979.

———. *The History of Sexuality: An Introduction.* Translated by Robert Hurley. New York: Penguin, 1978.

Fox, James Alan. *Trends in Juvenile Violence: A Report to the United States Attorney General on Current and Future Rates of Juvenile Offending.* Washington, DC: Bureau of Justice Statistics, U.S. Department of Justice, 1996.

Frazier, Charles E., and John C. Cochran. "Detention of Juveniles: Its Effect on Subsequent Juvenile Court Processing Decisions." *Youth and Society* 17 (3) (1986): 286–305.

Fritze, David. "Symington Calls for War on State's Juvenile Crime: Offers $31.7 Million Crackdown, Might Call Out Guard." *Arizona Republic*, 3 November 1993, p. A1.

Gilligan, James. *Violence: Our Deadly Epidemic and Its Causes.* New York: G. P. Putnam's, 1996.

Giroux, Henry A. *Fugitive Cultures: Race, Violence and Youth*. New York: Routledge, 1996.

Goffman, Erving. *Asylums: Essays on the Social Situation of Mental Patients and Other Inmates*. Chicago: Aldine, 1961.

Goldstein, Arnold P., and Barry Glick. *Aggression Replacement Training: A Comprehensive Intervention for Aggressive Youth*. Champaign, IL: Research Press, 1987.

Goodwillie, Susan, ed. *Voices from the Future: Our Children Tell Us About Violence in America*. New York: Crown, 1993.

Gordon, Avery. *Ghostly Matters*. Minneapolis: University of Minnesota Press, 1996.

Governor's Task Force on Juvenile Corrections. *Arizona's Troubled Youth: A New Direction*. Phoenix, June 1993.

Greenwood, Peter W., and Franklin E. Zimring. *One More Chance: The Pursuit of Promising Intervention: Strategies for Chronic Juvenile Offenders*. Santa Monica, CA: Rand Corporation, 1985.

Greenwood, Peter W., Joan Petersilia, and Franklin E. Zimring. *Age, Crime, and Sanctions: The Transition from Juvenile to Adult Court*. Santa Monica, CA: Rand Corporation, 1980.

Halemba, Gregg J. *Profile Study of Juveniles Committed to the Arizona DOC During 1989*. Mesa, AZ: Research and Information Specialists, 1990.

Hamid, Ansley. "Drugs and Patterns of Opportunity in the Inner City: The Case of Middle-aged, Middle-income Cocaine Smokers." In *Drugs, Crime, and Social Isolation: Barriers to Urban Opportunity*, eds. Adele V. Harrell and George E. Peterson, 209–39. Washington, DC: Urban Institute Press, 1992.

Hamparian, Donna M., Linda K. Estep, Susan M. Muntean, Ramon R. Priestino, Robert G. Swisher, Paul L. Wallace, and Joseph L. White. *Major Issues in Juvenile Justice Information and Training/Youth in Adult Courts: Between Two Worlds*. Columbus, OH: Academy for Contemporary Problems, 1982.

Harker, Victoria. "'These Kids Want to Succeed': A New Education System for State's Juvenile Offenders." *Arizona Republic*, 7 December 1992.

———. "Young Department's Future Unclear: Debate on Role Fuels Confusion Among Officials Saving Arizona's Children." *Arizona Republic*, 31 January 1994.

Harrell, Adele V., and George E. Peterson, eds. *Drugs, Crime, and Social Iso-*

lation: *Barriers to Urban Opportunity*. Washington, DC: Urban Institute Press, 1992.

Hartstone, Eliot, and Karen V. Hansen. "The Violent Juvenile Offender: An Empirical Portrait." In *Violent Juvenile Offenders: An Anthology*, eds. Robert A. Mathias, Paul DeMuro, and Richard S. Allison, 83–112. San Francisco: National Council on Crime and Delinquency, 1984.

Hebdige, Dick. *Subculture: The Meaning of Style*. London: Methuen, 1979.

Hermann, William. "Gangs Fight Police for Neighborhoods." *Arizona Republic*, 11 March 1995.

Hogue, RuthAnn. "Gang Teenager Saw Death Coming." *Phoenix Gazette*, 5 December 1993.

Horowitz, Ruth. "Sociological Perspectives on Gangs: Conflicting Definitions and Concepts." In *Gangs in America*, ed. C. Ronald Huff, 37–54. Newbury Park, CA: Sage, 1990.

Huff, C. Ronald. "Denial, Overreaction, and Misidentification: A Postscript to Public Policy." In *Gangs in America*, ed. C. Ronald Huff, 308–34. Newbury Park, CA: Sage, 1981.

Huizinga, David H., Scott Menard, and Delbert S. Elliott, "Delinquency and Drug Use: Temporal and Developmental Patterns." *Justice Quarterly* 6 (3) (1989): 419–55.

Hunt, Geoffrey, Stephanie Riegel, Tomas Morales, and Dan Waldorf. "Changes in Prison Culture: Prison Gangs and the Case of the 'Pepsi Generation.'" *Social Problems* 40 (3) (1993): 398–409.

Inciardi, James A. "Drug Use Can Cause Youth Violence." In *Youth Violence*, eds. Michael D. Biskup and Charles P. Cozic, 97–102. San Diego: Greenhaven, 1992.

Inmates of the Boy's Training School v Affeck, 346 F. Supp. 1354 (D.R.I. 1972).

In re Gault. 387 U.S. 1 (1967).

Irwin, John. *Prisons in Turmoil*. Boston: Little, Brown, 1980.

Jacobs, James B. *Stateville: The Penitentiary in Mass Society*. Chicago: University of Chicago Press, 1977.

Jacobs, Mark D. *Screwing the System and Making It Work: Juvenile Justice in the No-Fault Society*. Chicago: University of Chicago Press, 1990.

James, Howard. *Children in Trouble: A National Scandal*. New York: McKay, 1970.

Jankowski, Martin Sanchez. *Islands in the Street: Gangs and American Urban Society*. Berkeley: University of California Press, 1991.

John L. v Adams. 969 F. 2d 228 (6th Cir. 1992).

Johns, Christopher. "Arizona Is Part of a Juvenile-Justice Crisis: It's Not Just

About Crime, It's About Kids Who Are Abused, Neglected and in Need of Help." *Arizona Republic*, 28 November 1993.

Johnson v Upchurch. CIV-86-195-TUC-RMB. "Fifth Amended Complaint" (D. Ariz., filed April 11, 1988; consent decree entered May 5, 1993).

"Juvenile Jail: State Defies Court, Logic." *Arizona Republic*, 15 February 1997.

Kent v United States. 383 U.S. 541 (1966).

Kerbo, Harold R. *Social Stratification and Inequality: Class Conflict in Historical and Comparative Perspective.* 2d ed. New York: McGraw-Hill, 1991.

Klingemann, Harald K.-H. "Goal Conflicts in Correction Institutions for Juvenile Delinquents." *British Journal of Criminology* 22 (2) (1982): 140–64.

Kotlowitz, Alex. *There Are No Children Here: The Story of Two Boys Growing Up in the Other America.* New York: Bantam Doubleday Dell, 1991.

Kozol, Jonathan. *Amazing Grace: The Lives of Children and the Conscience of a Nation.* New York: Crown, 1995.

———. *Savage Inequalities: Children in America's Schools.* New York: Crown, 1991.

Kuhn, Ronald, and Phyllis R. Antonelli. *Keys to Innervisions.* Scottsdale, AZ: Keys to Excellence, 1990.

Kwok, Abraham. "New Era Dawns for Juvenile-Justice System." *Arizona Republic*, 9 February 1993.

———. "State Near New Juvenile-Detention Era; Decree Forcing Upgraded Treatment." *Arizona Republic*, 4 April 1993.

Lab, Steven P., and John T. Whitehead. "An Analysis of Juvenile Correctional Treatment." *Crime and Delinquency* 34 (1) (January 1988): 60–83.

Lambert, David. "*Johnson v Upchurch* Victory Brings Big Reforms in Arizona Juvenile Institutions." *Youth Law News* 14 (2) (March–April 1993): 2.

Lattimore, Pamela K., Christy A. Visher, and Richard L. Linster. "Predicting Rearrest for Violence among Serious Youthful Offenders." *Journal of Research in Crime and Delinquency* 32 (1) (1995): 54–84.

Lerman, Paul. *Community Treatment and Social Control: A Critical Analysis of Juvenile Correctional Policy.* Chicago: University of Chicago Press, 1975.

Lewis, Robert A., Fred P. Piercy, Douglas H. Sprenkle, and Terry S. Trepper. "Family-based Interventions for Helping Drug-Abusing Adolescents." *Journal of Adolescent Research* 5 (1) (1990): 82–95.

Mauer, Marc. *Americans Behind Bars: A Comparison of International Rates of Incarceration.* Washington, DC: Sentencing Project, 1991.

Mays, G. Larry, ed. *Gangs and Gang Behavior.* Chicago: Nelson-Hall, 1997.

McArthur, A. Verne. *Coming Out Cold: Community Reentry from a State Reformatory*. Lexington, MA: Lexington Books, 1974.

McCarthy, Belinda R., and Brent L. Smith. "The Conceptualization of Discrimination in the Juvenile Justice Process: The Impact of Administrative Factors and Screening Decisions on Juvenile Court Dispositions." *Criminology* 24 (1) (1986): 41–64.

McKeiver v Pennsylvania. 403 U.S. 528 (1971).

McNulty, Elizabeth W. "Transfer of Juvenile Offenders to Adult Court: Panacea or Problem?" Phoenix, Arizona Supreme Court, Administrative Office of the Courts, 1995. Photocopy.

Miller, A. Therese, Colleen Eggertson-Tacon, and Brian Quigg. "Patterns of Runaway Behavior Within a Larger Systems Context: The Road to Empowerment." *Adolescence* 25 (98) (1990): 271–89.

Monti, Daniel J. "The Culture of Gangs in the Culture of School." *Qualitative Sociology* 16 (4) (1993): 383–404.

Moore, Joan W. *Going Down to the Barrio: Homeboys and Homegirls in Change*. Philadelphia: Temple University Press, 1991.

———. *Homeboys: Gangs, Drugs, and Prison in the Barrios of Los Angeles*. Philadelphia: Temple University Press, 1978.

Morales v Turman. 364 F. Supp. 166 (E.D. Tex 1973).

Morgan v Sproat. 432 F. Supp. 1130 (S.D. Miss 1977).

Morrison Institute for Public Policy. *Kids Count Factbook: Arizona's Children 1994*. Tempe: Arizona State University, 1994.

Myers, Martha A., "Symbolic Policy and the Sentencing of Drug Offenders." *Law and Society Review* 23 (2) (1989): 295–315.

National Center for Youth Law. "CMJI Proof of Facts." Submitted to the U.S. District Court on behalf of plaintiffs in *Johnson v Upchurch* case, San Francisco, CA, 1988.

Nelson v Heyne. 355 F. Supp. 451 (N.D. Ind. 1973).

Nilsson, Joel. "Juveniles 'Follow the Dollar' in Treatment." *Arizona Republic*, 10 April 1994.

Norland, Stephen, Randall C. Wessel, and Neal Shover. "Masculinity and Delinquency." *Criminology* 19 (3) (1981): 421–33.

Palmer, Ted. *A Profile of Correctional Effectiveness and New Directions for Research*. Albany: State University of New York Press, 1994.

Pawlak, Edward J. "Differential Selection of Juveniles for Detention." *Journal of Research in Crime and Delinquency* 14 (2) (1977): 152–65.

Pena v New York State Division for Youth. 419 F. Supp. 203 (S.D.N.Y. 1976).

People v Hana. 443 Mich. 202 (1993).

Pfohl, Stephen. *Death at the Parasite Cafe: Social Science (Fictions) and the Postmodern.* New York: St. Martin's Press, 1992.

Phoenix South Community Mental Health Center. *Arizona's Alarming Trends 1994.* Phoenix: Arizona Association of Behavioral Health Programs, 1994.

Podkopacz, Marcy Rasmussen, and Barry C. Feld. "Judicial Waiver Policy and Practice: Persistence, Seriousness, and Race." *Law & Inequality: A Journal of Theory and Practice* 14 (1) (December 1995): 73–178.

Postman, Neil. *The Disappearance of Childhood.* New York: Vintage, 1994.

"Prison Population at Record 1.5 Million in U.S." *Arizona Republic*, 10 August 1995.

"Prison Population Tops 1 Million: Arizona Houses 18,809 Inmates." *Tribune Newspapers*, 28 October 1994.

Pryor, Douglas W., and Edmund F. McGarrell. "Public Perceptions of Youth Gang Crime: An Exploratory Analysis." *Youth and Society* 24 (4) (1993): 399–418.

Quinn, James F., and William Downs. "Police Perceptions of the Severity of Local Gang Problems: An Analysis of Noncriminal Predictors." *Sociological Spectrum* 13 (2) (1993): 209–26.

Redl, Fritz, and David Wineman. *Children Who Hate: A Sensitive Analysis of the Anti-Social Behavior of Children in Their Response to the Adult World.* New York: Free Press, 1951.

Regnery, Alfred S. "Getting Away with Murder: Why the Juvenile Justice System Needs an Overhaul." *Policy Review* 34 (Fall 1985): 65–68.

Reyes, Linda, and Nicolas Carrasco. "Special Training in Treating Youth Who Exhibit Violent Behavior." Paper presented to Arizona Department of Youth Treatment and Rehabilitation clinical staff, Phoenix, 23 May and 7 July 1994.

Robertson, Stephanie. "Boys at Adobe Mountain Leave Lasting, Haunting Impression." *Arizona Republic*, 25 June 1993.

Rodriguez, Luis J. *Always Running: La Vida Loca, Gang Days in L.A.* Willimantic, CT: Curbstone Press, 1993.

Rothman, David J. *Conscience and Convenience: The Asylum and Its Alternatives in Progressive America.* Boston: Little, Brown, 1980.

Rubin, Lillian. *Families on the Fault Line: America's Working Class Speaks about the Family, the Economy, Race, and Ethnicity.* New York: HarperCollins, 1994.

———. *Worlds of Pain: Life in the Working Class Family.* New York: Basic Books, 1976.

Rudman, Cary, Eliot Hartstone, Jeffrey Fagan, and Melinda Moore. "Violent Youth in Adult Court: Process and Punishment." *Crime and Delinquency* 32 (1986): 75–96.

Ryan, Gail D., and Sandy L. Lane, eds. *Juvenile Sexual Offending: Causes, Consequences, Correction*. Lexington, MA: Lexington Books, 1991.

Ryerson, Ellen. *The Best-Laid Plans: America's Juvenile Court Experiment*. New York: Hill and Wang, 1978.

Schall, A., Commissioner of New York City Department of Juvenile Justice v Martin et al. 467 U.S. 253 (1984).

Schatt, Paul J. "A Picture of Delinquency." *Arizona Republic*, 24 March 1994.

Schneider, Anne L. *Deterrence and Juvenile Crime: Results from a National Policy Experiment*. New York: Springer-Verlag, 1990.

Schneider, Anne, and Helen Ingram. "Social Construction of Target Populations: Implications for Politics and Policy." *American Political Science Review* 87 (2) (1993): 334–47.

Schuster, Bob. "Glimmer of Hope: State May Give Juvenile Rehab a Chance." *Tribune Newspapers*, 3 April 1993.

Schuster, Richard L. "Violent Juveniles and Proposed Changes in Juvenile Justice: A Case of Overkill?" *Juvenile and Family Court Journal* 33 (4) (1982): 37–42.

Schwartz, Ira M. *(In)Justice for Juveniles: Rethinking the Best Interests of the Child*. Lexington, MA: Lexington Books, 1989.

Schwartz, Ira M., Gideon Fishman, Radene Rawson Hatfield, Barry A. Krisberg, and Zvi Eisikovits. "Juvenile Detention: The Hidden Closets Revisited." *Justice Quarterly* 4 (2) (June 1987): 219–35.

Senge, Peter M. *The Fifth Discipline: The Art and Practice of the Learning Organization*. New York: Doubleday/Currency, 1990.

Sennett, Richard, and Jonathan Cobb. *The Hidden Injuries of Class*. New York: Alfred A. Knopf, 1972.

Shakur, Sanyika. *Monster: The Autobiography of an L.A. Gang Member*. New York: Penguin, 1993.

Sheh, Kevin. "Tattoos Scar Future for Ex-Gang Members: Removal Could Aid in Break with Past." *Arizona Republic*, 18 June 1993.

Simon, Jonathan. *Poor Discipline: Parole and the Social Control of the Underclass, 1890–1990*. Chicago: University of Chicago Press, 1993.

Sklar, Holly. *Chaos or Community? Seeking Solutions, Not Scapegoats for Bad Economics*. Boston: South End Press, 1995.

Smart, Barry. *Foucault, Marxism, and Critique*. London: Routledge and Kegan Paul, 1983.

Sniffen, Michael J. "Record Numbers in Prison." *Arizona Republic*, 2 June 1994.

Snyder, Howard N., and Melissa Sickmund. *Juvenile Offenders and Victims: A National Report*. Washington, DC: Office of Juvenile Justice and Delinquency Prevention, 1995.

Snyder, Howard N., Terrence A. Finnegan, Ellen H. Nimick, Melissa H. Sickmund, Dennis P. Sullivan, and Nancy J. Tierney. *Juvenile Court Statistics 1986*. Pittsburgh: National Center for Juvenile Justice, 1990.

Soler, Mark. "Litigation on Behalf of Children in Adult Jails." *Crime and Delinquency* 34 (2) (1988): 190–208.

Sontheimer, Henry, and Lynne Goodstein. "An Evaluation of Juvenile Intensive Aftercare Probation: Aftercare versus System Response Effects." *Justice Quarterly* 10 (2) (1993): 197–227.

Sowers, Carol. "Minister Defends Violent Play: Says Ugly Truths of Gang Life Exposed." *Arizona Republic*, 3 January 1994.

Sowers, Carol, and Victoria Harker. "Shake-up at Youth Correction: Director, Chief Deputy Forced Out by Governor." *Arizona Republic*, 6 January 1994.

Spencer, Kelly E. "Juvenile Incarceration: Translating Policy to Practice." Master's thesis, Tempe, AZ: Arizona State University, 1991.

Spergel, Irving A. "Youth Gangs: Continuity and Change." In *Crime and Justice: A Review of Research 12*, eds. Michael Tonry and Norval Morris, 171–275. Chicago: University of Chicago Press, 1990.

Stapelton, Vaughan, David P. Aday Jr., and Jeanne A. Ito. "An Empirical Typology of American Metropolitan Juvenile Courts." *American Journal of Sociology* 88 (1982): 549–564.

State v Werner. 242 S.E. 2d 907 (W.Va. 1978).

Stiffman, Arlene Rubin. "Physical and Sexual Abuse in Runaway Youths." *Child Abuse and Neglect* 13 (3) (1989): 417–26.

Street, David, Robert D. Vinter, and Charles Perrow. *Organization for Treatment: A Comparative Study of Institutions*. New York: Free Press, 1966.

Superior Court of Arizona. *Maricopa County Juvenile Court Center: 1994 Annual Report*. Phoenix, 1995.

Surette, Ray. "Predator Criminals as Media Icons." In *Media Process and the Social Construction of Crime*, ed. Gregg Barak, 131–58. New York: Garland, 1994.

Symington, J. Fife III. "Address by Gov. Fife Symington to Arizona Town Hall." Address given at Grand Canyon, AZ, 2 November 1993. Photocopy.

Takata, Susan R., and Richard G. Zevitz. "Divergent Perceptions of Group Delinquency in a Midwestern Community: Racine's Gang Problem." *Youth and Society* 21 (3) (March 1990): 282–305.

Thomas, Piri. *Down These Mean Streets*. New York: Vintage, 1991.

Thornberry, Terence P., Marvin D. Krohn, Alan J. Lizotte, and Deborah Chard-Wierschem. "The Role of Juvenile Gangs in Facilitating Delinquent Behavior." *Journal of Research in Crime and Delinquency* 30 (1) (1993): 55–87.

Thornton, William E. "Gender Traits and Delinquency Involvement of Boys and Girls." *Adolescence* 17 (68) (1982): 749–68.

Turco, Frank, and Bill Muller. "Democrat May Be Hired to Revamp Juvenile Justice." *Arizona Republic*, 10 January 1995.

———. "Juvenile Justice in Limbo: Overhaul Idea Met by Lawmaker Static." *Arizona Republic*, 10 January 1995.

U.S. Department of Justice. *Profile of Jail Inmates, 1989* (BJS Special Report). Rockville, MD: U.S. Department of Justice, 1991.

Van Sickle, Larry. *The American Dream and the Impact of Class: Teaching Poor Kids to Labor*. New York: Irvington, 1985.

Watters, John K., Craig Reinarman, and Jeffrey Fagan, "Causality, Context, and Contingency: Relationship between Drug Abuse and Delinquency." *Contemporary Drug Problems* 12 (Fall 1985): 351–73.

West, Cornel. *Race Matters*. Boston: Beacon, 1993.

Whitbeck, Les B., and Ronald L. Simons. "Life on the Streets: The Victimization of Runaway and Homeless Adolescents." *Youth and Society* 22 (1) (1990): 108–25.

Wilkinson, Karen. "An Investigation of the Contribution of Masculinity to Delinquent Behavior." *Sociological Focus* 18 (3) (1985): 249–63.

Williams, Linda M. "Ethics Policy and Society: Responsibility, Repression, or Rhetoric?" Ph.D. diss., Tempe, AZ: Arizona State University, 1994.

Williams, Terry, and William Kornblum. *The Uptown Kids: Struggle and Hope in the Projects*. New York: G. P. Putnam's, 1994.

Windle, Michael. "Substance Use and Abuse Among Adolescent Runaways: A Four-Year Follow-up Study." *Journal of Youth and Adolescence* 18 (4) (1989): 331–44.

Winter, Anne. "More Than Scrawls: Tagging, Graffiti, Different Forms of Language." *Arizona Republic*, 19 March 1995.

Winton, Ben. "Justice for Juveniles: Director Pushes for Overhaul of Youth Treatment." *Phoenix Gazette*, 14 May 1993.

Young, Iris Marion. *Justice and the Politics of Difference*. Princeton, NJ: Princeton University Press, 1990.

"Youth Corrections Shake-up Raises Questions." *Arizona Republic*, 7 January 1994.

Zatz, Marjorie S. "Los Cholos: Legal Processing of Chicano Gang Members." *Social Problems* 33 (1) (October 1985): 13–30.

Zide, Marilyn R., and Andrew L. Cherry. "A Typology of Runaway Youths: An Empirically Based Definition." *Child and Adolescent Social Work Journal* 9 (2) (April 1992): 155–68.

Index

Hames, Marty Vellasco, 209
Hamid, Ansley, 198
Hamparian, Donna Martin, 194
Hansen, Karen V., 204
Harker, Victoria, 185, 209, 210, 211
Harrell, Adele V., 198, 204
Hartstone, Eliot, 204
Hatfield, Radene Rawson, 182
Hebdige, Dick, 206
Hermann, William, 201
Herrara, Norma C., 183
Hogue, RuthAnn, 213
Homeboys, 58, 100, 138, 169–170, 201
Horowitz, Ruth, 202
Huff, C. Ronald, 201, 202
Huizinga, David, 203, 204
Human agency, *xiv*, 14
Hunt, Geoffrey, 206
Hurley, Robert, 197

Ideology, *xii*, 70, 140, 175–180
Imprisoned youths, *xi*, *xiv–xv*, 2, 3, 13, 65, 78, 140, 141–143, 180, 182, 184
    abuse of, *x*, *xii*, 1–8, 11
    adult-like experiences, 68–71
    age of, 44–45, 63, 199
    alternatives, lack of, 33, 176
    commonalities, *xii–xiii*, 43, 68
    community-based alternatives to, 63, 161, 177, 178, 180

compliance with institutional regime, *xiv*, 14, 15, 108, 124
"cutting," 5, 186
diagnostic evaluation, 9–10, 12, 24, 63, 181, 187
drug use, 60–61, 69, 203
educational experiences, 9–10, 39, 66–67, 68, 95–96, 99, 207
family, 14, 45–46, 65, 67, 161
"first timers," 62, 119, 204
gender, 43, 44–48
images of youth, *xii–xiii*, 47, 64, 70, 78, 139–140, 175–176, 183, 195, 206
individualized treatment, 10, 12, 13, 16
inappropriate imprisonment, 10, 63, 161
lengths of stay, *xi*, 12, 110–111, 121, 164–165, 182
medical care, 7, 8, 9, 187
mental health needs/illnesses, *x*, 9, 66, 111, 181
moral and political justifications, *xii*, 145, 175–176, 178–180
offense histories, 62–64
poverty and, 43, 44, 45, 46, 48, 49–51, 65, 67, 68, 69, 178, 200
power and, 30, 46, 70, 114, 209–210
psychopathy and sociopathy, 64, 173

1306